FIRST THINGS FIRST

A Modern Coursebook on Free Speech Fundamentals

RONALD K.L. COLLINS
WILL CREELEY
& DAVID L. HUDSON JR.

Managing Editor, Jackie Farmer

FIRE
Foundation for Individual
Rights in Education

FIRST AMENDMENT LIBRARY

Philadelphia | 2019

Published by Foundation for Individual Rights in Education (FIRE)
510 Walnut Street | Suite 1250
Philadelphia, Pennsylvania 19106
https://www.thefire.org

Library of Congress Control Number: 2019955121

ISBN: 978-1-938938-42-9

Book design and distribution by Top Five Books, LLC

Special thanks to David Skover and Sam Chaltain.

CONTENTS

The court opinions featured in this coursebook have been abridged.

We Must Not Be Afraid to Be Free

"We must not be afraid to be free."
—*Justice Hugo L. Black*

THINK OF THOSE WORDS. Who would be afraid of freedom? Why? Now, consider the statement made by Supreme Court Justice Hugo L. Black on April 24, 1961:

> Too many men are being driven to become government-fearing and time-serving because the Government is being permitted to strike out at those who are fearless enough to think as they please and say what they think. This trend must be halted if we are to keep faith with the Founders of our Nation and pass on to future generations of Americans the great heritage of freedom, which they sacrificed so much to leave to us. The choice is clear to me. If we are to pass on that great heritage of freedom, we must return to the original language of the Bill of Rights. We must not be afraid to be free.

Freedom has its costs. That is why we fear it. The freedom guaranteed by the First Amendment is no different. Those who applaud it can all too easily ignore the risks posed by unchecked expression. Likewise, those who rally against it can ignore the fact that unchecked calls for security lead all too often to tyranny.

That is not to say we will argue for a "happy medium" in this book. For better or worse, America has committed itself to an unprecedented experiment in freedom—an experiment based on the principle that more speech is better and, subsequently:

- More debate will produce better judgments;
- More knowledge will make for more self-realized persons;
- More associations and beliefs will make us more open-minded;
- More press freedom will hold those with power accountable;
- More robust expression of all sorts will make us a freer people; and
- The more we allow for all of this, the better our chances to check government abuses, to discover truth, beauty, freedom, and something about ourselves as well.

Simply put: more speech is better. That, at any rate, is the basic principle—call it a collective hope. On that principle we have banked everything.

Justice Black's warning about fearing speech was penned for his dissent in the famous First Amendment case *In re Anastaplo* (1961). In 1950, a man named George Anastaplo dared to step forward when others stepped back. He dared to stand on his First Amendment rights and refused to state his political associations, even when he stood to lose much for his position—admission to the bar association and a career in law, to be precise. In *Anastaplo*, a mere five-Justice majority voted against his stance; in doing so, they voted for a way of life where conformity and security trump individuality and liberty. Justice Black attributed the decision, which cost George Anastaplo his career, to a society fearful of freedom—at least, the kind of robust freedom Justice Black endorsed. But why would anyone fear freedom?

We fear what we do not know. In other words, we fear that our world will fall apart, that the values we hold may collapse just as the Colossus of Rhodes crumbled when the earth shook. After all, ideas can change minds. What was gospel yesterday may become heresy tomorrow, and vice-versa. Whenever we allow anyone to speak freely, print freely, associate freely, petition freely, or believe freely, we risk change and jeopardize what we hold dear. Risk is the companion of liberty. Without it, there could be no freedom.

In re Anastaplo exemplifies the conflict between those who, like Justice Black, place uninhibited faith in the First Amendment and those who feel that its freedoms must be curbed in the name of societal well-being. Of course, this black-and-white divide is the boldest view of the debate. There is generally a measure of wiggle room in both camps, but such nuances tend to get lost when fear prevails.

So how does all of this pertain to your life? And why should free speech matter to you? Let us engage in a Socratic thought exercise.

Assume you're a senior at college. Life is good, most of your teachers and colleagues share your views, and you're all for free speech...*until*, one day, the university announces who will be speaking at your graduation ceremony. This man offends you deeply. He represents everything you loathe, and you see him as a racist, sexist, and homophobe. Should he be allowed to speak on your campus?

Now, assume you're a different student who attends a different college. For you, too, life is good, many of your teachers and colleagues share your views, and you're all for free speech...*until*, one day, a person you find reprehensible is invited to speak at your campus. This woman offends you deeply. She represents everything you loathe, and you see her as a religious bigot who supports killing babies, champions anti-family values, and opposes your Second Amendment freedoms. Should she be allowed to speak on your campus?

We all favor free speech until it bumps up against our values. "Free speech for me, but not for thee," is how the late journalist and First Amendment aficionado Nat Hentoff put it. We fear the freedom of those we don't understand. But consider this: If the First Amendment protected only those views with which we agree, only those values we hold dear, and only those people whose speech conforms to those values, why on earth would we need this constitutional guaranty?

The First Amendment is there to protect speech that we hate, expression that we despise, and speakers whose ideas we detest or even fear. Its message to us: Be brave and speak up! Supreme Court Justice Louis Brandeis issued that very challenge in his celebrated concurrence in *Whitney v. California* (1927):

> Those who won our independence by revolution were not cowards. They did not fear political change. They did not exalt order at the cost of liberty. To courageous, self-reliant men, with confidence in the power of free and fearless reasoning applied through the processes of popular government, no danger flowing from speech can be deemed clear and present, unless the incidence of the evil apprehended is so imminent that it may befall before there is opportunity for full discussion. If there be time to expose through discussion the falsehood and fallacies, to avert the evil by the processes of education, *the remedy to be applied is more speech, not enforced silence* [emphasis added].

Keep that admonition in mind as you read through our book. It will serve you well. Our hope is that this book will expand your understanding of what it means to be a free people. Mind you, our aim is not to promote a collective, chaotic pact to wage endless wars of words. Rather, it is to highlight the fact that our American commitment to liberty is rooted in risk, and the idea that we as a people are willing to experiment with freedom even when it worries us.

With that warning, we dare you to read on.

1.

Looking Back & Looking Forward

WHY DOES HISTORY matter?

The answer to that question depends upon whom one asks. Take, for instance, Henry Ford, the famed captain of American industry. In 1916, he told a reporter at the *Chicago Tribune* that he had little use for history:

> History is more or less bunk. It's tradition. We don't want tradition. We want to live in the present, and the only history that is worth a tinker's damn is the history that we make today.

In other words, the living should not be judged by the dead hand of the past. From this perspective, today's understanding of our Constitution, including the First Amendment, is not to be dictated by exactly what the Founders meant when they drafted it, even if we could discern their true and complete intentions. Historian Leonard W. Levy once wrote:

> We may even have to confront the possibility that the intentions of the Framers were not the most libertarian and their insights on the subject of freedom of expression not the most edifying....If the Revolution produced any radical libertarians on the meaning of freedom of speech and the press, they were not present at the Constitutional Convention or the First Congress.

Let us assume, for the sake of argument, that Levy was right—that the Framers' legacy is one of suppression when it comes to free speech and press. Does this mean that the dead hand of the past should rule over the living?

For two famous and influential American jurists—Supreme Court Justices Hugo Black and Antonin Scalia—history was determinative. They believed in the "originalist" view of the law. For them, a judge's interpretation of the Constitution is legitimate only if it is consistent with the text of the Constitution as understood by its drafters. From an originalist's perspective, the Constitution's meaning is static, absent a new constitutional amendment.

There is yet a third school of thought holding that history, while not determinative, may sometimes be a persuasive tool that judges should use to interpret the Constitution.

Against that backdrop, let's examine what we know about the words and actions of the Constitution's drafters regarding free expression towards the end of the eighteenth century (the First Amendment was ratified in 1791). As you will see, how they *practiced* freedom of speech and of the press was often different from what they *preached* about those rights in the law.

THE ROUGH AND TUMBLE OF THE TIMES

Dissent was always in the air in colonial America. That meant that things like freedom of speech and press, freedom of association, freedom to petition, and freedom of conscience were of the utmost importance. People would meet in taverns to hash out their thoughts about the politics of the day. Public houses were filled with copies of politically charged newspapers and pamphlets. Political clubs and town meetings convened in private homes, taverns, and other public places to engage in all kinds of robust discussion, sometimes even with a subversive flavor. At times—as in their opposition to the Stamp Act—colonists would engage in theatrical expression. For instance, they held "Funeral for Liberty" processions, replete with black-draped coffins with the words "Liberty" inscribed on them. Some newspaper editors would even use funeral motifs and black mourning borders to show support for the underlying message.

Before the revolution of 1776, colonists in Boston gathered under a large elm tree, dubbed the Liberty Tree, to air their hostility to the Stamp Act and, more broadly, to royal rule. The tree became a symbol of colonial resistance to the Crown. Under it, people assembled, made speeches, and engaged in various forms of symbolic expression. These gatherings became a kind of political theater, but theater with revolutionary implications. As the Liberty Tree's fame grew, rebellious attitudes swelled beneath its branches. In 1775, the Loyalist rulers had had enough and ordered British troops to chop it down.

But removing the tree did not stop the colonists, who erected a liberty pole in its place. Liberty poles were tall, wooden poles topped with a red conical

Phrygian cap, which became a symbol of liberty during the French Revolution. These poles were used throughout the colonies as gathering places for groups like the Sons of Liberty—an organization that vehemently opposed the Stamp Act—to rail against the Crown, oppose the Stamp Act, and push for independence from England.

In an interview about his book *Revolutionary Dissent: How the Founding Generation Created the Freedom of Speech*, Professor Stephen Solomon gave a glimpse of what political life and strife were like in colonial America:

> When the colonists started protesting the Stamp Act of 1765, it started with newspapers and pamphlets that were largely aimed at the educated classes—politicians, wealthy merchants, people who could not only read but also who were interested in and could understand arguments based on English law and Enlightenment thinkers. But they had to go beyond that to get widespread support, so they used every means possible to democratize protest. They used songs and verse and cartoons and sermons, and all kinds of symbolic speech that brought in a large number of people to a protest. Thousands of people came out: three or four thousand people in Boston in a town of 16 thousand—proportionally that would be the same as two million people coming to a protest in New York today....Some of the governors brought seditious libel cases against some of the more egregious protestors, typically the ones that were complaining in print, but they couldn't get juries or grand juries to bring in an indictment or convict. People did not want to indict or convict a neighbor.

When looking back in time, it is useful to remember that newspapers as we now know them are radically different from those of the colonial era. Print was very much in demand, but journalism, as we know it today, was largely nonexistent. *Printers* were the focus—they either authored and distributed the news once a week or printed short "broadsides"—the political flyer of colonial times—for others.

Now, it's not as if all of the colonists were political activists constantly debating philosophy and ideals. Yes, they were politically minded, but they also spent plenty of time earning a living, chatting with their neighbors, passing out in taverns, and chasing the occasional chicken. Like us, they could be boring or raucous, orthodox or heretical—*and* passionate about politics.

THE PROVOCATIVE PRINTER

The American tradition of political activism and dissent hardly ended with the Declaration of Independence. The entire period leading up to the ratification of the Constitution in 1787 (and much thereafter) was one of significant political strife. There were heated clashes over, among other things, the appropriate powers of the federal government, the question of slavery, and the absence of a bill of rights in the Constitution as ratified. After the revolution, the target of protests was not the King, but the American Federalist Party.

The Federalist (who favored a strong central government) and Anti-Federalist (who favored decentralized power) printers and newspaper editors tested the fiber of the First Amendment like no one since. During that time, there was a certain faith in the printed word and in the noisy clash of divergent views. This reflected the old Miltonian belief in the staying power of truth and in people's ability to discern it. Benjamin Franklin, the onetime editor of the *Pennsylvania Gazette*, held dearly to that sentiment. He wrote the following in the *Gazette* on June 10, 1731:

> Printers are educated in the belief that even when men differ in Opinion, both Sides ought equally to have the Advantage of being heard by the Publick; and that even when Truth and Error have fair play, the former is always an overmatch for the latter.
>
> As politics collided with principle in the 1790s, the nation grew increasingly divided and confidence in a free exchange of ideas began to wane. The newspapers of the day mirrored the stark dualism of Federalist and Anti-Federalist views, at a time when public interest in the press was increasing. In the 1790s, as historian Ron Chernow noted, "the number of American newspapers more than doubled." And many of those, he added, "specialized in vituperative character attacks."
>
> No one better exemplifies this trend than the controversial editor of Philadelphia's *American Aurora* newspaper, Benjamin Franklin Bache. Foe of George Washington and John Adams, and friend of Thomas Jefferson and Thomas Paine, this grandson of Benjamin Franklin was an Anti-Federalist crusader at a time when the prosecutorial winds blew strongly against dissent. When Bache's paper came on the scene on October 1, 1790, a graphic of the aurora borealis appeared on its nameplate. Below the word "Aurora" was the motto "SURGO UT PROSIM," meaning "I rise to be useful." The paper's circulation began at around 400 and increased to an impressive 1,700 within a few years.

Soon enough, Bache earned the nickname "Lightning Rod Junior," both because of his relation to Benjamin Franklin and due to the shocking attention his publications brought. Federalist officials and Federalist-supported causes quickly became targets in Bache's editorial crosshairs. For example, the *Aurora* joined ranks with tradesmen, manufacturers, and farmers in the fierce battle over excise taxes; led the charge against the Jay Treaty; railed against Alexander Hamilton, the Federalist bogeyman for Jeffersonian Republicans; and frequently and personally attacked George Washington. Historian Jeffrey Smith observed that, leading up to the 1796 election, the *Aurora* was chock full of "regular reminders that Washington was a slaveholder and…that he was servile to Britain and hostile to France."

Bache was delighted when George Washington declined to serve a third term as president. "If ever there was a period for rejoicing," the *Aurora* proclaimed on March 6, 1797, "this is the moment—every heart, in unison with the freedom and happiness of the people, ought to beat high with exultation that the name of WASHINGTON from this day ceases to give currency to political inequity and to legalize corruption."

The enmity seems to have been mutual; Washington had had it with the printer by that point. "His Calumnies are to be exceeded only by his Impudence, and both stand unrivaled," he complained to Jeremiah Wadsworth in a March 6, 1797, letter.

But Bache's editorial arrows were not limited to Washington and Hamilton. Like his grandfather, the young Bache held strong views about John Adams. "Old, querulous, Bald, blind, crippled, Toothless Adams" is how the editor of the *Aurora* described the president he loved to loathe. An infuriated Mrs. Adams declared that she hoped and prayed that "the wrath" of the people would one day "devour" this "lying wretch of a Bache." As the war of words escalated, it quickly became a fight for freedom itself.

PROSECUTED…THEN PARDONED

In this verbal warfare, a single word threatened to silence the others: sedition. Sedition is defined as speech or action designed to incite rebellion against the government. When sedition was levelled as a charge, truth was not a defense. It was the subversive criticism of the government—not the merit of the words—that lay at the heart of the crime. The ramifications were profound:

> *Freedom of press cannot thrive as it should if closeted with a time bomb, the concept of seditious libel, ticking away in the law.*
> —*Leonard W. Levy, Emergence of a Free Press (1985)*

The concept of seditious libel strikes at the very heart of democracy. Political freedom ends when government can use its powers and courts to silence its critics....[D]efamation of the government is an impossible notion for a democracy.

—Harry Kalven, Jr., The New York Times Case: A Note on "The Central Meaning of the First Amendment" (1964)

It is suffice to say that the law of seditious libel was alive and well in the colonies, and it was a potent weapon for the government. Of course, the colonists were a feisty and at times unruly bunch when it came to expressing their beliefs. The resulting clashes were explosive.

The Federalist-controlled Congress passed, and President John Adams signed into law, the Alien and Sedition Acts of 1798. Among other things, the Acts restricted people's ability to speak critically about the government, tightened citizenship requirements, and allowed for the imprisonment and deportation of those considered to be dangerous to "the peace." Essentially, the Sedition Acts were designed to silence dissent, namely the Democratic-Republican Party.

The Acts were one of the first tests of the fledgling nation's commitment to free speech. As Professor Solomon has observed:

> On the one hand, it was a blatantly political move by the Adams administration to punish its critics. But you can also look at it as the first example of many in American history where free speech rights were violated because of fears regarding national security. This of course happened during the Civil War, the two World Wars, and also during the Cold War. Unfortunately we tend to sacrifice civil liberties during times of crisis. The Adams administration defined that period of near war with France as one such time.

In 1798, the inflammatory Anti-Federalist printer Benjamin Franklin Bache was arrested under the Alien and Sedition Acts and charged with "libeling the President & the Executive Government, in a manner tending to excite sedition, and opposition to the laws, by sundry publications and republications." Bache was able to post bail and proceeded to rail against the charges in the *Aurora*. Although he died at 29 of yellow fever before receiving his day in court, he was eventually vindicated. Once Thomas Jefferson took office, he allowed the Acts to expire and pardoned those prosecuted under them.

THE FRAMERS' NOTION OF RIGHTS

> *The Founders, however, often disagreed about the precise relation-*
> *ship between natural rights and the common law, leading to a con-*
> *fusing array of statements about expressive freedom....*
>
> *Debates about expressive freedom also were wide ranging*
> *because the Founders often vehemently disagreed about which*
> *regulations of speech promoted the public good. Many viewed nar-*
> *rowly drawn sedition laws as enhancing public debate by combating*
> *efforts to mislead the public. Others thought that sedition laws cre-*
> *ated more harm than good by chilling too much useful speech. But*
> *properly understood, this conflict did not reflect profound divisions*
> *about the concept of expressive freedom. Rather, the Founders dis-*
> *agreed about how to apply that concept to sedition laws.*
>
> —Jud Campbell, *Natural Rights and the First Amendment*
> (2017)

The disagreements among the Framers about the proper scope of free speech reveals that they did not view rights in the same way as modern Americans. For them, free expression rights were:

- Natural rights (not dependent on government creation) and positive rights (created by government);
- Protected by the common law;
- Protected by state constitutional declarations of rights (e.g., 1776 Virginia Declaration of Rights);
- Developed by representatives of the people (i.e., duly elected lawmakers);
- *Not* to be subjected to prior restraints or licensing (*subsequent* prosecutions were allowed);
- Safeguarded by a local jury of one's peers; and
- Subject to limitations that advanced the public good.

This was largely consistent with the anti-monarchical and social-contract-based political philosophy of the times. With the advent of the Federalist/Anti-Federalist divide, the rights of dissidents came under attack, as evidenced by the Alien and Sedition Acts. As bias found its way into the common law, Federalist lawmakers restricted rights, Federalist officials handpicked jurors, and Federalist ideas prevailed in the courts. The debate over the meaning of free speech became quite fierce, with radically divergent views over what was and was not protected.

Ever since 1919 (see Chapter 7), the U.S. Supreme Court and lower courts have played the lead and almost exclusive role in protecting First Amendment expression rights. In the process, they have frequently overruled many federal and state laws. This kind of judicial involvement and dominance over the legislative branch would have been foreign to the Founders. "There is no evidence," noted Professor Campbell, "that the Founders denied legislative authority to regulate expressive conduct in promotion of the public good—a principle that runs contrary to countless modern decisions." Thus, whatever view one holds of the historical meaning of the First Amendment, it appears that the meaning did not include any active enforcement of rights by the judiciary, especially when such enforcement was contrary to laws enacted by the legislature.

WHY HISTORY? DOES IT MATTER?

You've just had a sampling of dissident life in the colonies both before and after the Revolution. It's just a snapshot, but it should give you a general idea of the kind of political expression that was prevalent when the Constitution and the First Amendment were ratified. As Justice Brandeis noted in *Whitney v. California*, our Founders were no cowards, and they were willing to sacrifice order for freedom.

But there is also more to the story. The Alien and Seditions Acts followed hard on the heels of the hard-won battle for liberty. The legal right to free speech was far more restrictive than the practice of free speech.

Lawyers turn to history to make their cases, and judges, especially appellate ones, do so when drafting their opinions. So should history, as we know it, be determinative? Should it be the first and final word when trying to discover the meaning of the First Amendment?

APPROACHES TO INTERPRETING THE CONSTITUTION

History is certainly informative in examining how the First Amendment applies to modern-day cases. But understanding that history and deciding what to do with it can be like wrestling with a tiger. Certain wrestling techniques have emerged over the years:

- *Textual approach*: Under a textual approach, the focus is on the 45 words of the First Amendment and what they meant in 1791. Justices

Antonin Scalia, Clarence Thomas, and Neil Gorsuch are known for this approach.

- *Historical contextual approach*: The focus of this approach is on how First Amendment freedoms were exercised in the era of the First Amendment.
- *Political philosophy approach*: Here, the focus is on understanding the Founders' political philosophy in order to discern their definition of free speech.
- *Living Constitution approach*: With this approach, the history of the First Amendment, whatever it might be, is *not* determinative. Rather, the First Amendment, like the Constitution itself, should be interpreted in ways sensitive to the needs of the times. Among others, Justices William Brennan and Ruth Bader Ginsburg are known for this school of thought.

As you think about the practices of the people and the intentions of the drafters of the First Amendment (circa 1791), consider what they might think of current judicial interpretations extending constitutional protection to:

- Pornographers (Chapter 6)
- Defamers (Chapter 9)
- Flag burners (Chapter 10)
- High school students (Chapter 11)
- Commercial corporations (Chapter 12)
- Corporate campaign donors (Chapter 13)
- Rock and rap musicians (Chapter 15)

At the end of the day, history and text matter, but only up to a point. If they could tell us more, not only about what the dead thought, but how those thoughts apply to modern issues, they would rule the living. So, yes, history and text matter, but we must be duly mindful of their shortcomings and also focus on the demands of the present and future.

2.

Forty-Five Words and How
to Understand Them

Congress shall make no law respecting an establishment of religion, or prohibiting the free exercise thereof; or abridging the freedom of speech, or of the press; or the right of the people peaceably to assemble, and to petition the Government for a redress of grievances.

—*U.S. Constitution, Amendment I*

THE ORIGINAL CONSTITUTION, that of 1787, did not contain the Bill of Rights. Thus, it had no explicit protection for freedom of speech, press, assembly, petition, and religion. Its passage was nearly defeated owing to this omission. When consensus to adopt the Constitution was finally reached, it was contingent on a promise to add a bill of rights by way of subsequent amendments.

DOES THE GOVERNMENT HAVE THE AUTHORITY TO ABRIDGE SPEECH?

Before there were explicit constitutional protections for the freedoms of speech and press, these rights were thought to be protected by strictly confining the federal government's authority to act. That was the argument advanced by the Federalist Party in defense of the draft of the Constitution that lacked a bill of rights. Others, however, feared that Congress had been granted too much power. Consider, for example, the concerns expressed by a writer echoing James Wilson in an October 24, 1787, statement in the *Freeman's Journal*:

Mr. Wilson asks, "What controul can proceed from the federal government to shackle or destroy that sacred palladium of national freedom, the liberty of the press?" What! Cannot Congress, when possessed of the immense authority proposed to be devolved, restrain the printers, and put them under regulation[?]

It was the massive grant to Congress of the Constitution's Article I power that struck fear into the republican hearts of Thomas Jefferson, James Madison, and those of similar beliefs. The "omission of a bill of rights providing clearly and without the aid of sophisms for freedom of religion [and] freedom of the press," among other rights, greatly troubled Jefferson, as he told Madison in a December 20, 1787, letter. Without an express bill of rights—"fetters against doing evil," as Jefferson tagged it in a February 7, 1788, letter—the government could all too readily deny liberty.

The Federalists countered by stating that those powers not expressly given to Congress were reserved to the people. Thus, since Congress (and the other two branches, as well) was not granted explicit power to abridge freedom of speech or the press, it lacked any authority to regulate in this area.

This claim did not convince the Anti-Federalists, who saw the potential for Congressional abuses of power. The Anti-Federalist pamphleteer known as the "Federal Farmer" issued such a warning on January 20, 1788, pointing out that the taxation power given to Congress under Article I, Section 8, of the Constitution could be used to stifle the press: "Printing, like all other business, must cease when taxed beyond its profits; and it appears to me, that a power to tax the press at discretion, is a power to destroy or restrain the freedom of it." The author argued that, since "[a]ll parties apparently agree, that the freedom of the press is a fundamental right, and ought not to be restrained by any taxes, duties, or in any manner whatever," they should protect it from those restraints. Since Congress' power was so vast, it could easily "annihilate the freedom of the press" and other rights, complained another pamphleteer known as "Cincinnatus."

What, then, could be done to stop this "engine of imposition and tyranny," as Cincinnatus put it? That concern, among others, led to the creation of the First Amendment, which expressly prohibits Congress from making laws abridging the freedoms of speech, religion, press, assembly, and petition.

EXPRESS LIMITATIONS

The period between the day that the Constitution was signed in 1787 and the day that the Bill of Rights was ratified in 1791 was a tense one. The drafting of the Bill of Rights was no easy task; the inalienable rights of the people had to be expressly delineated and the powers of the federal government had to be expressly limited. Without such assurances, the Constitution of 1787 might never have seen the light of day.

Thanks largely to James Madison of Virginia (the primary drafter of the First Amendment)—with inspiration by George Mason of Virginia and with some help from Charles Pinckney of South Carolina—the Anti-Federalist idea of an express limitation on legislative power caught on. By 1789, the Senate had considered a bill of rights proposal that declared:

> That Congress shall make no law, abridging the freedom of speech or of the press, or the right of the People peacefully to assemble and consult for their common good, and to petition the Government for a redress of grievances.

Though revisions were made, the "Congress shall make no law" language survived into the First Amendment and became the supreme law of the land. But what about abridgments of First Amendment freedoms by the executive and judicial branches of the federal government? Jefferson raised this concern in a March 13, 1789, letter to Francis Hopkinson: "What I disapproved of from the first moment…was the want of a bill of rights to guard liberty against the legislative as well as the executive branches of the government." Jefferson detailed the specific freedoms he had wanted the original Constitution to secure, with freedom of religion and freedom of the press at the top of the list.

Madison, for his part, was sensitive to the need to rein in the states' powers over fundamental freedoms. To that end, he had proposed that the following provision be included in Article I, Section 10 of the Constitution:

> No state shall infringe the equal rights of conscience, nor the freedom of speech, or of the press, nor of the right of trial by jury in criminal cases.

The proposal failed, and it was not until the twentieth century that the U.S. Supreme Court finally applied the protections of the First Amendment to the states by "incorporating" those protections into the Due Process Clause of the Fourteenth Amendment, which limits the power of the states.

CONGRESS SHALL MAKE NO LAW

The brevity of the First Amendment is a testament to the genius of its drafting:

> Congress shall make no law respecting an establishment of religion, or prohibiting the free exercise thereof; or abridging the freedom of speech, or of the press; or the right of the people peaceably to assemble, and to petition the Government for a redress of grievances.

This amendment, drafted mainly by Madison, was unlike others before it, either at home or abroad. The "make no law" prohibition of the First Amendment is unique; nowhere else in the Constitution and its 27 amendments are the powers of the government so boldly restrained. Even under the Third Amendment, soldiers can sometimes be quartered in our homes if "prescribed by law." And while other provisions of the Constitution permit the government to act only when expressly authorized, no other provision bans outright the making of a law.

Why was the First Amendment confined to one branch of the federal government? Today, the First Amendment applies to the executive and judicial branches, as well. If the word "Congress" was the textual touchstone, how in Madison's name could its provisions ever restrain the other branches? Though Supreme Court opinions offer little guidance on this account, a dollop of eighteenth-century constitutional logic might explain such a feat: A limit on Congress' powers is a limits on all other powers.

The logic relies on the relationship between the branches. The power to *make* laws is vested in the Congress; the power to *enforce* laws is left to the executive; and the power to *interpret* laws is for the judiciary. Thus, the executive branch cannot enforce a law that Congress cannot make. Since Congress is barred from making a law abridging any of the five freedoms protected by the First Amendment, the executive branch cannot enforce a law abridging those freedoms. Similarly, the judiciary cannot interpret and apply a law that Congress cannot make, such as a law that abridges First Amendment freedoms. By that measure, a restriction on Congress' lawmaking powers is a limitation on the powers of the other two branches of government, as well—or so the argument goes.

Justice Hugo Black believed deeply in those words: "no law." In his book *A Constitutional Faith*, he wrote that "[t]he First and Fourteenth Amendments take away from government, state and federal, all power to restrict freedom of speech...where people have a right to be for such purposes." But Black's absolutism (like that of Justice William O. Douglas, who served on the Supreme Court with Black for three decades) did not allow for exceptions for such things as obscenity (Chapter 6) and defamation (Chapter 9), although it did allow the government to regulate symbolic speech (Chapter 10).

The problem with Justice Black's so-called absolutism is that it seemed oblivious to certain widely accepted exceptions to the First Amendment, such as:

- Speech that solicits murder for hire
- Speech that perpetuates fraud in commercial dealings
- Speech that involves perjury in a court proceeding
- Speech that is tantamount to bribery
- Speech involving plagiarism

These are just a few of many examples (there are currently 43 exceptions to the First Amendment).

As a counter to Black's absolutism, some Supreme Court justices, such as John Marshall Harlan II, urged a "balancing approach" to the First Amendment in *Barenblatt v. United States* (1959):

> Where First Amendment rights are asserted to bar governmental interrogation, resolution of the issue always involves a balancing by the courts of the competing private and public interests at stake in the particular circumstances shown.

While the Black-Douglas absolutist approach never garnered a five-vote majority in any case, the Roberts Court has recently veered close to such absolutism in a number of its First Amendment cases.

DEFINING THE FREEDOMS PROMISED

The freedoms covered under the First Amendment—religion, speech, press, assembly, and petition—may seem easy to define at first glance, but in the over 200 years since the Bill of Rights was ratified, courts have grappled with what kinds of expression and activities receive this protection.

Freedom of speech. Think about it: Is protecting *freedom of speech* synonymous with protecting *speech*? Were the words "freedom of" meant to qualify or somehow explain what kinds of speech are to be protected? Consider these forms of communication:

- Expressive conduct (e.g. civil rights sit-in protests)
- Symbolic expression (e.g., flag burning, wearing armbands, and burning of draft cards)

- Exchange of computer data
- Robotic communication (See Epilogue)

Does the First Amendment apply to all of them?

Freedom of the press. Moving beyond traditional media such as newspapers, who qualifies for protection under this clause of the First Amendment? What about redistributors of the news such as the conservative *Drudge Report* or liberal *Huffington Post*? Or blogs such as *SCOTUSblog* and *The Volokh Conspiracy*—or even *Refinery 29* and *Barstool Sports*? Or social media accounts *for* media outlets? Might the advent of robotic expression prompt the Court to reconsider the role of the press clause in such cases? (See Epilogue.)

What does the press portion of the First Amendment add to what is already protected under the "freedom of speech" provision? The freedom from prior restraint (preventing the press from publishing certain material) is at the core of many press cases. As we'll discuss at length, the scope of this freedom has been much debated at the Supreme Court level.

The right to peaceably assemble. This section guarantees the right of the people to come together and collectively express, promote, pursue, and defend their ideas, subject to certain time, place, and manner restrictions. Note that the Court has granted some latitude regarding these restrictions in civil rights cases involving sits-ins at all-white restaurant counters and at a public library.

While the freedom of association is not directly covered by the First Amendment, this freedom has emerged from freedom of assembly cases. The Court first articulated this right in the case of *NAACP v. Alabama* (1958):

> Inviolability of privacy in group association may in many circumstances
> be indispensable to preservation of freedom of association, particularly
> where a group espouses dissident beliefs.

Freedom to petition the government for a redress of grievances. This is the right to contact one's government without fear of retaliation due solely to the act of contacting them. Common issues addressed by these cases include communicating with the government in order to express an opinion or to complain.

The Declaration of Independence cited King George's failure to redress the grievances listed in colonial petitions as a justification for the colonies' decision to declare independence from England:

> In every stage of these Oppressions We have Petitioned for Redress in
> the most humble terms: Our repeated Petitions have been answered only
> by repeated injury. A Prince, whose character is thus marked by every
> act which may define a Tyrant, is unfit to be the ruler of a free people.

The newly free colonists were quick to petition their new government. On February 3, 1790, Benjamin Franklin (then President of the Pennsylvania Society for Promoting the Abolition of Slavery) signed a petition to Congress to "devise means for removing the Inconsistency [slavery] from the Character of the American People," and to "promote mercy and justice toward this distressed Race."

Later, the First Amendment's right of petition played a significant role in the abolitionists' campaign to end slavery. In the 1830s, some 130,000 such petitions were sent to Congress, which put this right to the test. The House of Representatives passed a "gag rule" that effectively prevented any debate on the matter. John Quincy Adams (the former president and then Massachusetts congressman) and other representatives opposed this limitation. By 1844, the gag rule was repealed on the grounds that it conflicted with the right to petition the government.

THE FIRST AMENDMENT AND THE STATES

The freedoms of the First Amendment were eventually applied to the states by way of the Due Process Clause of the Fourteenth Amendment, which in relevant part provides that no state shall "deprive any person of life, liberty, or property, without due process of law." Under this wording, the notion of due process includes those rights contained in the Bill of Rights. That interpretative process (known as the incorporation doctrine), extended the following First Amendment obligations to state governments:

- Freedom of speech: *Gitlow v. New York* (1925) and *Stromberg v. California* (1931)
- Freedom of the press: *Near v. Minnesota* (1931)
- Freedom of assembly: *De Jonge v. Oregon* (1937)
- Free exercise of religion: *Cantwell v. Connecticut* (1940)
- Establishment of religion: *Everson v. Board of Education* (1947)
- Right to petition: *Edwards v. South Carolina* (1963)

3.

First Amendment Tool Kit

WHAT IS SPEECH?

FIRST AMENDMENT LAW can be labyrinthine, intricate, complex, convoluted, and disjointed. In short, it is not the easiest subject in the world to understand. But it is certainly one of the most interesting. This chapter provides you with the tools and terminology necessary to read and understand the majority of First Amendment cases and controversies regarding free expression.

The threshold issue in many First Amendment cases is determining whether something is expressive enough to even qualify as "speech"—as opposed to conduct, which isn't always protected by the First Amendment. Sometimes, it is obvious that we are dealing with speech. The spoken word and the printed word clearly qualify as speech. But what if a person displays a symbol or wears a piece of clothing to convey a message? What if a person engages in action to convey an idea? In examining First Amendment cases, it is useful to focus on the idea of expressing a message—which is why you often hear people referring to "freedom of expression."

Symbolic Speech and Expressive Conduct

Speech goes beyond the written and spoken word. Symbolic speech is generally defined as the passive display of a symbol—whether it be wearing pink to promote breast cancer awareness or placing a sign with the symbol of a political party in your window. The U.S. Supreme Court first recognized the concept of symbolic speech in *Stromberg v. California* (1931).

In this case, nineteen-year-old Yetta Stromberg worked as a camp counselor for the Youth Communist League in California, where she "supervised and directed the children in raising a red flag"—a common symbol of communism. Authorities charged her under a California law prohibiting the display of the red flag "as a sign, symbol or emblem of opposition to organized government." The Court, in an opinion written by Chief Justice Charles Evans Hughes, reversed her conviction and recognized that the display of the red flag was a form of symbolic speech.

The Court later recognized in *Tinker v. Des Moines Independent Community School District* (1969) that public school students' wearing of black peace armbands to protest U.S. involvement in the Vietnam War was "akin to pure speech" and thus protected by the First Amendment. (*Tinker* and other campus cases are covered at length in Chapter 11.)

Expressive conduct is similar in concept to symbolic speech. However, expressive conduct often refers to *behavior or actions*, as opposed to the passive display of a symbol. For example, defacing the American flag to make a political statement or participating in a day of silence to spread awareness about violence against the LGBTQ community are actions considered to be expressive conduct.

Not all forms of conduct are "expressive" enough to receive First Amendment protection. Chief Justice William Rehnquist famously wrote in *City of Dallas v. Stanglin* (1989): "It is possible to find some kernel of expression in almost every activity a person undertakes—for example, walking down the street or meeting one's friends at a shopping mall—but such a kernel is not sufficient to bring the activity within the protection of the First Amendment." In *Stanglin*, the Court determined that the act of attending recreational dancehalls did not involve the sort of expressive association that merits First Amendment protection. So *Footloose* wasn't too far from reality, after all!

The Court reached a different result that same year in *Texas v. Johnson* (1989) with regard to protestor Gregory Lee Johnson, who burned the American flag as a form of political protest. "The expressive, overtly political nature of [Johnson's] conduct was both intentional and overwhelmingly apparent," wrote Justice William Brennan for the Court. In this case, there was no verbal speech, but there was conduct that could be understood as conveying a message.

So let's take a moment to consider these two cases. In the same year, the Court found that flag burning was protected expression but that social dancing was not expressive enough to warrant protection. While the two rulings were reached based on different legal reasoning (in Chapter 10, we'll address the tests courts use to determine protections for expressive conduct and symbolic speech), they beg the question: How would *you* determine what conduct is expressive or meaningful enough to warrant First Amendment protection?

Unprotected Speech

The text of the First Amendment uses absolutist terms: "Congress shall make no law...abridging the freedom of speech." However, the First Amendment does not protect all forms of speech. For example, a person does not have a First Amendment right to offer perjured testimony in court or to extort money from another.

Justice Oliver Wendell Holmes used the famous "falsely shouting fire" metaphor to explain why certain speech is not protected in *Schenck v. United States* (1919): "The most stringent protection of free speech would not protect a man in falsely shouting fire in a theatre and causing a panic." The Court elaborated on the distinction between protected and unprotected speech in *Chaplinsky v. New Hampshire* (1942):

> There are certain well-defined and narrowly limited classes of speech, the prevention and punishment of which have never been thought to raise any Constitutional problem. These include the lewd and obscene, the profane, the libelous, and the insulting or "fighting" words—those which by their very utterance inflict injury or tend to incite an immediate breach of the peace. It has been well observed that such utterances are no essential part of any exposition of ideas, and are of such slight social value as a step to truth that any benefit that may be derived from them is clearly outweighed by the social interest in order and morality.

Ronald Collins, a coauthor of this book, has identified at least 43 unprotected categories of speech. We will address several of these, including defamation in Chapter 4; obscenity and child pornography in Chapter 6; and fighting words and true threats in Chapter 9. While there are many categories of unprotected speech, the traditional pattern in First Amendment law has been to narrow their application over time. For example, obscenity prosecutions were once brought against booksellers who sold D.H. Lawrence and James Joyce novels. Now, obscenity prosecutions normally are reserved for particularly hard-core violent sexual productions.

Fortunately, in recent years, the Court has resisted efforts to create any new unprotected categories. For instance, it made no new categories in cases involving violent video games (*Brown v. Entertainment Merchants Association* [2011]), funeral protests (*Snyder v. Phelps* [2011]), and images of animal cruelty (*United States v. Stevens* [2010]).

TOOLS FOR CONSTITUTIONAL LITIGATORS

Perhaps the two chief tools used to analyze speech restrictions for constitutional litigators are the concepts of overbreadth and vagueness. When a court strikes down a law, it often is because the court finds that the law is either too broad (could restrict protected speech or conduct) or too vague (unclear or undefined).

Sometimes, a law may be both. Take, for example, a public school dress code that prohibits students from wearing "any inappropriate clothing." This language is vague because the key term "inappropriate" is not defined. Students are left to guess at the meaning of what is appropriate or inappropriate. The dress code is also overbroad; it can apply to both clothing that displays unprotected speech, such as profanity, and clothing bearing protected political speech, like the message, "Don't tread on me." An administrator can subjectively deem that protected speech is "inappropriate."

Overbreadth

Many laws may have a valid purpose, but they are not written with sufficient precision and could be used to punish protected speech. This is the essence of the overbreadth doctrine.

The Court emphasizes that the overbreadth doctrine is "strong medicine." This means that the doctrine should be applied with some reservation because a finding that a law is overbroad means that it is unconstitutional—that the government can no longer enforce the law, even against people whose speech would be unprotected under a well-written law. Courts are often very reluctant to invalidate entire laws passed by elected representatives.

A key limitation on the doctrine is that the overbreadth must be substantial. The Supreme Court has never quantified what "substantial" means. Justice John Paul Stevens once wrote: "The concept of 'substantial overbreadth' is not readily reduced to an exact definition." That said, to be overbroad, a law must pose more than a minor or incidental threat to protected expression.

In *Airport Commissioners v. Jews for Jesus* (1987), the Supreme Court used the overbreadth doctrine to rule that public airport officials unconstitutionally prohibited "any First Amendment activity." The Court found that the regulation could be applied to protected speech such as wearing campaign buttons or even talking among friends about the hot topics of the day. The regulation clearly was substantially overbroad as it included *all* speech at the airport.

In the 2019 case *Iancu v. Brunetti*, the Supreme Court also used the overbreadth doctrine to invalidate a provision of the federal trademark law known as the Lanham Act. The provision prohibited the registration of marks that were "immoral or scandalous." Erik Brunetti challenged the provision after being denied the trademark for his clothing brand FUCT. For the majority, Justice Elena Kagan wrote: "There are a great many immoral and scandalous ideas in the world (even more than there are swearwords) and the Lanham Act covers them all. It therefore violates the First Amendment."

Vagueness

The concept of vagueness is rooted in due process. The idea is that it is unfair to punish people for violating laws when they don't know whether their conduct violates the law or not. These concerns are amplified when speech is involved, because people may avoid saying anything that may come close to crossing the line, which would reduce the quality of our national discussion by eliminating some voices from the democratic dialogue. Vague laws also pose a special danger because they invite the risk of discriminatory or selective enforcement.

Consider *Coates v. Cincinnati* (1971). At issue in this case was a city ordinance that made it a criminal offense for "three or more persons to assemble...on any of the sidewalks...and there conduct themselves in a manner annoying to persons passing by." The Court explained:

> In our opinion this ordinance is unconstitutionally vague because it subjects the exercise of the right of assembly to an unascertainable standard, and unconstitutionally broad because it authorizes the punishment of constitutionally protected conduct.
>
> Conduct that annoys some people does not annoy others. Thus, the ordinance is vague, not in the sense that it requires a person to conform his conduct to an imprecise but comprehensible normative standard, but rather in the sense that no standard of conduct is specified at all. As a result, "men of common intelligence must necessarily guess at its meaning."

The Chilling Effect

Vague and overbroad laws can cause a chilling effect on speech. If a person does not know whether or not his speech will be punished, they may steer clear of uttering the speech to avoid arrest or prosecution.

Justice Felix Frankfurter explained how requiring a loyalty oath for teachers educed a chilling effect in his concurring opinion in *Wieman v. Updegraff* (1952). The oath required teachers to declare they were not:

> [A]ffiliated directly or indirectly...with any foreign political agency, party, organization or Government, or with any agency, party, organization, association, or group whatever which has been officially determined by the United States Attorney General or other authorized agency of the United States to be a communist front or subversive organization.

Justice Frankfurter explained that the loyalty oath "has an unmistakable tendency to chill that free play of the spirit which all teachers ought especially to cultivate and practice; it makes for caution and timidity in their associations by potential teachers."

Vague laws produce chilling effects because individuals cannot reasonably be expected to know exactly when their expressive conduct or speech crosses the line and violates such rules.

Content Discrimination

Another key tool in examining First Amendment cases involves the content discrimination principle. Laws that treat speech differently based on content are called content-based. Laws that treat all speech the same are content-neutral. But what do we mean by "content?" It is helpful to think of content as the subject matter, as opposed to the specific view on that subject (which is discussed later on in this chapter). For instance, a prohibition on using a megaphone, no matter what the subject, would be content-neutral. But a prohibition on using a megaphone when discussing abortion, whether from a pro-life or pro-choice perspective, would be content-based.

This difference is important to First Amendment jurisprudence because we don't want the government to control what topics can be discussed. If the government can regulate content, then it can control speech, and perhaps even thought.

Content-based laws are presumptively unconstitutional. That means that a court will rule it unconstitutional unless the government can meet the highest form of judicial review, called "strict scrutiny." To do so, the government must show *both* that it has a compelling, or very strong, interest in the law, and that the law limits speech in the least restrictive way possible. This is sometimes called the "least restrictive means" test.

The Supreme Court explained the content discrimination principle in *Chicago Police Dept. v. Mosley* (1972)—a case challenging a Chicago ordinance that prohibited picketing near schools with the exception of "peaceful picketing of any school involved in a labor dispute." Thus, picketers protesting labor issues were treated better than picketers protesting racial discrimination. Prior to the ordinance, federal postal employee Earl Mosley would peacefully picket outside of Jones Commercial High School on a regular basis, contending that the school engaged in racial discrimination. When the ordinance was implemented, he stopped picketing since he was told it would violate the law. He subsequently challenged the ordinance and the Court found it to be an unconstitutional content-based restriction on speech.

The Court also found that the ordinance violated the Equal Protection Clause of the Fourteenth Amendment, requiring that government officials treat similarly situated individuals the same. Earl Mosley was punished for his picketing when labor picketers were not, but the government didn't have a defensible reason to treat them differently.

Content-Neutral Restrictions

As we see from the *Mosley* case, content-based laws are viewed with suspicion. The same does not hold for content-neutral laws. In fact, they are more likely to be considered constitutional. Government officials don't have to meet the strict scrutiny test to justify a content-neutral law—only "intermediate scrutiny."

Let's consider an example. Imagine a city ordinance that allows demonstrators to march on city streets but only within certain hours. This ordinance is content-neutral, because it treats all demonstrators equally, regardless of their message. This content-neutral law places what's known as a "time, place, and manner" restriction on speech. Such laws don't have to meet strict scrutiny. Instead, the question is whether the restriction is narrowly tailored to serve an important government interest, and leaves other channels open for communicating the speaker's message.

Viewpoint Discrimination

There is a special category of content-based laws that are considered especially problematic. These laws go beyond mere content discrimination into what is called viewpoint discrimination.

For example, let's say a city ordinance prohibited political speakers from giving speeches in public parks. This would be content discrimination, because the city is banning political speakers but presumably allowing other speakers who are not talking about politics. However, if city officials allowed Democratic Party speakers but not Republican Party speakers, that would be viewpoint discrimination. That law would not just look to what the *topic* of the speech was, but its *perspective*, too.

Justice Anthony Kennedy expressed it well in *Rosenberger v. University of Virginia* (1995) when he wrote: "Viewpoint discrimination is thus an egregious form of content discrimination."

The famous student-speech decision *Tinker v. Des Moines Independent Community School District* (1969), which was referenced earlier in this chapter regarding symbolic speech, also involved viewpoint discrimination. The Court noted that students in the district had been allowed to wear political campaign buttons and iron crosses (a Nazi symbol). By targeting the anti-Vietnam War black armbands, the district participated in viewpoint discrimination.

In the previously mentioned *Iancu v. Bruncetti*, Justice Alito wrote in his concurring opinion: "Viewpoint discrimination is poison to a free society."

Public Forum Doctrine

The Supreme Court has created a doctrine relevant to the content discrimination principle that judges the constitutionality of speech restrictions on government property. This concept is known as the public forum doctrine. Under this doctrine, courts determine whether speech takes place in a traditional public forum, a designated or limited public forum, or a non-public forum. The important thing to remember is that the government's ability to regulate speech often depends on the nature of the place where the expression takes place.

A traditional public forum refers to a place that historically has been open for free expression, such as a public park or a public sidewalk. The Supreme Court declared in *Hague v. Committee for Industrial Organization* (1939) that such places "have immemorially been held in trust for the use of the public."

A designated, or limited, public forum is one that has not historically been open for expressive activities, but that the government has, by policy or practice, opened up for expression—for instance, for expression related to a certain topic, or for a specific group of people. This could be a meeting room in a public library or the public comment period at a school board meeting.

A non-public forum is one that is not generally open for expression by the public. The Supreme Court, for example, ruled in *United States v. Kokinda* (1990) that a sidewalk leading from the parking lot to the post office was a non-public forum, despite public sidewalks traditionally being deemed public forums. Explaining the difference between a traditional public sidewalk and the post office sidewalk, the Court stated: "The postal sidewalk was constructed solely to assist postal patrons to negotiate the space between the parking lot and the front door of the post office, not to facilitate the daily commerce and life of the neighborhood or city."

Speech restrictions in a traditional or designated public forum are more stringent, while the government generally has a freer hand in regulating speech in a non-public forum.

Doctrinal Exceptions

There are some exceptions to the general principle against content and viewpoint discrimination. Two chief exceptions are the secondary effects doctrine and the government speech doctrine.

Under the secondary effects doctrine, patently content-based restrictions on adult entertainment are treated as content-neutral. The idea is that when government officials regulate, let's say, how close an adult entertainment business like a strip club can be to a school, they are not punishing the speech because of its offensiveness but because they believe that the adult business causes harmful secondary effects—such as increased crime and decreased property values. Sadly, some lower courts have used the secondary effects doctrine to restrict many types of speech, not just adult entertainment.

Under the government speech doctrine, the government has its own rights to engage in speech, immune from First Amendment challenge, particularly when promoting a public interest. For example, the government could engage in a "Say No to Smoking" campaign without having to fund or support a "Support Smoking" campaign. This doctrine is controversial. Often times it is debatable whether the government is expressing its own message or censoring private speech. Take the case of specialized license plates. Many believe that specialty license plates are the speech of the vehicle owner. However, the U.S. Supreme Court ruled in *Sons of Confederate Veterans v. Walker* (2015) that such specialty license plates are a form of government speech.

4.

Equality & Free Speech: Civil Rights & Gay Rights

SOME THINK THE First Amendment is the enemy of people of color and the LGBTQ community.

Fair enough. After all, when the First Amendment flag is waved in defense of the white supremacists marching in Charlottesville or on behalf of a baker who won't make a wedding cake for a gay couple, it's easy for many to feel that something is amiss, even terribly wrong. Again, fair enough. But many First Amendment advocates and people of faith see the matter quite differently. So where does that leave us? Does it mean that we should cabin the First Amendment so as to restrict the free speech rights of these individuals? Some people think so.

Here is how UCLA professor of law K-Sue Park sized up the matter in a 2017 *New York Times* op-ed she wrote titled, "The A.C.L.U. Needs to Rethink Free Speech." From where she stood, the ACLU was on the wrong side: "Sometimes standing on the wrong side of history in defense of a cause you think is right is still just standing on the wrong side of history."

Reporter Jeremy Peters, writing in the *New York Times*, added a similar sentiment to the mix: "The First Amendment has become the most powerful weapon of social conservatives fighting to limit the separation of church and state and to roll back laws on same-sex marriage and abortion rights."

Yes, racial bigots and religious dogmatists can wrap themselves up in the First Amendment's flag, but we want to take you back in time to show you how courageous Americans turned to the First Amendment to *vindicate* the civil rights of minority communities. In all of this, there is a lesson to be learned:

The First Amendment, like life, is what we make it.

WHEN THE NAACP REFUSED TO TURN OVER ITS MEMBERSHIP LISTS

Let's go back some sixty years ago to segregated Alabama, where bigotry thrived thanks to a legal system largely indifferent to the appalling plight of people of color. Even so, one man believed enough in the rule of law—buttressed by the First Amendment—to challenge racism at its roots. That man was Robert L. Carter. After graduating from Howard Law School, he pursued an advanced law degree at Columbia Law School. Bearing the burden of being the first African-American enrolled in the graduate department, the young man completed his thesis on the importance of the First Amendment for the preservation of a democratic society.

In 1944, Carter joined the staff of Thurgood Marshall's National Association for the Advancement of Colored People (NAACP). Fourteen years later, the ideas contained in his Columbia Law School thesis helped Carter frame the novel arguments that expanded the legal protections of the First Amendment and helped the NAACP strike back against the segregationist impulses of the South.

That landmark case, which he won, is set out below.

OPINION

National Association for the Advancement of Colored People
v. Alabama

(Abridged.)

357 U.S. 449 (1958)
Vote: 9–0

JUSTICE HARLAN delivered the opinion of the Court.

We review from the standpoint of its validity under the Federal Constitution a judgment of civil contempt entered against petitioner, the National Association for the Advancement of Colored People, in the courts of Alabama.

[Issue] The question presented is whether Alabama can compel petitioner to reveal to the State's Attorney General the names and addresses of all its Alabama members and agents, without regard to their positions or functions in the Association. The judgment of contempt was based upon petitioner's refusal to comply fully with a court order requiring in part the production of membership lists.

Petitioner's claim is that the order, in the circumstances shown by this record, violated rights assured to petitioner and its members under the Constitution.

[**State law**] Alabama has a statute similar to those of many other States which requires a foreign corporation, except as exempted, to qualify before doing business by filing its corporate charter with the Secretary of State and designating a place of business and an agent to receive service of process. The statute imposes a fine on a corporation transacting intrastate business before qualifying and provides for criminal prosecution of officers of such a corporation.

[**Corporate status of NAACP**] The National Association for the Advancement of Colored People is a nonprofit membership corporation organized under the laws of New York. Its purposes, fostered on a nationwide basis, are those indicated by its name, and it operates through chartered affiliates which are independent unincorporated associations, with membership therein equivalent to membership in petitioner. The first Alabama affiliates were chartered in 1918. The Association has never complied with the qualification statute, from which it considered itself exempt.

[**Facts**] In 1956 the Attorney General of Alabama brought a lawsuit to prevent the Association from conducting further activities within, and to oust it from, the State. Among other things the lawsuit alleged that the Association had opened a regional office and had organized various affiliates in Alabama; had recruited members and solicited contributions within the State; had given financial support and furnished legal assistance to Negro students seeking admission to the state university; and had supported a Negro boycott of the bus lines in Montgomery to compel the seating of passengers without regard to race. The suit recited that the Association, by continuing to do business in Alabama without complying with the qualification statute, was "...causing irreparable injury to the property and civil rights of the residents and citizens of the State of Alabama for which criminal prosecution and civil actions at law afford no adequate relief...." On the day the complaint was filed, the Circuit Court issued an order restraining the Association from engaging in further activities within the State and forbidding it to take any steps to qualify itself to do business therein.

Petitioner contended that its activities did not subject it to the qualification requirements of the statute and that in any event what the State sought to accomplish by its suit would violate rights to *freedom of speech and assembly* guaranteed under the Fourteenth Amendment to the Constitution of the United States. Before the date set for a hearing on this motion, the State moved for the production of a large number of the Association's records and papers, including bank statements, leases, deeds, and records containing the names and addresses of all Alabama "members" and "agents" of the Association. It alleged that all such documents were necessary for adequate preparation for the hearing, in view of petitioner's denial of the conduct of intrastate business within the meaning of the qualification statute. Over petitioner's objections, the court ordered the production of a substantial part of the requested records, including the membership lists, and postponed the hearing on the restraining order to a date later than the time ordered for production.

[**Fines**] Thereafter petitioner admitted its Alabama activities substantially as alleged in the complaint and that it had not qualified to do business in the State. Although still disclaiming the statute's application to it, petitioner offered to qualify if the bar from qualification made part of the restraining order were lifted, and it submitted with the answer an executed set of the forms required by the statute. However petitioner did not comply with the production order, and for this failure was adjudged in civil contempt and fined $10,000. The contempt judgment provided that the fine would be subject to reduction or remission if compliance were forthcoming within five days but otherwise would be increased to $100,000.

At the end of the five-day period petitioner produced substantially all the data called for by the production order except its membership lists, as to which it contended that Alabama could not constitutionally compel disclosure, and moved to modify or vacate the contempt judgment, or stay its execution pending appellate review. This motion was denied. While a similar stay application, which was later denied, was pending before the Supreme Court of Alabama, the Circuit Court made a further order adjudging petitioner in continuing contempt and increasing the fine already imposed to $100,000. The effect of the contempt order was to foreclose petitioner from obtaining a hearing on the merits of the underlying ouster action, or from taking any steps to dissolve the temporary restraining order which had been issued until it purged itself of contempt.

The Alabama State Supreme Court thereafter twice dismissed petitions to review this final contempt judgment, the first time for insufficiency of the petition's allegations and the second time on procedural grounds. We granted certiorari because of the importance of the constitutional questions presented.

We thus reach petitioner's claim that the production order in the state litigation trespasses upon fundamental freedoms protected by the Due Process Clause of the Fourteenth Amendment. Petitioner argues that in view of the facts and circumstances shown in the record, the effect of compelled disclosure of the membership lists will be to abridge the rights of its rank-and-file members to engage in lawful association in support of their common beliefs. It contends that governmental action which, although not directly suppressing association, nevertheless carries this consequence, can be justified only upon some overriding valid interest of the State.

Effective advocacy of both public and private points of view, particularly controversial ones, is undeniably enhanced by group association, as this Court has more than once recognized by remarking upon the close nexus between the freedoms of speech and assembly. It is beyond debate that freedom to engage in association for the advancement of beliefs and ideas is an inseparable aspect of the "liberty" assured by the Due Process Clause of the Fourteenth Amendment, which embraces freedom of speech. Of course, it is immaterial whether the beliefs sought to be advanced by association pertain to political, economic, religious or cultural matters, and state action which may have the effect of curtailing the freedom to associate is subject to the closest scrutiny.

The fact that Alabama, so far as is relevant to the validity of the contempt judgment presently under review, has taken no direct action to restrict the right of petitioner's members to associate freely, does not end inquiry into the effect of the production order. In the domain of these indispensable liberties, whether of speech, press, or association, the decisions of this Court recognize that abridgment of such rights, even though unintended, may inevitably follow from varied forms of governmental action.

It is hardly a novel perception that compelled disclosure of affiliation with groups engaged in advocacy may constitute as effective a restraint on freedom of association. This Court has recognized the vital relationship between freedom to associate and privacy in one's associations. When referring to the varied forms of governmental action which might interfere with freedom of assembly, it said in *American Communications Assn. v. Douds* (1950): "A requirement that adherents of particular religious faiths or political parties wear identifying arm-bands, for example, is obviously of this nature." Compelled disclosure of membership in an organization engaged in advocacy of particular beliefs is of the same order. Inviolability of privacy in group association may in many circumstances be indispensable to preservation of freedom of association, particularly where a group espouses dissident beliefs.

[Impact of compelled disclosure] We think that the production order, in the respects here drawn in question, must be regarded as entailing the likelihood of a substantial restraint upon the exercise by petitioner's members of their right to freedom of association. Petitioner has made an uncontroverted showing that on past occasions revelation of the identity of its rank-and-file members has exposed these members to economic reprisal, loss of employment, threat of physical coercion, and other manifestations of public hostility. Under these circumstances, we think it apparent that compelled disclosure of petitioner's Alabama membership is likely to affect adversely the ability of petitioner and its members to pursue their collective effort to foster beliefs which they admittedly have the right to advocate, in that it may induce members to withdraw from the Association and dissuade others from joining it because of fear of exposure of their beliefs shown through their associations and of the consequences of this exposure.

It is not sufficient to answer, as the State does here, that whatever repressive effect compulsory disclosure of names of petitioner's members may have upon participation by Alabama citizens in petitioner's activities follows not from state action but from private community pressures. The crucial factor is the interplay of governmental and private action, for it is only after the initial exertion of state power represented by the production order that private action takes hold.

[Compelling interest test] We turn to the final question—whether Alabama has demonstrated an interest in obtaining the disclosures it seeks from petitioner which is sufficient to justify the deterrent effect which we have concluded these disclosures may well have on the free exercise by petitioner's members of their constitutionally protected right of association. Such a "...subordinating interest of the State must be compelling," *Sweezy v. New Hampshire* (1957).

It is important to bear in mind that petitioner asserts no right to absolute immunity from state investigation, and no right to disregard Alabama's laws. As shown by its substantial compliance with the production order, petitioner does not deny Alabama's right to obtain from it such information as the State desires concerning the purposes of the Association and its activities within the State. Petitioner has not objected to divulging the identity of its members who are employed by or hold official positions with it. It has urged the rights solely of its ordinary rank-and-file members.

[Adequacy of state's interest] Whether there was "justification" in this instance turns solely on the substantiality of Alabama's interest in obtaining the membership lists. During the course of a hearing before the Alabama Circuit Court, the State Attorney General presented at length, under examination by petitioner, the State's reason for requesting the membership lists. The exclusive purpose was to determine whether petitioner was conducting intrastate business in violation of the Alabama foreign corporation registration statute, and the membership lists were expected to help resolve this question. The issues in the litigation were whether the character of petitioner and its activities in Alabama had been such as to make petitioner subject to the registration statute, and whether the extent of petitioner's activities without qualifying suggested its permanent ouster from the State. Without intimating the slightest view upon the merits of these issues, we are unable to perceive that the disclosure of the names of petitioner's rank-and-file members has a substantial bearing on either of them. As matters stand in the state court, petitioner (1) has admitted its presence and conduct of activities in Alabama since 1918; (2) has offered to comply in all respects with the state qualification statute, although preserving its contention that the statute does not apply to it; and (3) has apparently complied satisfactorily with the production order, except for the membership lists, by furnishing the Attorney General with varied business records, its charter and statement of purposes, the names of all of its directors and officers, and with the total number of its Alabama members and the amount of their dues. These last items would not on this record appear subject to constitutional challenge and have been furnished, but whatever interest the State may have in obtaining names of ordinary members has not been shown to be sufficient to overcome petitioner's constitutional objections to the production order.

[**Holding**] We hold that the immunity from state scrutiny of membership lists which the Association claims on behalf of its members is here so related to the right of the members to pursue their lawful private interests privately and to associate freely with others in so doing as to come within the protection of the Fourteenth Amendment. And we conclude that Alabama has fallen short of showing a controlling justification for the deterrent effect on the free enjoyment of the right to associate which disclosure of membership lists is likely to have. Accordingly, the judgment of civil contempt and the $100,000 fine which resulted from petitioner's refusal to comply with the production order in this respect must fall.

[**Ruling**] For the reasons stated, the judgment of the Supreme Court of Alabama must be reversed and the case remanded for proceedings not inconsistent with this opinion.

Points to Consider

1. *The aftermath.*

Unanimous judgment? Carter, as he would later recall, never saw it coming, though he was hopeful that he could prevail by way of a divided ruling. Newspapers in the North applauded the decision. "All Americans, no less than the members of the NAACP, can applaud this decision," editorialized the *Washington Post*. "It keeps open arteries of association and expression through which the lifeblood of the democratic process can flow."

But in the South, things were different. The Alabama state courts did all they could to thwart the Supreme Court ruling. More litigation, more trips to the Supreme Court, more delay—but in the end, Carter prevailed. In the years that followed, he continued to win a series of important First Amendment civil rights cases in the Supreme Court. In 1972, President Richard Nixon appointed him as a federal judge.

2. *Reflecting on the decision 47 years later.*

On the Monday following Thanksgiving in 2005, people filed into the National Archives auditorium in Washington to hear the latest in a series of public conversations about the First Amendment. The topic that day concerned freedom of association and assembly, past and present. The featured guests were Judge Carter and University of Chicago Law School professor Geoffrey R. Stone. Judge Carter, then 88 years old and retired, reflected on the First Amendment cases he argued on behalf of the NAACP and answered questions like: "Why is it that you feel that the First Amendment is still not an important issue in the minority community, especially among civil rights activists?" As the C-SPAN cameras captured his words and body language, Carter answered such questions with vital vigor. Summing up his thoughts on the importance of the First Amendment as a viewpoint-neutral tool that today's activists should embrace, he stated:

> My feeling about it is that you can't have it one way.... You've got to tolerate the business of allowing people in this country to be able to dissent. And it's whole hard. But you can't have it for one side and not have it for the other. That's why I don't accept the view that—this business about hate speech—that somehow that is the kind of speech that we ought to curb.
>
> You don't curb speech, you curb action. When speech turns to action, then that's the time to stop it. But as long as it is speech, if you're going to have First Amendment rights in this country, then you've got to

calm yourself down…you've got to breathe, breathe, breathe and then say: "Okay, I've got to let that go, too. Because I've got to allow that in order to have my right to do it."

THE CIVIL RIGHTS ACTIVISTS SUED FOR BOYCOTTING RACIST STORES

In 1966, the NAACP—along with other groups and numerous individuals—organized a boycott of white merchants in Claiborne County, Mississippi. Those who organized the boycott hoped to secure their demands for racial justice by urging others to engage in non-violent picketing of local businesses. The demands called for the desegregation of all public schools and public facilities, the hiring of black police officers, public improvements in black residential areas, the selection of black people for jury duty, the integration of segregated bus stations, and an end to verbal abuse by law enforcement officers.

Charles Evers, the Field Secretary of the NAACP, was one of the key players in organizing these efforts. Evers was a noted figure in the Civil Rights Movement, as was his younger brother, Medgar Evers, who was murdered by a member of the White Citizens' Council. After Medgar's death, Charles took over his position as field director of the NAACP in Mississippi.

Public speeches and organizing efforts were conducted by the NAACP to foster compliance with its boycott. Citing threats and acts of violence on the part of some supporters of the boycott, seventeen white merchants sued in Mississippi courts seeking to stop the boycott and to secure monetary damages for lost profits.

OPINION

National Association for the Advancement of Colored People v. Claiborne Hardware Co.

(Abridged.)

458 U.S. 886 (1982)
Vote: 8–0

JUSTICE STEVENS delivered the opinion of the Court.

[Facts] The boycott of white merchants in Claiborne County, Miss., that gave rise to this litigation included elements of criminality and elements of majesty.

Evidence that fear of reprisals caused some black citizens to withhold their patronage from respondents' businesses convinced the Supreme Court of Mississippi that the entire boycott was unlawful and that each of the 92 petitioners was liable for all of its economic consequences.

[**Issue**] Evidence that persuasive rhetoric, determination to remedy past injustices, and a host of voluntary decisions by free citizens were the critical factors in the boycott's success presents us with the question of whether the state court's civil damages judgment against Petitioners for malicious interference with Respondents' businesses is consistent with the Constitution of the United States.

We consider first whether petitioners' activities are protected in any respect by the Federal Constitution and, if they are, what effect such protection has on a lawsuit of this nature.

The boycott of white merchants at issue in this case took many forms. The boycott was launched at a meeting of a local branch of the NAACP attended by several hundred persons. Its acknowledged purpose was to secure compliance by both civic and business leaders with a lengthy list of demands for equality and racial justice. The boycott was supported by speeches and nonviolent picketing. Participants repeatedly encouraged others to join in its cause.

Each of these elements of the boycott is a form of speech or conduct that is ordinarily entitled to protection under the First and Fourteenth Amendments. The black citizens named as defendants in this action banded together and collectively expressed their dissatisfaction with a social structure that had denied them rights to equal treatment and respect. As we so recently acknowledged in *Citizens Against Rent Control/Coalition for Fair Housing v. Berkeley* (1981), "the practice of persons sharing common views banding together to achieve a common end is deeply embedded in the American political process." We recognized that "by collective effort individuals can make their views known, when, individually, their voices would be faint or lost." In emphasizing "the importance of freedom of association in guaranteeing the right of people to make their voices heard on public issues," we noted the words of Justice Harlan, writing for the Court in *NAACP v. Alabama* (1958):

> "Effective advocacy of both public and private points of view, particularly controversial ones, is undeniably enhanced by group association, as this Court has more than once recognized by remarking upon the close nexus between the freedoms of speech and assembly."

The Chief Justices stated for the Court in *Citizens Against Rent Control*: "There are, of course, some activities, legal if engaged in by one, yet illegal if performed in concert with others, but political expression is not one of them."

The right to associate does not lose all constitutional protection merely because some members of the group may have participated in conduct or advocated doctrine that itself is not protected. In *De Jonge v. Oregon* (1937) the Court unanimously held that an individual could not be penalized simply for assisting in the conduct of an otherwise lawful meeting held under the auspices of the Communist Party, an organization that advocated "criminal syndicalism." After reviewing the rights of citizens "to meet peaceably for consultation in respect to public affairs and to petition for a redress of grievances," Chief Justice Hughes, writing for the Court, stated:

> "It follows from these considerations that, consistently with the Federal Constitution, peaceable assembly for lawful discussion cannot be made a crime. The holding of meetings for peaceable political action cannot be proscribed. Those who assist in the conduct of such meetings cannot be branded as criminals on that score. The question, if the rights of free speech and peaceable assembly are to be preserved, is not as to the auspices under which the meeting is held but as to its purpose; not as to the relations of the speakers, but whether their utterances transcend the bounds of the freedom of speech which the Constitution protects. If the persons assembling have committed crimes elsewhere, if they have formed or are engaged in a conspiracy against the public peace and order, they may be prosecuted for their conspiracy or other violation of valid laws. But it is a different matter when the State, instead of prosecuting them for such offenses, seizes upon mere participation in a peaceable assembly and a lawful public discussion as the basis for a criminal charge."

Of course, the petitioners in this case did more than assemble peaceably and discuss among themselves their grievances against governmental and business policy. Other elements of the boycott, however, also involved activities ordinarily safeguarded by the First Amendment. In *Thornhill v. Alabama* (1940), the Court held that peaceful picketing was entitled to constitutional protection, even though, in that case, the purpose of the picketing "was concededly to advise customers and prospective customers of the relationship existing between the employer and its employees and thereby to induce such customers not to patronize the employer."

Speech itself also was used to further the aims of the boycott. Nonparticipants repeatedly were urged to join the common cause, both through public address and through personal solicitation. These elements of the boycott involve speech in its most direct form. In addition, names of boycott violators were read aloud at meetings at the First Baptist Church and published in a local black newspaper. Petitioners admittedly sought to persuade others to join the boycott through social pressure and the "threat" of social ostracism. Speech does not lose its protected character, however, simply because it may embarrass others or coerce them into action. As Justice Rutledge, in describing the protection afforded by the First Amendment, explained:

> "It extends to more than abstract discussion, unrelated to action. The First Amendment is a charter for government, not for an institution of learning. 'Free trade in ideas' means free trade in the opportunity to persuade to action, not merely to describe facts." *Thomas v. Collins* (1945).

In sum, the boycott clearly involved constitutionally protected activity. The established elements of speech, assembly, association, and petition, "though not identical, are inseparable." *Thomas v. Collins.* Through exercise of these First Amendment rights, petitioners sought to bring about political, social, and economic change. Through speech, assembly, and petition—rather than through riot or revolution—petitioners sought to change a social order that had consistently treated them as second-class citizens.

While States have broad power to regulate economic activity, we do not find a comparable right to prohibit peaceful political activity such as that found in the boycott in this case. This Court has recognized that expression on public issues "has always rested on the highest rung of the hierarchy of First Amendment values." *Carey v. Brown* (1980). "[S]peech concerning public affairs is more than self-expression; it is the essence of self-government." *Garrison v. Louisiana* (1964). There is a "profound national commitment" to the principle that "debate on public issues should be uninhibited, robust, and wide-open." *New York Times Co. v. Sullivan* (1964).

Petitioners sought to vindicate rights of equality and of freedom that lie at the heart of the Fourteenth Amendment itself. The right of the States to regulate economic activity could not justify a complete prohibition against a nonviolent, politically motivated boycott designed to force governmental and economic change and to effectuate rights guaranteed by the Constitution itself.

[**Holding**] We hold that the nonviolent elements of Petitioners' activities are entitled to the protection of the First Amendment.

The First Amendment does not protect violence. "Certainly violence has no sanctuary in the First Amendment, and the use of weapons, gunpowder, and gasoline may not constitutionally masquerade under the guise of 'advocacy.'" *Samuels v. Mackell* (1971). Although the extent and significance of the violence in this case are vigorously disputed by the parties, there is no question that acts of violence occurred. No federal rule of law restricts a State from imposing tort liability for business losses that are caused by violence and by threats of violence. When such conduct occurs in the context of constitutionally protected activity, however, "precision of regulation" is demanded. *NAACP v. Button* (1963). Specifically, the presence of activity protected by the First Amendment imposes restraints on the grounds that may give rise to damages liability and on the persons who may be held accountable for those damages.

[**Damages and liability**] The careful limitation on damages liability imposed by our precedents resulted from the need to accommodate state law with federal labor policy. That limitation is no less applicable, however, to the important First Amendment interests at issue in this case. Petitioners withheld their patronage from the white establishment of Claiborne County to challenge a political and economic system that had denied them the basic rights of dignity and equality that this country had fought a Civil War to secure. While the State legitimately may impose damages for the consequences of violent conduct, it may not award compensation for the consequences of nonviolent, protected activity. Only those losses proximately caused by unlawful conduct may be recovered.

The First Amendment similarly restricts the ability of the State to impose liability on an individual solely because of his association with another. In *Scales v. United States* (1961) the Court noted that a "blanket prohibition of association with a group having both legal and illegal aims" would present "a real danger that legitimate political expression or association would be impaired."

[**Test**] The Court suggested that to punish association with such a group, there must be "clear proof that a defendant 'specifically intend[s] to accomplish [the aims of the organization] by resort to violence.'" (quoting *Noto v. United States* [1961]) Moreover, in *Noto v. United States* (1961) the Court emphasized that this intent must be judged "according to the strictest law," for "otherwise there is a danger that one in sympathy with the legitimate aims of such an organization, but not specifically intending to accomplish them by resort to violence, might be punished for his adherence to lawful and constitutionally protected purposes, because of other and unprotected purposes which he does not necessarily share."

In *Healy v. James* (1972) the Court applied these principles in a noncriminal context. In that case the Court held that a student group could not be denied recognition at a state-supported college merely because of its affiliation with a national organization associated with disruptive and violent campus activity. It noted that "the Court has consistently disapproved governmental action imposing criminal sanctions or denying rights and privileges solely because of a citizen's association with an unpopular organization." The Court stated that "it has been established that 'guilt by association alone, without [establishing] that an individual's association poses the threat feared by the Government,' is an impermissible basis upon which to deny First Amendment rights." (quoting *United States v. Robel* [1967]) "The government has the burden of establishing a knowing affiliation with an organization possessing unlawful aims and goals, and a specific intent to further those illegal aims."

[**Test**] For liability to be imposed by reason of association alone, it is necessary to establish that the group itself possessed unlawful goals and that the individual held a specific intent to further those illegal aims. "In this sensitive field, the State may not employ 'means that broadly stifle fundamental personal liberties when the end can be more narrowly achieved.' *Shelton v. Tucker* (1960)." *Carroll v. Princess Anne* (1968).

[**Fighting words**] It is clear that "fighting words"—those that provoke immediate violence—are not protected by the First Amendment. *Chaplinsky v. New Hampshire* (1942). Similarly, words that create an immediate panic are not entitled to constitutional protection. *Schenck v. United States* (1919). This Court has made clear, however, that mere advocacy of the use of force or violence does not remove speech from the protection of the First Amendment. In *Brandenburg v. Ohio* (1969), we reversed the conviction of a Ku Klux Klan leader for threatening "revengeance" if the "suppression" of the white race continued; we relied on "the principle that the constitutional guarantees of free speech and free press do not permit a State to forbid or proscribe advocacy of the use of force or of law violation except where such advocacy is directed to inciting or producing imminent lawless action and is likely to incite or produce such action."

The emotionally charged rhetoric of Charles Evers' speeches did not transcend the bounds of protected speech set forth in *Brandenburg*. The lengthy addresses generally contained an impassioned plea for black citizens to unify, to support and respect each other, and to realize the political and economic power available to them. In the course of those pleas, strong language was used. If that language had been followed by acts of violence, a substantial question would be presented whether Evers could be held liable for the consequences of that unlawful conduct. In this case, however—with the possible exception of the Cox incident—the acts of violence identified in 1966 occurred weeks or months after the April 1, 1966, speech; the chancellor made no finding of any violence after the challenged 1969 speech. Strong and effective extemporaneous rhetoric cannot be nicely channeled in purely dulcet phrases. An advocate must be free to stimulate his audience with spontaneous and emotional appeals for unity and action in a common cause. When such appeals do not incite lawless action, they must be regarded as protected speech. To rule otherwise would ignore the "profound national commitment" that "debate on public issues should be uninhibited, robust, and wide-open." *New York Times Co. v. Sullivan.*

For these reasons, we conclude that Evers' addresses did not exceed the bounds of protected speech. If there were other evidence of his authorization of wrongful conduct, the references to discipline in the speeches could be used to corroborate that evidence. But any such theory fails for the simple reason that there is no evidence—apart from the speeches themselves—that Evers authorized, ratified, or directly threatened acts of violence. The chancellor's findings are not sufficient to establish that Evers had a duty to "repudiate" the acts of violence that occurred. The findings are constitutionally inadequate to support the damages judgment against him.

The liability of the NAACP derived solely from the liability of Charles Evers. Of course, to the extent that Charles Evers' acts are insufficient to impose liability upon him, they may not be used to impose liability on his principal. On the present record, however, the judgment against the NAACP could not stand in any event.

The associational rights of the NAACP and its members have been recognized repeatedly by this Court. The NAACP—like any other organization—of course may be held responsible for the acts of its agents throughout the country that are undertaken within the scope of their actual or apparent authority. Moreover, the NAACP may be found liable for other conduct of which it had knowledge and specifically ratified.

To impose liability without a finding that the NAACP authorized—either actually or apparently—or ratified unlawful conduct would impermissibly burden the rights of political association that are protected by the First Amendment.

In litigation of this kind the stakes are high. Concerted action is a powerful weapon. History teaches that special dangers are associated with conspiratorial activity. And yet one of the foundations of our society is the right of individuals to combine with other persons in pursuit of a common goal by lawful means.

At times the difference between lawful and unlawful collective action may be identified easily by reference to its purpose. In this case, however, petitioners' ultimate objectives were unquestionably legitimate. The charge of illegality—like the claim of constitutional protection—derives from the means employed by the participants to achieve those goals. The use of speeches, marches, and threats of social ostracism cannot provide the basis for a damages award. But violent conduct is beyond the pale of constitutional protection.

The taint of violence colored the conduct of some of the petitioners. They, of course, may be held liable for the consequences of their violent deeds.

[**Burden of proof**] The burden of demonstrating that it colored the entire collective effort, however, is not satisfied by evidence that violence occurred or even that violence contributed to the success of the boycott. A massive and prolonged effort to change the social, political, and economic structure of a local environment cannot be characterized as a violent conspiracy simply by reference to the ephemeral consequences of relatively few violent acts. Such a characterization must be supported by findings that adequately disclose the evidentiary basis for concluding that specific parties agreed to use unlawful means, that carefully identify the impact of such unlawful conduct, and that recognize the importance of avoiding the imposition of punishment for constitutionally protected activity. The burden of demonstrating that fear rather than protected conduct was the dominant force in the movement is heavy. A court must be wary of a claim that the true color of a forest is better revealed by reptiles hidden in the weeds than by the foliage of countless freestanding trees.

[**Ruling**] The judgment is reversed. The case is remanded for further proceedings not inconsistent with this opinion. It is so ordered.

Points to Consider

1. The aftermath.

After the Supreme Court handed down its decision, many celebrated it as much-needed and overdue. Writing for the *New York Times*, law professor Leonard Orlando argued:

> The boycott of commercial goods is firmly ingrained in American history as an effective form of political protest. Long before the Rev. Dr. Martin Luther King Jr. made the Montgomery, Ala., bus boycott the spearhead of the desegregation movement, colonial boycotts had forced repeal of the Stamp Act, antebellum abolitionists had refused to buy slave-made wares, and early 20th century Progressives organized boycotts of sweatshop industries.... The Supreme Court's opinion in the Claiborne County case fills a constitutional vacuum.

Others, however, frowned upon the outcome. In a 1983 volume of *Duke Law Journal*, Gordon M. Orloff called political boycotting "a coercive *mode* of expression that, regardless of its goals, deprives its victims of their freedom to speak and to associate as they please." In 1984, George C. Covington wrote for the *North Carolina Law Review*:

> Although the decision legally endorses the historical acceptance protest boycotts have enjoyed, several factors suggest that this potentially far reaching holding was not the product of a great deal of judicial scrutiny. Specifically, the social and historical backdrop to the case very nearly dictated its outcome and thus discouraged serious examination of the conflicting interests at stake.
>
> Had the Court faced the first amendment question in a different boycott case it might have felt obligated to identify and weigh more carefully the difficult, conflicting interests involved. As it was, the hard facts of *Claiborne* may have made the answer seem too clear, leading the Court to announce the kind of broad protection that ultimately will demand extensive qualification.

2. Backdrop of violence.

Although the boycott was generally a peaceful act of protest, some supporters resorted to violence, property destruction, and threats to intimidate store owners and those noncompliant with the boycott. How did the violence surrounding this boycott affect the outcome? Do you think the Supreme Court properly balanced concerns over violence and free speech?

THE CASE OF THE MAGAZINE THAT BROUGHT GAY LIFE OUT OF THE CLOSET

Imagine being gay in 1956. You live in a secret world. If discovered, your intimate life could get you arrested and thrown in jail—or worse. If outed, you could lose your job. Sharing time with other gay people often means going to a dark and dingy bar on the outskirts of town. And if your parents and trusted friends know about your orientation, it is all kept very secret. In other words, you live in the closet.

That America was once the reality for nearly all gay people. Even publishing and mailing a non-obscene "pro-homosexual" magazine could trigger an FBI investigation and U.S. Postal censorship. Again, we're talking about non-obscene material, even by 1957–58 legal standards. (See *Roth v. United States* (1957), discussed in Chapter 6). The government took aim at such magazines, preventing them from being sent in the mail—a death sentence for most periodicals. *The Masses*, an avant-garde leftist magazine, shut down in 1917 after the post office refused to send it (see Chapter 7).

This brings us to *ONE*, a trailblazing LGBTQ magazine. As author, journalist, and activist Jonathan Rauch recounted, "ONE was the country's first openly gay magazine of ideas. It debuted in 1953 with serious articles on subjects like 'homosexual marriage.' (In 1953!) It did not publish explicitly sexual content or anything that approached the boundaries of pornography."

ONE took its name from a line in a poem by Thomas Carlyle, a Scottish philosopher and writer: "A mystic bond of brotherhood makes all men one." To be "one," then, meant to be "one of us"—a proud gay, lesbian, or transgender person.

Back then, to print such a publication, and to house an office where it was produced, was to risk trouble. And trouble came in 1954, when the postmaster in Los Angeles tagged *ONE*'s October issue as "obscene, lewd, lascivious and filthy." In other words, it could not be sent in the U.S. mail—which, in an era without alternative methods of correspondence, like FedEx or e-mail, essentially meant it couldn't be sent at all. And why? To start with, it contained a poem about gay cruising ("Lord Samuel and Lord Montagu"), a short lesbian love story ("Sappho Remembered"), and an ad for *The Circle* magazine, which printed gay romance stories. But there was more to it, as Rauch has aptly noted: "[T]he banned issue's cover article was a critique of, you guessed it, the government's censorship. The cover announced 'You Can't Print It!' and the article walked through the many restrictions imposed on the magazine. The government censored the article objecting to government censorship."

When censorship came, the ACLU did not come to the rescue of *ONE*. In a statement released by its board of directors in 1957, the ACLU stated:

> The ACLU national Board (sic.) in 1957 considered the occasional demands which are made upon the Union to defend the civil liberties of homosexuals. The Board held it was not the function of the ACLU to evaluate the social validity of laws aimed at the suppression or elimination of homosexuals, and that overt acts of homosexuality constitute a common law felony.

It fell to *ONE*'s in-house counsel and the unnamed author of "You Can't Print It!," Eric Julber, to take the government to federal court in *ONE v. Olesen*. Jonathan Rauch's account of the results paints a dismal picture:

> Federal district and appellate courts delivered defeats in stinging terms, leaving no doubt that the government's censorship was message-specific. The district court's decision held, "The suggestion advanced that homosexuals should be recognized as a segment of our people and be accorded special privilege as a class is rejected."

When the Court of Appeals for the Ninth Circuit weighed in, it focused on the "Sappho Remembered" short story and the impact the tale might have on society: "[T]he young girl gives up her chance for a normal married life to live with the lesbian. This article is nothing more than cheap pornography calculated to promote lesbianism."

But when the case went to the Supreme Court, something very unexpected happened. On January 13, 1958, the Court reversed the lower-court holding by way of a *per curiam* opinion (meaning that it was signed by the Court, without identifying the author of the opinion) which read, in its entirety:

> The petition for writ of certiorari is granted and the judgment of the United States Court of Appeals for the Ninth Circuit is reversed. *Roth v. United States*, 354 U.S. 476.

Think about it: Julber's First Amendment victory on behalf of free speech rights for the LGBTQ community took place:

- 11 years before the Stonewall riots
- 15 years before Lambda Legal was founded
- 15 years before the American Psychiatric Association removed homosexuality from its list of mental disorders in the DSM-II Diagnostic and Statistical Manual of Mental Disorders
- 20 years before San Francisco elected Harvey Milk to office (who made history as the first openly gay man to be elected to a political office in California…shortly before he was murdered.)
- 21 years before first
- National March on Washington for Lesbian and Gay Rights occurred
- 45 years before Paul M. Smith convinced the Supreme Court to strike down a "homosexual conduct" sodomy law in *Lawrence v. Texas*
- 57 years before Mary L. Bonauto persuaded the Supreme Court to strike down anti-same-sex marriage laws in *Obergefell v. Hodges*

This early victory was a First Amendment victory—and at a time when everyone, save *ONE* and Julber, thought it impossible.

Points to Consider

1. Projecting dissent.

In 2017, the Human Rights Campaign protested the Trump administration's ban on the use of seven words in Centers for Disease Control publications by projecting the words onto the Trump International Hotel in Washington, D.C. The projection ended with a final message from the LGBTQ advocacy group: "We will not be erased."

Was this an act of civil disobedience? Should First Amendment protections be applied to projection protests?

THE RELIGIOUS BAKER WHO REFUSED TO DESIGN AND SELL A WEDDING CAKE TO A GAY COUPLE

It all began in the summer of 2012, three years before the Supreme Court's ruling in *Obergefell v. Hodges* (2015) that state bans on same-sex marriages violated the Constitution. Back then, Charlie Craig and Dave Mullins had arranged to be married outside of Colorado, where they lived, since same-sex marriages had not yet been legally recognized in the state. Like other couples, they wanted a lovely wedding cake. So they went to one of the best cake makers around: Jack Phillips, owner of the Masterpiece Cakeshop. They requested that he make a cake for their wedding. Phillips refused. Since he was a devout Christian, he opposed same-sex marriages as a matter of faith. He felt that designing such a cake would be seen as an endorsement of same-sex marriage.

The couple was outraged. The ACLU filed a discrimination complaint on their behalf with the Colorado Civil Rights Division. The Division conducted an investigation and concluded that the cake shop had denied Mullins and Craig the full and equal enjoyment of a place of public accommodation, in violation of the Colorado Anti-Discrimination Act. The baker countered that to force him to provide a wedding cake for this couple would violate his First Amendment rights of freedom of religion and freedom of speech. "[C]ompelling him to exercise his artistic talents to express a message with which he disagreed," Phillips argued, was unconstitutional. The state administrative judge ruled for the couple and against the baker. The Civil Rights Commission affirmed the judgment. It then ordered Phillips to conduct comprehensive staff training on public accommodations and prepare quarterly compliance reports—a decision that the Colorado Court of Appeals affirmed.

The baker took his case to the Supreme Court, where he won by a 7–2 margin, but on very narrow grounds. The ruling for *Masterpiece Cakeshop, Ltd. v. Colorado Civil Rights* was confined to the particular facts of this case, in which there was evidence of actual animus directed against the baker based on his religious beliefs. This hostility, said the majority, was manifest in certain statements made by two members of the Colorado Civil Rights Commission. This, Justice Anthony Kennedy wrote for the Court, violated Phillips' First Amendment right to the free exercise of his religion.

Since the majority confined its ruling to the First Amendment free exercise claim, it did *not* reach the First Amendment free expression claim—although seven justices did discuss that issue in four different opinions either concurring with the majority opinion or dissenting from it.

In an op-ed in the *Washington Post*, the ACLU's David Cole, who argued the case on the couple's behalf, summed up the ruling this way:

> In the Supreme Court, the baker won, but not on the ground he principally advanced. His main argument was that where a business offers expressive products, the First Amendment prohibition on "compelled speech" bars the government from requiring the business to provide that product when it objects to doing so. The Trump administration backed that argument, maintaining that when businesses provide expressive products or services for "expressive events" such as weddings, the First

Amendment bars states from requiring them to provide them to gay and lesbian customers on the same terms as heterosexual customers.

Justice Anthony M. Kennedy, writing the majority opinion, could not have been more clear in rejecting the argument that there is a First Amendment right to discriminate. He wrote that "it is a general rule that [religious and philosophical] objections do not allow business owners... to deny protected persons equal access to goods and services under a neutral and generally applicable public accommodations law."

As for Jack Phillips, he was just happy that he'd won, however narrow the ruling: "I'm profoundly thankful that the court saw the injustice that the government inflicted on me," he said in a statement. "This is a great day for our family, our shop, and for people of all faiths who should not fear government hostility or unjust punishment."

Points to Consider

1. Designing.

Is *designing* a cake expressive conduct under the First Amendment? How about baking bread? In what ways are they similar and different for First Amendment freedom of expression purposes?

If such conduct were indeed speech under the First Amendment, it would be symbolic speech unless there were also words involved.

2. Purchasing.

What about *purchasing* generic wedding cakes? Assume that Dave and Charlie came into a cake shop and asked to purchase one of the generic cakes for their wedding, but the baker refuses to sell them one based on his religious beliefs. Does his making of generic cakes qualify as expressive conduct under the First Amendment?

3. Another context.

What if a person of color and his white fiancée walked into a wedding cake shop and asked for a cake with their photo on it? The baker refuses on religious grounds and argues that forcing him to design such a cake would amount to compelling him to express a view contrary to his religious beliefs. Does it make any difference that one case involved racial rights while the other involved gay rights?

5.

Hate Speech: Is It Protected?

WHAT IS HATE SPEECH?

[I]f there is any principle of the Constitution that more impera-
tively calls for attachment than any other, it is the principle of free
thought—not free thought for those who agree with us but freedom
for the thought that we hate.

—*Justice Oliver Wendell Holmes,*
dissenting in United States v. Schwimmer (1929)

THOSE WORDS, issued by Justice Holmes nearly ninety years ago, resonate deeply in America's free speech tradition. In *Matal v. Tam* (2017), a case involving the denial of an offensive trademark, Justice Samuel Alito, Jr., called Holmes' protection for the "thought that we hate" the "proudest boast of our free speech jurisprudence."

Other countries ban certain forms of "hate speech." In France, "public insults" based on race, religion, or ethnicity can lead to prosecution. Closer to home, Section 319 of the Canadian Criminal Code prohibits the willful promotion of hatred:

> Every one who, by communicating statements, other than in private conversation, wilfully promotes hatred against any identifiable group is guilty of (**a**) an indictable offence and is liable to imprisonment for a term not exceeding two years; or (**b**) an offence punishable on summary conviction.

Article 10 of the European Convention of Human Rights protects freedom of expression, but Section 2 provides that with such rights come "responsibilities," which are broadly defined to include:

[S]uch formalities, conditions, restrictions or penalties as are prescribed by law and are necessary in a democratic society, in the interests of national security, territorial integrity or public safety, for the prevention of disorder or crime, for the protection of health or morals, for the protection of the reputation or rights of others, for preventing the disclosure of information received in confidence, or for maintaining the authority and impartiality of the judiciary.

Article 20 of the United Nation's International Covenant on Civil and Political Rights provides: "Any advocacy of national, racial or religious hatred that constitutes incitement to discrimination, hostility or violence shall be prohibited by law."

Critical race theorists argue that free speech protection should not apply to hateful speech. They contend that American jurisprudence has unnecessarily elevated the liberty interests of the First Amendment over the equality interests of the First Amendment.

A problem with hate speech is that it is hard, if not impossible, to define. And the process of defining hate speech naturally leads to the suppression of ideas. Is inflammatory speech about a religion or nationality hate speech? Does context matter, or are some words completely off the table? Is it okay for a stigmatized group to use a racial slur but not okay for a non-stigmatized group? What about comedy? Can someone repeat inflammatory remarks in jest to make a point about using those very same words?

Under the First Amendment, Hate Speech—Standing Alone— Is Protected

Many laws banning hate speech suffer from inherent problems of vagueness and overbreadth. Nadine Strossen argued in her book *Hate: Why We Should Resist It with Free Speech, Not Censorship* that "the term 'hate speech' is not a legal term of art, with a specific definition; rather it is deployed to stigmatize and to suppress widely varying expression."

Consider the term "slants," which has long been used as a derogatory term referring to Asian people. It is a word with a lengthy history of animus against Asian people and continues to have hateful connotations. So, if someone were to use that term to refer to Asian Americans, would that automatically be hate speech?

The Asian-American members of a Portland, Oregon, rock band thought not. They even named their band "The Slants." Why? They wanted to reclaim the name and infuse it with a new meaning—one of pride in their Asian heritage. But when they tried to trademark the name, the U.S. Patent and Trademark Office refused their request, ostensibly on the grounds that it was racist. The litigation in *Matal v. Tam* (2017) went all the way to the Supreme Court, which unanimously reversed the Patent and Trademark Office's decision and sustained the band's First Amendment claim.

Not All Hateful Speech in the United States Is Protected

It is important to keep in mind that not all hateful speech is protected expression in the United States. If such speech falls into one of the narrow categories of speech unprotected by the First Amendment, the speaker may be punished. Thus, hateful speech is unprotected when it is:

- An incitement to imminent lawless action (Chapter 7);
- A true threat (Chapter 8);
- Fighting words (Chapter 8); or
- Defamatory remarks (Chapter 9).

Campus Speech Codes

In the 1980s and 1990s, a variant of the hate speech controversy took college campuses by storm: campus speech codes. Such codes broadly prohibit speech that could be deemed demeaning to others based on race, sex, age, and other protected criteria. The problem is that many of these speech codes are overbroad. Federal courts have invalidated campus speech codes in a large number of cases, such as *Doe v. University of Michigan* (1989) and *UMW Post v. Regents of the University of Wisconsin* (1991).

Despite their repeated defeat in court, speech codes on college campuses still exist. Read Chapter 11 on student speech for more.

NAZIS MARCHING IN SKOKIE

Controversy over hate speech reached center stage in the American body politic in the 1970s when the National Socialist Party (better known as the Nazi Party) sought to organize a march through the town of Skokie, Illinois—home to thousands of Jewish survivors of the Nazi Holocaust. Frank Collin, the head of the group, declared that his group had a First Amendment right to march in support of white supremacy.

The village of Skokie responded by passing three ordinances to thwart Collin's demonstration. One ordinance created a permit scheme for public assemblies and parades. A second prohibited the "dissemination of any materials" in the town that "promotes and incites hatred against persons by reason of their race, national origin, or religion." A third ordinance prohibited public demonstrations by persons wearing "military-style uniforms."

A federal district court invalidated all of the ordinances on the grounds that they violated the First Amendment. The case reached the U.S. Court of Appeals for the Seventh Circuit.

OPINION

Collin v. Smith

(Abridged.)

578 F.2d 1197 (7th Cir. 1978)
Vote: 2–1

WILBUR PELL, Circuit Judge.

[**Facts**] Plaintiff appellee, the National Socialist Party of America (NSPA) is a political group described by its leader, plaintiffappellee Frank Collin, as a Nazi party. Among NSPA's more controversial and generally unacceptable beliefs are that black persons are biologically inferior to white persons, and should be expatriated to Africa as soon as possible; that American Jews have "inordinate...political and financial power" in the world and are "in the forefront of the international Communist revolution." NSPA members affect a uniform reminiscent of those worn by members of the German Nazi Party during the Third Reich, and display a swastika thereon and on a red, white, and black flag they frequently carry.

[**Procedural history**] The Village of Skokie, Illinois, a defendantappellant, is a suburb north of Chicago. It has a large Jewish population, including as many as several thousand survivors of the Nazi holocaust in Europe before and during World War II.

When Collin and NSPA announced plans to march in front of the Village Hall in Skokie on May 1, 1977, Village officials responded by obtaining in state court a preliminary injunction against the demonstration. On May 2, 1977, the Village enacted three ordinances to prohibit demonstrations such as the one Collin and NSPA had threatened. This lawsuit seeks declaratory and injunctive relief against enforcement of the ordinances.

[**The ordinances**] Village Ordinance No. 77-5-N-994 (994) is a comprehensive permit system for all parades or public assemblies of more than 50 persons. It requires permit applicants to obtain $300,000 in public liability insurance and $50,000 in property damage insurance. One of the prerequisites for a permit is a finding by the appropriate (officials) that the assembly:

> will not portray criminality, depravity or lack of virtue in, or incite violence, hatred, abuse or hostility toward a person or group of persons by reason of reference to religious, racial, ethnic, national or regional affiliation.

Another is a finding that the permit activity will not be conducted "for an unlawful purpose." None of this ordinance applies to activities of the Village itself or of a governmental agency, and any provision of the ordinance may be waived by unanimous consent of the Board of Trustees of the Village. To parade or assemble without a permit is a crime, punishable by fines from $5 to $500.

Village Ordinance No. 77-5-N-995 (995) prohibits:

> the dissemination of any materials within the Village of Skokie which promotes and incites hatred against persons by reason of their race, national origin, or religion, and is intended to do so

Violation is a crime punishable by fine of up to $500, or imprisonment of up to six months. Village Ordinance No. 77-5-N-996 (996) prohibits public demonstrations by members of political parties while wearing "military-style" uniforms, and violation is punishable as in 995.

The conflict underlying this litigation has commanded substantial public attention, and engendered considerable and understandable emotion. We would hopefully surprise no one by confessing personal views that NSPA's beliefs and goals are repugnant to the core values held generally by residents of this country, and, indeed, to much of what we cherish in civilization. As judges sworn to defend the Constitution, however, we cannot decide this or any case on that basis. Ideological tyranny, no matter how worthy its motivation, is forbidden as much to appointed judges as to elected legislators.

The record in this case contains the testimony of a survivor of the Nazi holocaust in Europe. Shortly before oral argument in this case, a lengthy and highly publicized citizenship revocation trial of an alleged Nazi war criminal was held in a federal court in Chicago, and in the week immediately after argument here, a fourpart "docudrama" on the holocaust was nationally televised and widely observed. We cannot then be unmindful of the horrors associated with the Nazi regime of the Third Reich, with which to some real and apparently intentional degree appellees associate themselves.

But our task here is to decide whether the First Amendment protects the activity in which appellees wish to engage, not to render moral judgment on their views or tactics. No authorities need be cited to establish the proposition, which the Village does not dispute, that First Amendment rights are truly precious and fundamental to our national life. Nor is this truth without relevance to the saddening historical images this case inevitably arouses. It is, after all, in part the fact that our constitutional system protects minorities unpopular at a particular time or place from governmental harassment and intimidation, that distinguishes life in this country from life under the Third Reich.

These activities involve the "cognate rights" of free speech and free assembly. See *Thomas v. Collins* (1945). Standing alone, at least, it is "closely akin to 'pure speech' which, we have repeatedly held, is entitled to comprehensive protection under the First Amendment." *Tinker v. Des Moines* (1969). Likewise, although marching, parading, and picketing, because they involve conduct implicating significant interests in maintaining public order, are less protected than pure speech, they are nonetheless subject to significant First Amendment protection. Indeed, an orderly and peaceful demonstration, with placards, in the vicinity of a seat of government, is "an exercise of (the) basic constitutional rights of (speech, assembly, and petition) in their most pristine and classic form." *Edwards v. South Carolina* (1963).

No doubt, the Nazi demonstration could be subjected to reasonable regulation of its time, place, and manner. Although much of the permit system of 994 is of that nature, the provisions attacked here are not. No objection is raised by the Village, in ordinances or in their proofs and arguments in this case, to the suggested time, place, or manner of the demonstration, except the general assertion that in the place of Skokie, in these times, *given the content of appellees' views and symbols*, the demonstration and its symbols and speech should be prohibited. Because the ordinances turn on the content of the demonstration, they are necessarily not time, place, or manner regulations.

Legislating against the content of First Amendment activity, however, launches the government on a slippery and precarious path:

> Above all else, the First Amendment means that government has no power to restrict expression because of its message, its ideas, its subject matter, or its content. To permit the continued building of our politics and culture, and to assure selffulfillment for each individual, our people are guaranteed the right to express any thought, free from government censorship. The essence of this forbidden censorship is content control. Any restriction on expressive activity because of its content would completely undercut the "profound national commitment to the principle that debate on public issues should be uninhibited, robust, and wideopen."

We first consider ordinance 995, prohibiting the dissemination of materials which would promote hatred towards persons on the basis of their heritage. The Village would apparently apply this provision to NSPA's display of swastikas, their uniforms, and, perhaps, to the content of their placards.

[**Not obscenity or incitement**] The ordinance cannot be sustained on the basis of some of the more obvious exceptions to the rule against content control. While some would no doubt be willing to label appellees' views and symbols obscene, the constitutional rule that obscenity is unprotected applies only to material with erotic content. Furthermore, although the Village introduced evidence in the district court tending to prove that some individuals, at least, might have difficulty restraining their reactions to the Nazi demonstration, the Village tells us that it does not rely on a fear of responsive violence to justify the ordinance, and does not even suggest that there will be any physical violence if the march is held. This confession takes this case out of the scope of *Brandenburg v. Ohio* (1969) and *Feiner v. New York* (1951) (intentional "incitement to riot" may be prohibited). The Village does not argue otherwise.

[**Not fighting words**] The concession also eliminates any argument based on the fighting words doctrine of *Chaplinsky v. New Hampshire* (1942). The Court in

Chaplinsky affirmed a conviction under a statute that, as authoritatively construed, applied only to words with a direct tendency to cause violence by the persons to whom, individually, the words were addressed. A conviction for less than words that at least tend to incite an immediate breach of the peace cannot be justified under *Chaplinsky*.

Four basic arguments are advanced by the Village to justify the content restrictions of 995. First, it is said that the content criminalized by 995 is "totally lacking in social content," and that it consists of "false statements of fact" in which there is "no constitutional value." We disagree that, if applied to the proposed demonstration, the ordinance can be said to be limited to "statements of fact," false or otherwise. No handbills are to be distributed; no speeches are planned. To the degree that the symbols in question can be said to assert anything specific, it must be the Nazi ideology, which cannot be treated as a mere false "fact."

We may agree with the district court that if any philosophy should be regarded as completely unacceptable to civilized society, that of plaintiffs, who, while disavowing on the witness stand any advocacy of genocide, have nevertheless deliberately identified themselves with a regime whose record of brutality and barbarism is unmatched in modern history, would be a good place to start. But there can be no legitimate start down such a road.

Under the First Amendment there is no such thing as a false idea. However pernicious an opinion may seem, we depend for its correction not on the conscience of judges and juries but on the competition of other ideas. The asserted falseness of Nazi dogma, and, indeed, its general repudiation, simply do not justify its suppression.

The Village's second argument, and the one on which principal reliance is placed, centers on *Beauharnais v. Illinois* (1952). There a conviction was upheld under a statute prohibiting, in language substantially (and perhaps not unintentionally) similar to that used in the ordinance here, the dissemination of materials promoting racial or religious hatred. The closely-divided Court stated that the criminal punishment of libel of an Individual raised no constitutional problems.

That being so, the Court reasoned that the state could constitutionally extend the prohibition to utterances aimed at groups.

In our opinion *Beauharnais* does not support ordinance 995, for two independent reasons. First, the rationale of that decision turns quite plainly on the strong tendency of the prohibited utterances to cause violence and disorder. The Court also pointed out that the tendency to induce breach of the peace was the traditional justification for the criminal libel laws which had always been thought to be immune from the First Amendment.

The Village's third argument is that it has a policy of fair housing, which the dissemination of racially defamatory material could undercut. We reject this argument without extended discussion. That the effective exercise of First Amendment rights may undercut a given government's policy on some issue is, indeed, one of the purposes of those rights. No distinction is constitutionally admissible that turns on the intrinsic justice of the particular policy in issue.

The Village's fourth argument is that the Nazi march, involving as it does the display of uniforms and swastikas, will create a substantive evil that it has a right to prohibit: the infliction of psychic trauma on resident holocaust survivors and other Jewish residents. The Village points out that Illinois recognizes the "new tort" of intentional infliction of severe emotional distress, the coverage of which may well include personally directed racial slurs. Assuming that specific individuals could proceed in tort under this theory to recover damages provably occasioned by the proposed march, and that a First Amendment defense would not bar the action, it is nonetheless quite a different matter to criminalize protected First Amendment conduct in anticipation of such results.

It would be grossly insensitive to deny, as we do not, that the proposed demonstration would seriously disturb, emotionally and mentally, at least some, and probably many of the Village's residents. The problem with engrafting an exception on the First Amendment for such situations is that they are indistinguishable in principle from speech that "invite(s) dispute ....induces a condition of unrest, creates dissatisfaction with conditions as they are, or even stirs people to anger." *Terminiello v. Chicago* (1949). Yet these are among the "high purposes" of the First Amendment. It is perfectly clear that a state many not "make criminal the peaceful expression of unpopular views." *Edwards v. South Carolina*. Where, as here, a crime is made of a silent march, attended only by symbols and not by extrinsic conduct offensive in itself, we think the words of the Court in *Street v. New York* (1969) are very much on point:

> Any shock effect...must be attributed to the content of the ideas expressed.
> It is firmly settled that under our Constitution the public expression of

ideas may not be prohibited merely because the ideas are themselves offensive to some of their hearers.

It is said that the proposed march is not speech, or even "speech plus," but rather an invasion, intensely menacing no matter how peacefully conducted. The Village's expert psychiatric witness, in fact, testified that the effect of the march would be much the same regardless of whether uniforms and swastikas were displayed, due to the intrusion of self-proclaimed Nazis into what he characterized as predominately Jewish "turf." There is room under the First Amendment for the government to protect targeted listeners from offensive speech, but only when the speaker intrudes on the privacy of the home, or a captive audience cannot practically avoid exposure.

This case does not involve intrusion into people's homes. There need be no captive audience, as Village residents may, if they wish, simply avoid the Village Hall for thirty minutes on a Sunday afternoon which no doubt would be their normal course of conduct on a day when the Village Hall was not open in the regular course of business. Absent such intrusion or captivity, there is no justifiable substantial privacy interest to save 995 from constitutional infirmity, when it attempts, by fiat, to declare the entire Village, at all times, a privacy zone that may be sanitized from the offensiveness of Nazi ideology and symbols.

[**Holding**] We conclude that 995 may not be applied to criminalize the conduct of the proposed demonstration. Because it is susceptible to such an application, we also conclude that it suffers from substantial overbreadth, even if some of the purposes 995 is said to serve might constitutionally be protectable by an appropriate and narrower ordinance.

Although we would have thought it unnecessary to say so, it apparently deserves emphasis in the light of the dissent's reference to this court apologizing as to the result, that our Regret at the use appellees plan to make of their rights is not in any sense an Apology for upholding the First Amendment. The result we have reached is dictated by the fundamental proposition that if these civil rights are to remain vital for all, they must protect not only those society deems acceptable, but also those whose ideas it quite justifiably rejects and despises.

[**Ruling**] The judgment of the district court is

AFFIRMED.

Points to Consider

1. Lawyer for Frank Collin.

The case for NSPA was argued in the court of appeals by David Goldberger of the ACLU. Due to its involvement in the case, the ACLU lost 15 percent of its membership. Goldberger later argued a First Amendment case before the U.S. Supreme Court involving anonymous speech—*McIntyre v. Ohio Elections Commission* (1995).

2. Supreme Court denies review.

The Village of Skokie appealed to the U.S. Supreme Court. In October 1978, the Court declined to review the matter. Justices Harry Blackmun and Byron White dissented and voted to hear the case. Blackmun opened with strong words: "It is a matter of regret for me that the Court denies certiorari in this case, for this is litigation that rests upon critical, disturbing, and emotional facts, and the issues cut down to the very heart of the First Amendment." He argued that "the present case afford[ed] the Court an opportunity to consider whether, in the context of the facts that this record appears to present, there is no limit whatsoever to the exercise of free speech"—noting that "[t]here indeed may be no such limit."

3. Did the Nazis ever march in Skokie?

Even though Collin prevailed before the 7th Circuit, the planned march never took place in the Village of Skokie. Instead, Collin and about 20 of his followers marched in a Chicago park on July 9, 1978. Collin explained that his purpose had been to engage in "pure agitation."

4. Intentional infliction of emotional distress.

One of the arguments advanced by the Village of Skokie was that allowing the Nazis to march in Skokie would cause psychological trauma on many of the village's residents. This is akin to a claim that the hate speech will cause intentional infliction of emotional distress—a claim that requires a plaintiff to show that a defendant engaged in intentional or reckless conduct that was outrageous or beyond the bounds of social decency. The federal appeals court emphasized that the expression in question was protected speech.

Note that the Supreme Court set a high bar for recovering damages for intentional infliction of emotional distress nearly a decade later in *Hustler Magazine Co. v. Falwell* (1988), which we will discuss in Chapter 9.

5. Beauharnais v. Illinois (1952)

The village argued that it could ban the hateful expression of the Nazis based on *Beauharnais v. Illinois.* In that decision, the Supreme Court ruled 5–4 that Joseph

Beauharnais could be punished under a group libel law for disseminating racist literature that denigrated African Americans. In the majority opinion, Justice Felix Frankfurter reasoned that the Illinois group libel law could prevent disorder and breaches of the peace. Justice Hugo Black wrote a powerful dissent, accusing the majority of upholding the discredited notion of "seditious libel."

6. What would you have done in response to the proposed Nazi march in Skokie?
One wisdom you'll hear First Amendment advocates repeat time and time again is that the answer to speech you don't like is more speech. With that in mind, think about what you would do to oppose hateful speech or other ideas you find distasteful. Consider how LGBTQ activists in the city of Philadelphia responded in 2016 when the Westboro Baptist Church came to protest one of the city's LGBTQ health providers, the Mazzoni Center. Instead of calling for the silencing of the Westboro members, the activist threw a pride parade—dwarfing the handful of Westboro members with their large numbers, vibrant displays, and music.

WHAT ABOUT BURNING A CROSS?

In the early 1990s, the U.S. Supreme Court examined another interesting case involving hateful expression. It concerned the actions of a juvenile named Robert Alan Victoria (referred to by his initials, R.A.V., as is common in court proceedings involving juveniles), who burned a cross in the yard of the Jones family, the only African-American family in the neighborhood. Instead of charging the youth with terroristic threats, vandalism, trespassing, or other criminal charges, prosecutors charged him under the city of St. Paul's bias-motivated ordinance:

> Whoever places on public or private property, a symbol, object, appellation, characterization or graffiti, including, but not limited to, a burning cross or Nazi swastika, which one knows or has reasonable grounds to know arouses anger, alarm or resentment in others on the basis of race, color, creed, religion or gender commits disorderly conduct and shall be guilty of a misdemeanor.

Victoria's attorney contended that the ordinance violated the First Amendment. The Supreme Court agreed unanimously in *R.A.V. v. City of St. Paul* (1992), though the justices disagreed on the rationale.

Writing for the majority, Justice Antonin Scalia reasoned that the law violated the First Amendment because it targeted only certain types of fighting words—one that "arouses anger, alarm or resentment" on certain bases. Scalia wrote that the "ordinance goes even beyond mere content discrimination, to actual viewpoint discrimination."

"Let there be no mistake about our belief that burning a cross in someone's front yard is reprehensible," Scalia concluded. "But St. Paul has sufficient means at its disposal to prevent such behavior without adding the First Amendment to the fire."

While the Court invalidated St. Paul's ordinance, more than a decade later, the Supreme Court upheld the bulk of a Virginia law that outlawed cross burnings done with an "intent to intimidate" others. In *Virginia v. Black* (2003), the Court reasoned that those cross burnings done to intimidate others were a form of a true threat and, thus, such conduct could be criminalized without violating the First Amendment.

Note: The attorney who represented Victoria was Edward J. Cleary, who was a public defender at the time. Cleary later became a judge on the Minnesota Court of Appeals, where he currently serves as Chief Judge. He wrote a book about the case entitled *Beyond the Burning Cross: A Landmark Case of Race, Censorship and the First Amendment* (1995).

Protected Hate Speech or Hate Crime?

One year after its historic decision in *R.A.V. v. City of St. Paul*, the Supreme Court upheld a Wisconsin hate crime law that allowed for the increase of penalties if the perpetrator selected his victim because of race, sex, age, or other protected criteria. The case involved a 19-year-old African-American defendant named Todd Mitchell, who allegedly selected 14-year-old victim Greggory Reddick because Reddick was white.

Evidence in the case reflected that Mitchell and some friends had finished discussing a scene from the civil rights movie *Mississippi Burning* where several white men beat a young African-American boy. When Mitchell saw Reddick across the street, he allegedly said: "You all want to fuck somebody up? There goes a white boy; go get him." Mitchell and others proceeded to severely beat Reddick.

Mitchell faced prosecution under the state's penalty enhancement law—a type of hate crime law that allows for the increase of criminal punishment for selecting a victim because of race. Mitchell argued that the law violated his First Amendment rights because it punished him for a thought crime.

The Supreme Court disagreed in *Wisconsin v. Mitchell* (1993), distinguishing between speech and conduct. "The First Amendment, moreover, does not prohibit the evidentiary use of speech to establish the elements of a crime or to prove motive or intent," wrote Chief Justice William Rehnquist for a unanimous Court.

6.

Sexual Expression & Moralism

Now we talk about sex on the radio and video shows
Many will know, anything goes
Let's tell it like it is, and how it could be
How it was, and of course, how it should be
Those who think it's dirty have a choice
Pick up the needle, press pause, or turn the radio off.
　　　　　　　　　　—Salt-N-Pepa, "Let's Talk About Sex"

SALT-N-PEPA'S "Let's Talk About Sex" arrived on America's airwaves in 1991—
and it was a hit, earning the hip-hop trio a Grammy nomination and selling more
than 500,000 copies nationwide. The song's success is remarkable given the fact
that just a few decades earlier, its frank lyrics about sexuality would almost certainly have been subject to censorship. While perhaps tame by today's standards,
Salt-N-Pepa's "dirty" rhymes most certainly wouldn't have reached the public in
1891 or 1951, and perhaps not in 1971, either.

That's because sexual expression has long served as a legal, moral, and cultural battleground. Over the years, would-be censors from both the left and the
right have sought to restrict and punish sexual expression in the United States,
whether in the form of novels, paintings, movies, records, or websites. Very few
subjects engender more calls for censorship than sex.

This is not surprising given how central sexuality is to the human experience.
As evidenced by ancient texts from the *Bhagavad Gita* to the Bible, our intense
fascination with sex is hardly new. Justice William Brennan articulated this point
in *Roth v. United States* (1957):

> Sex, a great and mysterious motive force in human life, has indisputably
> been a subject of absorbing interest to mankind through the ages; it is
> one of the vital problems of human interest and public concern.

Accordingly, the seemingly infinite variety of ways in which we experience sexuality inevitably provokes passionate debate about how we may (or may not) express ourselves on the subject.

Here in the United States, that debate centers around the First Amendment and its evolving protection for sexual expression. Over the decades, judges, attorneys, artists, actors, retailers, broadcasters, parents, advocacy groups, and the general public have wrestled with difficult questions about free speech and sex:

- Is all sexual expression fair game, or should there be limits on the sexual content we may say, see, or hear?
- What is "obscenity," anyways? Is it the same as "indecency"?
- What about moral or social considerations—should our neighbors' attitudes about sex determine what sexual content we may access?
- What about the impact of sexual content on children?
- Does the Internet change our understanding of what speech should be protected?

No easy answers here. And what answers we do have from the courts could fill their own book. As you'll read in the opinions and commentary below, determining the boundaries of the First Amendment's protection for sexual expression has been an exceedingly difficult task—and every technological, social, or artistic advance reminds us that it may never be completed.

To get a sense of how the law governs sexual expression today, we'll first review the restrictions in place nearly 150 years ago.

THE *HICKLIN* TEST & THE COMSTOCK ERA

Regina v. Hicklin

Early American regulation of sexual expression took its direction from legal reasoning imported across the Atlantic Ocean. In 1868, an English judge issued a Victorian-era test for obscenity that came to be cited by American jurists evaluating the legality of sexual expression for many decades thereafter.

Sir Alexander Cockburn, chief justice of the Court of Queen's Bench, announced the Crown's operative definition of obscenity in *Regina v. Hicklin* (1868), a case involving an anti-Catholic publication. The pamphlet, which featured a characteristically unwieldy Victorian title (*The Confessional Unmasked: Shewing the Depravity of the Romish Priesthood, the Iniquity of the Confessional, and the Questions Put to Females in Confession*), was seized and destroyed under the Obscene Publications Act passed in 1857.

Chief Justice Cockburn ruled that the pamphlet "was, to a considerable extent, an obscene publication...calculated to produce a pernicious effect in depraving and debauching the minds of the persons into whose hands it might come." Cockburn reasoned that the publisher's intent (here, to "expose the errors and practices of the Roman Catholic Church") was immaterial, nor was he moved by the publisher's argument that "a great many publications of high repute" might also be punished as "immodest" and "immoral." Instead, Cockburn insisted, "[t]he law says, you shall not publish an obscene work"—and that was that. So what did the court consider obscene?

According to the *Hicklin* test, a publication is obscene if it contains any material that tends to "deprave and corrupt those whose minds are open to such immoral influences, and into whose hands a publication of this sort may fall."

Anthony Comstock

Back in the United States, a young Union Army veteran named Anthony Comstock championed a similar "moral" view of obscenity. While working at the Young Men's Christian Association, Comstock met New York City philanthropists who shared his moral disdain for American society's changing views of marriage and reproduction. With their support, he founded the New York Society for the Suppression of Vice, which advocated for laws targeting a wide range of sexual speech and conduct. Working with law enforcement, Comstock mounted campaigns against saloons, booksellers, abortion providers, and sellers of contraceptives and sex toys, among other "immoral" targets.

Comstock's crusading found a powerful audience. In 1873, he successfully lobbied Congress to pass "An Act for the Suppression of Trade in, and Circulation of, Obscene Literature and Articles of Immoral Use"—better known simply as the Comstock Law. As amended in 1876, the law prohibited the mailing of:

> *Every obscene, lewd, or lascivious book, pamphlet, picture, paper, writing, print or other publication of an indecent character*, and every article or thing designed or intended for the prevention of conception or procuring of abortion, and every article or thing intended or adapted for any indecent or immoral use, and every written or printed card, circular, book, pamphlet, advertisement, or notice of any kind giving information, directly or indirectly, where, or how, or of whom, or by what means, any of the hereinbefore mentioned matters, articles, or things may be obtained or made, and *every letter upon the envelope of which, or postal card upon which, indecent, lewd, obscene, or lascivious delineations, epithets, terms, or language may be written or printed*...[emphases added].

The law's broad ban was influential, and its effects were widely felt. All states eventually passed their own legislation inspired by the Comstock Law, and Comstock himself was named a special agent for the U.S. Postal Services. In this position, which he held until his death in 1915, he was authorized to inspect the mail, destroy publications, and arrest suspected violators—making him a powerful censor.

Though backed by the United States Government, Comstock's vigorous moralizing and aggressive prosecution earned him many critics, including, among many others, playwright George Bernard Shaw and feminist activists Margaret Sanger and Victoria Woodhull. The puritanical zeal of "Comstockery" was unsparing and cruel; Comstock boasted that fifteen subjects of his investigations had committed suicide.

Here's Comstock in his own words, from his book *Morals Versus Art*, on the relationship between morals and artistic sexual expression:

> In the guise of art, this foe of moral purity comes in its most insidious, fascinating and seductive form.
>
> Obscenity may be produced by the pen of the ready writer in prose; it may come upon the flowery wing of poetry; or, as in this instance, by the gilded touch of the brush of the man of genius in art. Prose, poetry and art all have been employed to charm and entrance the human mind and to picture beautiful and seductive things. They have each of them also been prostituted to the production of the most base, obscene and lewd ideas. There is no conflict, however, between either, of prose, poetry or art, and morals or law, until some person prostitutes some one of them to reproduce the impure conceptions of the individual mind.

MAILING OBSCENITY

The Victorian conception of morality empowered by the *Hicklin* test and Comstock's crusading eventually lost significant social, political, and legal support. By the 1950s, as social mores evolved and new telecommunications media emerged, the U.S. Supreme Court found itself forced to wrestle anew with the question of sexual expression and "obscenity." If Hicklin's broad, subjective prohibition of "immoral influences" was no longer persuasive or practical, then what would replace it?

In explicitly rejecting the *Hicklin* test in the case below, the Court began to figure out its answer.

OPINION

Roth v. United States

(Abridged.)

354 U.S. 476 (1957)
Vote: 6–3

JUSTICE BRENNAN delivered the opinion of the Court.

[**Issue**] The constitutionality of a criminal obscenity statute is the question in each of these cases. In *Roth*, the primary constitutional question is whether the federal obscenity statute violates the provision of the First Amendment that "Congress shall make no law…abridging the freedom of speech, or of the press." In *Alberts*, the primary constitutional question is whether the obscenity provisions of the California Penal Code invade the freedoms of speech and press as they may be incorporated in the liberty protected from state action by the Due Process Clause of the Fourteenth Amendment.

[**Facts of *Roth***] Samuel Roth conducted a business in New York in the publication and sale of books, photographs and magazines. He used circulars and advertising matter to solicit sales. He was convicted by a jury in the District Court for the Southern District of New York upon 4 counts of a 26-count indictment charging him with mailing obscene circulars and advertising, and an obscene book, in violation of the federal obscenity statute.

[**Facts of *Alberts***] Alberts conducted a mail-order business from Los Angeles. He was convicted by the Judge of the Municipal Court of the Beverly Hills Judicial District (having waived a jury trial) under a misdemeanor complaint which charged him with lewdly keeping for sale obscene and indecent books, and with writing, composing and publishing an obscene advertisement of them, in violation of the California Penal Code. The conviction was affirmed by the Appellate Department of the Superior Court of the State of California in and for the County of Los Angeles. We noted probable jurisdiction.

[**Issue restated**] The dispositive question is whether obscenity is utterance within the area of protected speech and press. Although this is the first time the question has been squarely presented to this Court, either under the First Amendment or under the Fourteenth Amendment, expressions found in numerous opinions indicate that this Court has always assumed that obscenity is not protected by the freedoms of speech and press.

[**Analysis**] In light of this history, it is apparent that the unconditional phrasing of the First Amendment was not intended to protect every utterance. At the time of the adoption of the First Amendment, obscenity law was not as fully developed as libel law, but there is sufficiently contemporaneous evidence to show that obscenity, too, was outside the protection intended for speech and press.

The protection given speech and press was fashioned to assure unfettered interchange of ideas for the bringing about of political and social changes desired by the people.

[**Sex v. obscenity**] All ideas having even the slightest redeeming social importance—unorthodox ideas, controversial ideas, even ideas hateful to the prevailing climate of opinion—have the full protection of the guaranties, unless excludable because they encroach upon the limited area of more important interests. But implicit in the history of the First Amendment is the rejection of obscenity as utterly without redeeming social importance. This is the same judgment expressed by this Court in *Chaplinsky v. New Hampshire* (1942):

> "...There are certain well-defined and narrowly limited classes of speech, the prevention and punishment of which have never been thought to raise any Constitutional problem. *These include the lewd and obscene....It has been well observed that such utterances are no essential part of any exposition of ideas, and are of such slight social value as a step to truth that any benefit that may be derived from them is clearly outweighed by the social interest in order and morality....*" (Emphasis added.)

We hold that obscenity is not within the area of constitutionally protected speech or press.

It is strenuously urged that these obscenity statutes offend the constitutional guaranties because they punish incitation to impure sexual *thoughts*, not shown to be related to any overt antisocial conduct which is or may be incited in the persons stimulated to such *thoughts*. In *Roth*, the trial judge instructed the jury: "The words 'obscene, lewd and lascivious' as used in the law, signify that form of immorality which has relation to sexual impurity and has a tendency to excite lustful *thoughts*." (Emphasis added.) It is insisted that the constitutional guaranties are violated because convictions may be had without proof either that obscene material will perceptibly create a clear and present danger of antisocial conduct, or will probably induce its recipients to such conduct. But, in light of our holding that obscenity is not protected speech, the complete answer to this argument is in the holding of this Court in *Beauharnais v. Illinois* (1952):

> "Libelous utterances not being within the area of constitutionally protected speech, it is unnecessary, either for us or for the State courts, to consider the issues behind the phrase 'clear and present danger.' Certainly no one would contend that obscene speech, for example, may be punished only upon a showing of such circumstances. Libel, as we have seen, is in the same class."

However, sex and obscenity are not synonymous. Obscene material is material which deals with sex in a manner appealing to prurient interest. The portrayal of sex (e.g., in art, literature and scientific works) is not itself sufficient reason to deny material the constitutional protection of freedom of speech and press. Sex, a great and mysterious motivational force in human life, has indisputably been a subject of absorbing interest to mankind through the ages; it is one of the vital problems of human interest and public concern.

The fundamental freedoms of speech and press have contributed greatly to the development and well-being of our free society and are indispensable to its continued growth. Ceaseless vigilance is the watchword to prevent their erosion by Congress or by the States. The door barring federal and state intrusion into this area cannot be left ajar; it must be kept tightly closed and opened only the slightest crack necessary to prevent encroachment upon more important interests. It is therefore vital that the standards for judging obscenity safeguard the protection of freedom of speech and press for material which does not treat sex in a manner appealing to prurient interest.

[**Rejecting *Hicklin***] The early leading standard of obscenity allowed material to be judged merely by the effect of an isolated excerpt upon particularly susceptible persons. *Regina v. Hicklin*, [1868]. Some American courts adopted this standard but later decisions have rejected it and substituted this test: whether to the average person, applying contemporary community standards, the dominant theme of the material taken as a whole appeals to prurient interest. The *Hicklin* test, judging obscenity by the effect of isolated passages upon the most susceptible persons, might well encompass material legitimately treating with sex, and so it must be rejected as unconstitutionally restrictive of the freedoms of speech and press. On the other hand, the substituted standard provides safeguards adequate to withstand the charge of constitutional infirmity.

[**Accepting *Roth* test**] In *Roth*, the trial judge instructed the jury as follows:

> "The test in each case is [1] the effect of the book, picture or publication considered as a whole, not upon any particular class, but upon all those whom it is likely to reach. In other words, you determine its [2] impact upon the average person in the community. [3] The books, pictures and circulars must be judged as a whole, in their entire context, and you are not to consider detached or separate portions in reaching a conclusion. You judge the circulars, pictures and publications which have been put in evidence by [4] present-day standards of the community. You may ask yourselves does it offend the common conscience of the community by present-day standards."

[**Ruling**] In summary, then, we hold that these statutes, applied according to the proper standard for judging obscenity, do not offend constitutional safeguards against convictions based upon protected material, or fail to give men in acting adequate notice of what is prohibited.

The judgments are

Affirmed.

Points to Consider

1. The aftermath.

The Court's decision in *Roth* had an immediate impact on the obscenity cases winding their way through the appellate courts. One clear example is presented by the *One, Inc.*, case discussed earlier in Chapter 4. Review the stark difference between the Ninth Circuit's application of *Hicklin* to those facts in 1957 and the Supreme Court's reliance on its opinion in *Roth* one year later:

- *One, Inc. v. Olesen*, 241 F.2d 772 (9th Cir., Feb. 27, 1957), *rehearing denied*, Apr. 12, 1957: "The test for obscenity is whether the tendency of the matter is to deprave and corrupt the morals of those whose minds are open to such influence and into whose hands a publication of this sort may fall."

- *One, Inc. v. Olesen* (1958): "The petition for writ of *certiorari* is granted and the judgment of the United States Court of Appeals for the Ninth Circuit is reversed."

2. Poetry on trial.

Not long after *Roth* came down, a trial court in San Francisco had to decide if a publisher and poet, Lawrence Ferlinghetti, could be criminally prosecuted for publishing and selling Allen Ginsberg's poem "Howl." Why? It contained "dirty" words. In a seminal opinion, the trial judge ruled that the poem was protected under the First Amendment as interpreted in *Roth v. United States*.

3. Comedy on trial.

Before the Supreme Court declared a difference between obscenity and indecency, the two were treated the same. Thus, the comedian Lenny Bruce was prosecuted for obscenity in San Francisco, Chicago, Los Angeles, and New York for using colorful language in comedy clubs for adults. Following *Roth*, either Bruce was found not guilty or his convictions were reversed on appeal. His New York conviction, however, stood since he died before he could appeal it. In 2003, the Governor of New York posthumously pardoned Lenny Bruce.

ROTH DIDN'T SETTLE THE QUESTION OF OBSCENITY

While clearer than *Hicklin*, in practice, the *Roth* decision didn't resolve the Court's struggle to produce a clear definition of obscenity. As detailed in this excerpt from noted First Amendment lawyer Robert Corn-Revere, the task splintered the Court:

> Justice Harlan noted that the 13 obscenity cases at the Supreme Court between 1957 and 1968 produced a total of 55 separate opinions, and that the quest to find a coherent test for obscenity had only "produced a variety of views among the members of the Court unmatched in any other course of constitutional adjudication."…
>
> If at least five justices, applying their respective tests, decided that the material was not obscene, the conviction was reversed without opinion, typically with the unadorned statement: "The petition for a writ of certiorari is granted and the judgment of the [court below] is reversed." By

1964, Chief Justice Warren complained that most of the Court's obscenity decisions since *Roth* had been issued without opinion. Nevertheless, the practice became more prominent after the Court's 1967 decision in *Redrup v. New York*, in which the Court summarily reversed convictions in three consolidated cases. The Court issued 31 similar reversals between 1967 and 1971, and countless other decisions denying review and upholding lower court convictions.

The result was a confusing maze of rulings with no suitable legal test. As Corn-Revere observed:

> The practice was wholly unsatisfactory for many reasons, not the least of which is that it turned the justices into censors of last resort. Justice Harlan complained that the members of the Court were tied to "the absurd business of perusing and viewing the miserable stuff that pours into the Court." Justice Brennan observed that the material may have varying degrees of social importance, but complained "it is hardly a source of edification to the members of this Court who are compelled to view it before passing on its obscenity." Justice Douglas, on the other hand, who never subscribed to the majority position that obscenity could be denied constitutional protection, always refused to look at the material because, he said, "I have thought the First Amendment made it unconstitutional for me to act as a censor."

Corn-Revere also noted that most of the justices screened the material in question—surely a bizarre scene for all involved. In their 1979 book *The Brethren*, Bob Woodward and Scott Armstrong describe an aging Justice Harlan reviewing the movies at issue:

> During his later years, Harlan watched the films from the first row, a few feet from the screen, able only to make out the general outlines. His clerk or another Justice would describe the action. "By Jove," Harlan would exclaim. "Extraordinary."

The inherent subjectivity of the justices' review was famously articulated by Justice Potter Stewart in his concurring opinion in *Jacobellis v. Ohio* (1964):

> I shall not today attempt further to define the kinds of material I understand to be embraced within that shorthand description; and perhaps I

could never succeed in intelligibly doing so. But *I know it when I see it* [emphasis added], and the motion picture involved in this case is not that.

That motion picture was *Les Amants*, a French film screened by Nico Jacobellis, the manager of the Heights Art Theatre in Cleveland Heights, Ohio. For showing the film, Jacobellis was fined $2,500 in total—roughly $20,000 after inflation in 2018 dollars—and "was sentenced to the workhouse if the fines were not paid."

THE "SEX ORGIES ILLUSTRATED" AD CASE

Imagine opening up your mailbox and finding, in between all of the regular spam mail (credit card applications, new customer deals for the Internet provider you already use, and coupons for the new takeout restaurants down the street), an advertisement for "adult" content. The unsolicited ad contains explicit drawings of individuals engaging in sex.

While finding pornographic images in your mail may seem far-fetched, that's exactly what happened to certain California residents in 1973. After a recipient of the advertisement complained to the police, the individual responsible for the mass mailing, Marvin Miller, was convicted for distributing obscenity under California state law. The Supreme Court case that followed is below.

OPINION

Miller v. California

(Abridged.)

413 U.S. 15 (1973)
Vote: 5–4

CHIEF JUSTICE BURGER delivered the opinion of the Court.

[**Facts**] Appellant conducted a mass mailing campaign to advertise the sale of illustrated books, euphemistically called "adult" material. After a jury trial, he was convicted of a misdemeanor, by knowingly distributing obscene matter, and the Appellate Department, Superior Court of California summarily affirmed the judgment without opinion. Appellant's conviction was specifically based on his conduct in causing five unsolicited advertising brochures to be sent through the mail in an envelope addressed to a restaurant in Newport Beach, California. The envelope was opened by the manager of the restaurant and his mother. They had not requested the brochures; they complained to the police.

The brochures advertise four books entitled *Intercourse, Man-Woman, Sex Orgies Illustrated*, and *An Illustrated History of Pornography*, and a film entitled "Marital Intercourse." While the brochures contain some descriptive printed material, primarily they consist of pictures and drawings very explicitly depicting men and women in groups of two or more engaging in a variety of sexual activities, with genitals often prominently displayed.

[**Issue**] This case involves the application of a State's criminal obscenity statute to a situation in which sexually explicit materials have been thrust by aggressive sales action upon unwilling recipients who had in no way indicated any desire to receive such materials. This Court has recognized that the States have a legitimate interest in prohibiting dissemination or exhibition of obscene material when the mode of dissemination carries with it a significant danger of offending the sensibilities of unwilling recipients or of exposure to juveniles. It is in this context that we are called on to define the standards which must be used to identify obscene material that a State may regulate without infringing on the First Amendment as applicable to the States through the Fourteenth Amendment.

[Obscenity holdings following *Roth*] Apart from the initial formulation in the *Roth* case, no majority of the Court has at any given time been able to agree on a standard to determine what constitutes obscene, pornographic material subject to regulation under the States' police power. See, *e. g., Redrup v. New York* (1967). We have seen "a variety of views among the members of the Court unmatched in any other course of constitutional adjudication." *Interstate Circuit, Inc. v. Dallas* (1968). This is not remarkable, for in the area of freedom of speech and press the courts must always remain sensitive to any infringement on genuinely serious literary, artistic, political, or scientific expression. This is an area in which there are few eternal verities.

[**Analysis**] This much has been categorically settled by the Court, that obscene material is unprotected by the First Amendment. We acknowledge, however, the inherent dangers of undertaking to regulate any form of expression. State statutes designed to regulate obscene materials must be carefully limited. As a result, we now confine the permissible scope of such regulation to works which depict or describe sexual conduct. That conduct must be specifically defined by the applicable state law, as written or authoritatively construed. A state offense must also be limited to works which, taken as a whole, appeal to the prurient interest in sex, which portray sexual conduct in a patently offensive way, and which, taken as a whole, do not have serious literary, artistic, political, or scientific value.

[***Miller* test**] The basic guidelines for the trier of fact must be: (a) whether "the average person, applying contemporary community standards" would find that the work, taken as a whole, appeals to the prurient interest; *Kois v. Wisconsin* (1972) quoting *Roth v. United States* (1957); (b) whether the work depicts or describes, in a patently offensive way, sexual conduct specifically defined by the applicable state law; and (c) whether the work, taken as a whole, lacks serious literary, artistic, political, or scientific value.

[**Serious merit or value**] Sex and nudity may not be exploited without limit by films or pictures exhibited or sold in places of public accommodation any more than live sex and nudity can be exhibited or sold without limit in such public places. At a minimum, prurient, patently offensive depiction or description of sexual conduct must have serious literary, artistic, political, or scientific value to merit First Amendment protection. For example, medical books for the education of physicians and related personnel necessarily use graphic illustrations and descriptions of human anatomy.

Under the holdings announced today, no one will be subject to prosecution for the sale or exposure of obscene materials unless these materials depict or describe patently offensive "hard core" sexual conduct specifically defined by the regulating state law, as written or construed. We are satisfied that these specific prerequisites will provide fair notice to a dealer in such materials that his public and commercial activities may bring prosecution.

["**Community standards**"] Under a National Constitution, fundamental First Amendment limitations on the powers of the States do not vary from community to community, but this does not mean that there are, or should or can be, fixed, uniform national standards of precisely what appeals to the "prurient interest" or is "patently offensive." These are essentially questions of fact, and our Nation is simply too big and too diverse for this Court to reasonably expect that such standards could be articulated for all 50 States in a single formulation, even assuming the prerequisite consensus exists. To require a State to structure obscenity proceedings around evidence of a *national* "community standard" would be an exercise in futility.

It is neither realistic nor constitutionally sound to read the First Amendment as requiring that the people of Maine or Mississippi accept public depiction of conduct found tolerable in Las Vegas, or New York City. People in different States vary in their tastes and attitudes, and this diversity is not to be strangled by the absolutism of imposed uniformity.

[**Answering the dissent's charge of "repression"**] The dissenting Justices sound the alarm of repression. But, in our view, to equate the free and robust exchange of ideas and political debate with commercial exploitation of obscene material demeans the grand conception of the First Amendment and its high purposes in the historic struggle for freedom. The First Amendment protects works which, taken as a whole, have serious literary, artistic, political, or scientific value, regardless of whether the government or a majority of the people approve of the ideas these works represent. "The protection given speech and press was fashioned to assure unfettered interchange of *ideas* for the bringing about of political and social changes desired by the people," *Roth* v. *United States* (emphasis added). But the public portrayal of hard-core sexual conduct for its own sake, and for the ensuing commercial gain, is a different matter.

There is no evidence, empirical or historical, that the stern 19th century American censorship of public distribution and display of material relating to sex, see *Roth* v. *United States*, in any way limited or affected expression of serious literary, artistic, political, or scientific ideas. On the contrary, it is beyond any question that the era following Thomas Jefferson to Theodore Roosevelt was an "extraordinarily vigorous period," not just in economics and politics, but in *belles lettres* and in "the outlying fields of social and political philosophies." We do not see the harsh hand of censorship of ideas—good or bad, sound or unsound—and "repression" of political liberty lurking in every state regulation of commercial exploitation of human interest in sex.

One can concede that the "sexual revolution" of recent years may have had useful byproducts in striking layers of prudery from a subject long irrationally kept from needed ventilation. But it does not follow that no regulation of patently offensive "hard core" materials is needed or permissible; civilized people do not allow unregulated access to heroin because it is a derivative of medicinal morphine.

Vacated and remanded.

Points to Consider

1. Defining community standards.

The *Miller* ruling still left unanswered questions. For example, take this observation from the majority opinion: "It is neither realistic nor constitutionally sound to read the First Amendment as requiring that the people of Maine or Mississippi accept public depiction of conduct found tolerable in Las Vegas or New York City." What does this distinction mean in practice? Is the notion of "community standards" still relevant in the Internet age?

2. The dissent.

Remember, *Miller* was a 5–4 ruling. Writing in dissent in another obscenity case issued the same day as *Miller*, Justice Brennan all but threw up his hands in annoyance. His frustration with the Court's search for a workable definition of obscenity is palpable:

> I am forced to conclude that the concept of "obscenity" cannot be defined with sufficient specificity and clarity to provide fair notice to persons who create and distribute sexually oriented materials, to prevent substantial erosion of protected speech as a byproduct of the attempt to suppress unprotected speech, and to avoid very costly institutional harms.

Justice William O. Douglas voiced similar concerns in his own *Miller* dissent. "The use of the standard 'offensive' gives authority to government that cuts the very vitals out of the First Amendment," he wrote. "As is intimated by the Court's opinion, the materials before us may be garbage. But so is much of what is said in political campaigns, in the daily press, on TV, or over the radio. By reason of the First Amendment—and solely because of it—speakers and publishers have not been threatened or subdued because their thoughts and ideas may be 'offensive' to some."

Do you agree with the dissent's criticisms? Can "obscenity" be usefully defined, or is the consideration of it an invitation to censorship? In short, does the *Miller* test work?

3. The Internet.

Has the Internet functionally legitimated most types of obscene expression (save for child pornography, discussed below)? Given the post-*Miller* communications technologies, does the law of obscenity matter much anymore?

SEXUAL EXPRESSION AND THE CREATION OF NEW UNPROTECTED CATEGORIES OF SPEECH

The Special Case of Child Pornography

Nine years after *Miller*, the Supreme Court confronted the unique problem of child pornography in 1982's *New York v. Ferber*. The defendant, the proprietor of an adult bookstore in Manhattan, had been found guilty of violating a New York state statute that criminalized, among other acts, selling recordings of "any performance which includes sexual conduct by a child less than sixteen years of age."

The New York Court of Appeals found that the statute violated the First Amendment—but when the case reached the Supreme Court, all nine justices disagreed, "persuaded that the States are entitled to greater leeway in the regulation of pornographic depictions of children."

What was the Court's reasoning? Simply put, children are different. Because the "evil to be restricted so overwhelmingly outweighs the expressive interests, if any, at stake," and because the material "bears so heavily and pervasively on the welfare of children engaged in its production," the Court had little difficulty in finding that the First Amendment's protections do not extend to child pornography.

The Court explained its rationale by noting: (1) the compelling state interest in prohibiting child pornography; (2) that child pornography continues to hurt children involved in its production indefinitely; (3) that advertising and selling child pornography means a continuing market for its illegal production; and (4) the "exceedingly modest, if not *de minimis*" literary, scientific, or educational value in the material.

What About "Virtual" Child Pornography?

In *Ashcroft v. Free Speech Coalition* (2002), the Supreme Court considered the constitutionality of the federal Child Pornography Prevention Act of 1996, which prohibited computer-generated "virtual child pornography" involving images of adults digitally altered to look like children engaged in sexual activity. The Court found that the Act violated the First Amendment by "prohibit[ing] speech despite its serious literary, artistic, political, or scientific value." Justice Kennedy penned the majority opinion:

> Both themes—teenage sexual activity and the sexual abuse of children—have inspired countless literary works. William Shakespeare created the most famous pair of teenage lovers, one of whom is just 13 years of age. See *Romeo and Juliet*, act I, sc. 2, l. 9 ("She hath not seen the change of fourteen years"). In the drama, Shakespeare portrays the

relationship as something splendid and innocent, but not juvenile. The work has inspired no less than 40 motion pictures, some of which suggest that the teenagers consummated their relationship. *E.g., Romeo and Juliet* (B. Luhrmann director, 1996). Shakespeare may not have written sexually explicit scenes for the Elizabethan audience, but were modern directors to adopt a less conventional approach, that fact alone would not compel the conclusion that the work was obscene.

Contemporary movies pursue similar themes. Last year's Academy Awards featured the movie, *Traffic*, which was nominated for Best Picture....The film portrays a teenager, identified as a 16-year-old, who becomes addicted to drugs. The viewer sees the degradation of her addiction, which in the end leads her to a filthy room to trade sex for drugs. The year before, *American Beauty* won the Academy Award for Best Picture....In the course of the movie, a teenage girl engages in sexual relations with her teenage boyfriend, and another yields herself to the gratification of a middle-aged man. The film also contains a scene where, although the movie audience understands the act is not taking place, one character believes he is watching a teenage boy performing a sexual act on an older man.

Our society, like other cultures, has empathy and enduring fascination with the lives and destinies of the young. Art and literature express the vital interest we all have in the formative years we ourselves once knew, when wounds can be so grievous, disappointment so profound, and mistaken choices so tragic, but when moral acts and self-fulfillment are still in reach. Whether or not the films we mention violate the CPPA, they explore themes within the wide sweep of the statute's prohibitions. If these films, or hundreds of others of lesser note that explore those subjects, contain a single graphic depiction of sexual activity within the statutory definition, the possessor of the film would be subject to severe punishment without inquiry into the work's redeeming value. This is inconsistent with an essential First Amendment rule: The artistic merit of a work does not depend on the presence of a single explicit scene.... *For this reason, and the others we have noted, the CPPA cannot be read to prohibit obscenity, because it lacks the required link between its prohibitions and the affront to community standards prohibited by the definition of obscenity* [emphasis added].

The *Ashcroft* Court was particularly cognizant of artistic merit. But in *Ferber*, the Court noted that "a work which, taken on the whole, contains serious literary, artistic, political, or scientific value may nevertheless embody the hardest core of child pornography." After all, "[i]t is irrelevant to the child [who has been abused] whether or not the material...has a literary, artistic, political or social value." How does *Ashcroft* square with that observation?

"Crush Videos" and New Exceptions to the First Amendment

The Court's holding in *Ferber* was also noteworthy because it announced an entire category of speech, child pornography, to lie beyond the First Amendment's protection—a very rare step. In 2010's *United States v. Stevens*, the Court reminded the government just how extraordinary such an action was.

Stevens involved a First Amendment challenge to a federal statute that banned "any...depiction" in which "a living animal is intentionally maimed, mutilated, tortured, wounded, or killed." The law was intended to target so-called "crush videos," which "depict women slowly crushing animals to death 'with their bare feet or while wearing high heeled shoes,' sometimes while 'talking to the animals in a kind of dominatrix patter' over '[t]he cries and squeals of the animals, obviously in great pain.'" The defendant had been convicted of violating the statute for selling videos depicting dogfights and dogs hunting wild boar.

The government argued that the federal statute "necessarily complies with the Constitution because the banned depictions of animal cruelty, as a class, are categorically unprotected by the First Amendment," but the Court disagreed.

Proclaiming that *Ferber* "cannot be taken as establishing a freewheeling authority to declare new categories of speech outside the scope of the First Amendment," the Court determined that the statute was overbroad. For example, the Court reasoned, the law's ban could extend to non-obscene material designed primarily for entertainment or recreation, like hunting magazines or videos. The government's assurances to the Court that it would use the law only to prosecute "extreme" cruelty were unavailing; as the Court wrote, "the First Amendment protects against the Government; it does not leave us at the mercy of *noblesse oblige*."

SEVEN DIRTY WORDS, INDECENCY, AND EXPLICIT BUT NON-OBSCENE EXPRESSION

Now that we've covered obscenity, child pornography, and "crush videos," you may be wondering about the really important issues: Why are curse words and nudity available only on premium cable channels? And what about regular old pornography—does it enjoy any special legal status? To answer these good questions, let's head back to the case law.

OPINION

FCC v. Pacifica Foundation

(Abridged.)

438 U.S. 726 (1978)
Vote: 5–4

JUSTICE STEVENS delivered the opinion of the Court.

[**Issue**] This case requires that we decide whether the Federal Communications Commission has any power to regulate a radio broadcast that is indecent but not obscene.

[**Facts**] A satiric humorist named George Carlin recorded a 12-minute monologue entitled "Filthy Words" before a live audience in a California theater. He began by referring to his thoughts about "the words you couldn't say on the public, ah, airwaves, um, the ones you definitely wouldn't say, ever." He proceeded to list those words and repeat them over and over again in a variety of colloquialisms. The transcript of the recording, which is appended to this opinion, indicates frequent laughter from the audience.

At about 2 o'clock in the afternoon on Tuesday, October 30, 1973, a New York radio station, owned by respondent Pacifica Foundation, broadcast the "Filthy Words" monologue. A few weeks later a man, who stated that he had heard the broadcast while driving with his young son, wrote a letter complaining to the Commission. He stated that, although he could perhaps understand the "record's being sold for private use, I certainly cannot understand the broadcast of same over the air that, supposedly, you control."

The complaint was forwarded to the station for comment. In its response, Pacifica explained that the monologue had been played during a program about contemporary society's attitude toward language and that, immediately before its broadcast, listeners had been advised that it included "sensitive language which might be regarded as offensive to some." Pacifica characterized George Carlin as "a significant social satirist" who "like Twain and Sahl before him, examines the language of ordinary people....Carlin is not mouthing obscenities, he is merely using words to satirize as harmless and essentially silly our attitudes towards those words." Pacifica stated that it was not aware of any other complaints about the broadcast.

[**The FCC's response**] On February 21, 1975, the Commission issued a declaratory order granting the complaint and holding that Pacifica "could have been the subject of administrative sanctions." The Commission concluded that certain words depicted sexual and excretory activities in a patently offensive manner, noted that they "were broadcast at a time when children were undoubtedly in the audience (i.e., in the early afternoon)," and that the prerecorded language, with these offensive words "repeated over and over," was "deliberately broadcast." In summary, the Commission stated: "We therefore hold that the language as broadcast was indecent and prohibited by [the law]."

[**Analysis**] In this case it is undisputed that the content of Pacifica's broadcast was "vulgar," "offensive," and "shocking." Because content of that character is not entitled to absolute constitutional protection under all circumstances, we must consider its context in order to determine whether the Commission's action was constitutionally permissible.

[**The power of broadcast**] First, the broadcast media have established a uniquely pervasive presence in the lives of all Americans. Patently offensive, indecent material presented over the airwaves confronts the citizen, not only in public, but also in the privacy of the home, where the individual's right to be left alone plainly outweighs the First Amendment rights of an intruder. *Rowan v. Post Office Dept* (1970). Because the broadcast audience is constantly tuning in and out, prior warnings cannot completely protect the listener or viewer from unexpected program content. To say that one may avoid further offense by turning off the radio when he hears indecent language is like saying that the remedy for an assault is to run away after the first blow. One may hang up on an indecent phone call, but that option does not give the caller a constitutional immunity or avoid a harm that has already taken place.

[**Impact on children**] Second, broadcasting is uniquely accessible to children, even those too young to read. Although Cohen's written message might have been incomprehensible to a first grader, Pacifica's broadcast could have enlarged a child's vocabulary in an instant. Other forms of offensive expression may be withheld from the young without restricting the expression at its source. Bookstores and motion picture theaters, for example, may be prohibited from making indecent material available to children. We held in *Ginsberg v. New York* (1968), that the government's interest in the "well-being of its youth" and in supporting "parents' claim to authority in their own household" justified the regulation of otherwise protected expression. The ease with which children may obtain access to broadcast material, coupled with the concerns recognized in *Ginsberg*, amply justify special treatment of indecent broadcasting.

[**Ruling**] It is appropriate, in conclusion, to emphasize the narrowness of our holding. This case does not involve a two-way radio conversation between a cab driver and a dispatcher, or a telecast of an Elizabethan comedy. We have not decided that an occasional expletive in either setting would justify any sanction or, indeed, that this broadcast would justify a criminal prosecution. The Commission's decision rested entirely on a nuisance rationale under which context is all-important. The concept requires consideration of a host of variables. The time of day was emphasized by the Commission. The content of the program in which the language is used will also affect the composition of the audience, and differences between radio, television, and perhaps closed-circuit transmissions, may also be relevant. As Mr. Justice Sutherland wrote, a "nuisance may be merely a right thing in the wrong place,—like a pig in the parlor instead of the barnyard." *Euclid v. Ambler Realty Co.* (1926). We simply hold that when the Commission finds that a pig has entered the parlor, the exercise of its regulatory power does not depend on proof that the pig is obscene.

The judgment of the Court of Appeals is reversed.

Points to Consider

1. *Changing the channel.*

What do you think of the majority's reasoning? Couldn't the parent have simply turned the radio dial? How persuasive does the Court's rationale strike you in today's media environment?

2. *The dissent.*

Is the majority opinion relying on certain assumptions about a given broadcast's audience? Justice William Brennan's dissent, joined by Justice Thurgood Marshall, makes the case:

> Yet there runs throughout the opinions of my Brothers POWELL and STEVENS another vein I find equally disturbing: a depressing inability to appreciate that in our land of cultural pluralism, there are many who

think, act, and talk differently from the Members of this Court, and who do not share their fragile sensibilities. It is only an acute ethnocentric myopia that enables the Court to approve the censorship of communications solely because of the words they contain.

"A word is not a crystal, transparent and unchanged, it is the skin of a living thought and may vary greatly in color and content according to the circumstances and the time in which it is used." *Towne v. Eisner* (1918). The words that the Court and the Commission find so unpalatable may be the stuff of everyday conversations in some, if not many, of the innumerable subcultures that compose this Nation. Academic research indicates that this is indeed the case....As one researcher concluded, "[words] generally considered obscene like 'bullshit' and 'fuck' are considered neither obscene nor derogatory in the [black] vernacular except in particular contextual situations and when used with certain intonations." C. Bins, "Toward an Ethnography of Contemporary African American Oral Poetry," Language and Linguistics Working Papers No. 5, p. 82 (Georgetown Univ. Press 1972)...

In confirming Carlin's prescience as a social commentator by the result it reaches today, the Court evidences an attitude toward the "seven dirty words" that many others besides Mr. Carlin and Pacifica might describe as "silly." Whether today's decision will similarly prove "harmless" remains to be seen. One can only hope that it will.

Did Justice Brennan's hope that the *Pacifica* ruling would prove "harmless" bear out?

PROTECTING AGAINST THE "HARMS" OF PORNOGRAPHY

The Court's holdings in both *Ferber* and *Pacifica* rely on a judicial desire to protect children from harm, albeit of different degrees. But what if a legislature, not the judicial branch, sought to protect not just children, but *adult* citizens, from the alleged harms of pornographic material?

Professor Catharine MacKinnon (a renowned feminist, scholar, lawyer, teacher and activist) authored the path-breaking *Sexual Harassment of Working Women: A Case of Sex Discrimination* in 1979. In 1983, the city of Indianapolis hired MacKinnon and Andrea Dworkin to draft an anti-pornography civil rights ordinance. The law defined pornography as a civil rights violation against women and allowed women who claimed harm from pornography to sue the producers and distributors for damages in civil court. After the city of Indianapolis enacted the statute, the U.S. Court of Appeals for the Seventh Circuit had the opportunity to confront the very question posed above in the following case.

OPINION

American Booksellers Association, Inc. v. Hudnut

(Abridged.)

771 F.2d 323 (7th Cir. 1985), aff'd mem., 475 U.S. 1001 (1986)

EASTERBROOK, Circuit Judge.

[**Facts**] Indianapolis enacted an ordinance defining "pornography" as a practice that discriminates against women. "Pornography" is to be redressed through the administrative and judicial methods used for other discrimination. The City's definition of "pornography" is considerably different from "obscenity," which the Supreme Court has held is not protected by the First Amendment.

[**Statute**] "Pornography" under the ordinance is "the graphic sexually explicit subordination of women, whether in pictures or in words, that also includes one or more of the following:

(1) Women are presented as sexual objects who enjoy pain or humiliation; or
(2) Women are presented as sexual objects who experience sexual pleasure in being raped; or
(3) Women are presented as sexual objects tied up or cut up or mutilated or bruised or physically hurt, or as dismembered or truncated or fragmented or severed into body parts; or
(4) Women are presented as being penetrated by objects or animals; or
(5) Women are presented in scenarios of degradation, injury abasement, torture, shown as filthy or inferior, bleeding, bruised, or hurt in a context that makes these conditions sexual; or
(6) Women are presented as sexual objects for domination, conquest, violation, exploitation, possession, or use, or through postures or positions of servility or submission or display."

The statute provides that the "use of men, children, or transsexuals in the place of women in paragraphs (1) through (6) above shall also constitute pornography under this section."

The Indianapolis ordinance does not refer to the prurient interest, to offensiveness, or to the standards of the community. It demands attention to particular depictions, not to the work judged as a whole. It is irrelevant under the ordinance whether the work has literary, artistic, political, or scientific value. The City and many amici point to these omissions as virtues. They maintain that pornography influences attitudes, and the statute is a way to alter the socialization of men and women rather than to vindicate community standards of offensiveness. And as one of the principal drafters of the ordinance has asserted, "if a woman is subjected, why should it matter that the work has other value?" Catharine A. MacKinnon, *Pornography, Civil Rights, and Speech.*

[**Analysis**] Civil rights groups and feminists have entered this case as amici on both sides. Those supporting the ordinance say that it will play an important role in reducing the tendency of men to view women as sexual objects, a tendency that leads to both unacceptable attitudes and discrimination in the workplace and violence away from it. Those opposing the ordinance point out that much radical feminist literature is explicit and depicts women in ways forbidden by the ordinance and that the ordinance would reopen old battles. It is unclear how Indianapolis would treat works from James Joyce's *Ulysses* to Homer's *Iliad*; both depict women as submissive objects for conquest and domination.

We do not try to balance the arguments for and against an ordinance such as this. The ordinance discriminates on the ground of the content of the speech. Speech treating women in the approved way—in sexual encounters "premised on equality" (MacKinnon)—is lawful no matter how sexually explicit. Speech treating women in the disapproved way—as submissive in matters sexual or as enjoying humiliation—is unlawful no matter how significant the literary, artistic, or political qualities of the work taken as a whole. The state may not ordain preferred viewpoints in this way. The Constitution forbids the state to declare one perspective right and silence opponents.

Under the ordinance graphic sexually explicit speech is "pornography" or not depending on the perspective the author adopts. Speech that "subordinates" women and also, for example, presents women as enjoying pain, humiliation, or rape, or even simply presents women in "positions of servility or submission or display" is forbidden, no matter how great the literary or political value of the work taken as a whole. Speech that portrays women in positions of equality is lawful, no matter how graphic the sexual content. This is thought control. It establishes an "approved" view of women, of how they may react to sexual encounters, of how the sexes may relate to each other. Those who espouse the approved view may use sexual images; those who do not, may not.

In *Pacifica* the FCC sought to keep vile language off the air during certain times. The Court held that it may; but the Court would not have sustained a regulation prohibiting scatological descriptions of Republicans but not scatological descriptions of Democrats, or any other form of selection among viewpoints.

At all events, "pornography" is not low value speech within the meaning of these cases. Indianapolis seeks to prohibit certain speech because it believes this speech influences social relations and politics on a grand scale, that it controls attitudes at home and in the legislature. This precludes a characterization of the speech as low value. True, pornography and obscenity have sex in common. But Indianapolis left out of its definition any reference to literary, artistic, political, or scientific value. The ordinance applies to graphic sexually explicit subordination in works great and small. The Court sometimes balances the value of speech against the costs of its restriction, but it does this by category of speech and not by the content of particular works. Indianapolis has created an approved point of view and so loses the support of these cases.

Any rationale we could imagine in support of this ordinance could not be limited to sex discrimination. Free speech has been on balance an ally of those seeking change. Governments that want stasis start by restricting speech. Culture is a powerful force of continuity; Indianapolis paints pornography as part of the culture of power. Change in any complex system ultimately depends on the ability of outsiders to challenge accepted views and the reigning institutions. Without a strong guarantee of freedom of speech, there is no effective right to challenge what is.

An attempt to repair this ordinance would be nothing but a blind guess.

No amount of struggle with particular words and phrases in this ordinance can leave anything in effect. The district court came to the same conclusion. Its judgment is therefore

AFFIRMED.

Points to Consider

1. The role of the state.

Was Indianapolis choosing sides in the debate over the harms of pornography in a way that threatened speech more generally? Was Indianapolis trying to engage in "thought control"? Even if legislators were trying to protect women, should the state be able to determine what is "good" for women in this context?

2. Other examples?

What kind of legislative efforts do you think are permissible in the arena of sexuality and morality? How should speech rights be balanced with other societal interests? Consider the concerns raised by civil libertarians about recent federal legislation aimed at combating sex trafficking online. For example, in opposing the federal Allow States and Victims to Fight Online Sex Trafficking Act of 2017, the Electronic Frontier Foundation, a civil liberties group, argued that while the law was intended to fight sex trafficking, it included "broad language" that "makes criminals of those who advocate for and provide resources to adult, consensual sex workers and actually hinders efforts to prosecute sex traffickers and aid victims."

3. The feminist debate: MacKinnon v. Strossen.

Pornography and its impact on women has historically been a point of debate among different wings of the feminist movement. Catherine MacKinnon, as noted in the opinion intro, has been a leading voice in the anti-pornography movement. On the other side, former ACLU president Nadine Strossen has long defended the right to make and distribute pornography. Read their opposing opinions to inform your own opinion.

7.

Fighting Faiths:
Free Speech in Perilous Times

ADVOCACY OF ILLEGAL ACTION

SEDITION. Let us start there, with that word—a word heavy with free speech implications. Here is how the editors of "Black's Law Dictionary" define sedition:

> An insurrectionary movement tending towards treason, but wanting an overt act; attempts made by meetings or speeches, or by publications, to disturb the tranquility of the state. The distinction between "sedition" and "treason" consists in this: that though the ultimate object of sedition is a violation of the public peace, or at least such a course of measures as evidently engenders it, yet it does not aim at direct and open violence against the laws or the subversion of the constitution.

In other words, sedition or seditious libel is strong criticism of the government. It may be activists protesting military intervention in Syria, union workers protesting labor conditions, women protesting against Congress for being lax on sexual harassment, or even protests against how immigration policies are enforced. Below is a list of the major federal laws involving sedition and related offences:

- The Sedition Act of 1798 was passed by a Federalist-controlled Congress to deal with widespread and vocal Anti-Federalist opposition to the Quasi-War with France.

- The Espionage Act of 1917 was passed shortly after the U.S. entry into World War I. It was intended to prohibit interference with military operations or recruitment, insubordination in the military, and the support of United States enemies during wartime.
- The Sedition Act of 1918 expanded limitations on speech beyond those set out in the Espionage Act of 1917 by outlawing speech opposing the government, including speech targeting the flag, military, and Constitution. Additionally, this act outlawed speech supporting labor strikes and those countries with which the United States was at war. Speech that incited disloyalty within the military was also made illegal.

Under any of these laws (or their state-law equivalents), radicals, rabble-rousers, and activists of all stripes could readily be charged with sedition or seditious libel for being stridently critical of government or business entities.

JUDGE LEARNED HAND & *THE MASSES* CASE

On April 6, 1917, the United States declared war on Germany and entered World War I. World War I drew considerable opposition from many progressive groups and individuals. Such opposition was on open display in 1917 in *The Masses* magazine. The New York–based monthly publication was a cutting-edge, collectively owned magazine that championed socialist politics and artistic freedom. Max Eastman was the radical editor of the bohemian magazine, and various Greenwich Village artists and writers contributed to it.

With the advent of the war, the magazine went into high gear to voice its opposition to the military-industrialist-capitalist war. Following the passage of the Espionage Act of 1917, the monthly magazine published four cartoons and four articles critical of the war effort. Relying on the Espionage Act, the postmaster of New York informed the business manager of *The Masses* in July of 1917 that its August issue could not be mailed. Later, the magazine's second-class mailing privileges were revoked altogether. The Masses Publishing Company then went to federal court to enjoin the postmaster from banning the mailing of its publication.

Judge Learned Hand presided over the federal district court case, titled *Masses Publishing Co. v. Patten* (1917). In the course of his opinion, Hand conceded that there were legitimate limits on free expression. He did so by way of drawing a distinction between "direct incitement to violent resistance," which may be punished, and "political agitation," which is "a safeguard of free government." Hand deemed that political agitation did not violate the Espionage Act if the speaker "stops short of urging upon others that it is their duty or their interest to resist the law." In stating this, Judge Hand stressed that only direct advocacy of resistance to the war effort could be punished. Although Hand's opinion was grounded in statutory law and not in First Amendment law, it very much influenced the latter.

On the free speech side of the equation, Hand emphasized people's ability to express those opinions included antiwar protests, which:

> fall within the scope of the right to criticize either by temperate reasoning, or by immoderate and indecent invective, which is normally the privilege of the individual in countries dependent upon free expression of opinion as the ultimate source of authority.

Hand stressed that the Espionage Act did not prohibit the mere "criticism" of existing laws or the War. Since such criticism was all that was at issue in what *The Masses* published, the postmaster was without authority to prohibit the magazine's distribution in the mail.

While Judge Hand's opinion proved very influential, it was never formally adopted. Four months after the opinion was handed down, it was reversed by the Court of Appeals for the Second Circuit.

The Masses folded after its loss in the circuit court. Nonetheless, it was quickly resurrected as *The Liberator*, which published from 1918 to 1924. *The Liberator* featured the following opening statement: "Never was the moment more auspicious to issue a great magazine on liberty."

THE ANARCHISTS AND THEIR "SILLY" LEAFLETS

In 1919, after Justice Oliver Wendell Holmes discussed the matter of sedition first on a train ride and then in a series of letters with Judge Learned Hand, the Supreme Court considered the First Amendment in two notable wartime cases: *Schenck v. United States* and *Abrams v. United States*.

Persuaded by Hand's more speech-protective views of sedition, Holmes began to fight for the Supreme Court to adopt legal tests that would better respect First Amendment rights in wartime.

While Holmes denied the First Amendment claim and upheld the convictions of the petitioners in *Schenck*, he did not rely on the existing "bad tendency" test of constitutionality introduced by the Ninth Circuit in 1919's *Shaffer v. United States*, which focused on "whether the natural and probable tendency and effect of the words are such as are calculated to produce the result condemned by law."

Instead, Holmes crafted the new "clear and present danger" test to determine the reach of First Amendment protections for speech:

> The question in every case is whether the words used are used in such circumstances and are of such a nature as to create a clear and present danger that they will bring about the substantive evils that Congress has a right to prevent.

While the clear and present danger test became law in *Schenck* and its progeny, a majority of the court refused to embrace it. Just a few months later, they returned to the bad tendency test in *Abrams*. As we'll see from Holmes' dissent in *Abrams*, Holmes refined his clear and present danger test and made it even more speech protective.

In *Abrams*, the defendants consisted of Jacob Abrams and four other Russian immigrants indicted by a federal grand jury for violating the Sedition Act of 1918 and sentenced to terms of up to 20 years. They were tried under the Espionage Act after tossing leaflets in English and Yiddish from a rooftop in New York City. The leaflets stated their opposition to the intervention of American troops in Russia during World War I and called for a general strike to prevent shipments of ammunition to Russia.

The lawyer for the petitioners, Harry Weinberger, argued that the "discussion of public questions is absolutely immune under the First Amendment." Overt illegal acts alone—not mere speech—could be punished under the Espionage Act.

Counsel for the government, Assistant Attorney General Robert P. Stewart, countered by arguing that no liberty "was conceived of which included the unlimited right to publish a seditious libel [i.e. criticizing the government]. No claim of that sort was ever made by a respectable person."

Nineteen days after oral arguments, the Court, per Justice John H. Clarke, rendered its opinion against the defendants. The vote was 7–2 with Justices Holmes and Brandeis dissenting.

OPINION

Abrams v. United States

(Abridged.)

250 U.S. 616 (1919)
Vote: 7–2

JUSTICE CLARKE delivered the opinion of the court.

[**Facts**] All of the five defendants were born in Russia. They were intelligent, had considerable schooling, and at the time they were arrested they had lived in the United States terms varying from five to ten years, but none of them had applied for naturalization. Four of them testified as witnesses in their own behalf and of these, three frankly avowed that they were "rebels," "revolutionists," "anarchists," that they did not believe in government in any form, and they declared that they had no interest whatever in the Government of the United States. The fourth defendant testified that he was a "socialist" and believed in "a proper kind of government, not capitalistic," but in his classification the Government of the United States was "capitalistic."

It was admitted on the trial that the defendants had united to print and distribute the described circulars and that five thousand of them had been printed and distributed about the 22nd day of August, 1918. The group had a meeting place in New York City, in rooms rented by defendant Abrams, under an assumed name, and there the subject of printing the circulars was discussed about two weeks before the defendants were arrested. The defendant Abrams, although not a printer, on July 27, 1918, purchased the printing outfit with which the circulars were printed and installed it in a basement room where the work was done at night. The circulars were distributed some by throwing them from a window of a building where one of the defendants was employed and others secretly, in New York City.

While the immediate occasion for this particular outbreak of lawlessness, on the part of the defendant alien anarchists, may have been resentment caused by our Government sending troops into Russia as a strategic operation against the Germans on the eastern battle front, yet the plain purpose of their propaganda was to excite, at the supreme crisis of the war, disaffection, sedition, riots, and, as they hoped, revolution, in this country for the purpose of embarrassing and if possible defeating the military plans of the Government in Europe.

[**Ruling**] The language of these circulars was obviously intended to provoke and to encourage resistance to the United States in the war, and the defendants, in terms, plainly urged and advocated a resort to a general strike of workers in ammunition factories for the purpose of curtailing the production of ordnance and munitions necessary and essential to the prosecution of the war as is charged in the fourth count. Thus it is clear not only that some evidence but that much persuasive evidence was before the jury tending to prove that the defendants were guilty as charged in both the third and fourth counts of the indictment and under the long established rule of law hereinbefore stated the judgment of the District Court must be

Affirmed.

JUSTICE HOLMES, dissenting.

This indictment is founded wholly upon the publication of two leaflets. The first of these leaflets says that the President's cowardly silence about the intervention in Russia reveals the hypocrisy of the plutocratic gang in Washington. It intimates that "German militarism combined with allied capitalism to crush the Russian revolution"—goes on that the tyrants of the world fight each other until they see a common enemy—working class enlightenment, when they combine to crush it; and that now militarism and capitalism combined, though not openly, to crush the Russian revolution. It says that there is only one enemy of the workers of the world and that is capitalism; that it is a crime for workers of America, etc., to fight the workers' republic of Russia, and ends "Awake! Awake, you workers of the world! Revolutionists." A note adds: "It is absurd to call us pro-German. We hate and despise German militarism more than do you hypocritical tyrants. We have more reason for denouncing German militarism than has the coward of the White House."

The other leaflet, headed "Workers—Wake Up," with abusive language says that America together with the Allies will march for Russia to help the Czecko-Slovaks in their struggle against the Bolsheviki, and that this time the hypocrites shall not fool the Russian emigrants and friends of Russia in America. It tells the Russian emigrants that they now must spit in the face of the false military propaganda by which their sympathy and help to the prosecution of the war have been called forth and says that with the money they have lent or are going to lend "they will make bullets not only for the Germans but also for the Workers Soviets of Russia," and further, "Workers in the ammunition factories, you are producing bullets, bayonets, cannon to murder not only the Germans, but also your dearest, best, who are in Russia fighting for freedom." It then appeals to the same Russian emigrants at some length not to consent to the "inquisitionary expedition to Russia," and says that the destruction of the Russian revolution is "the politics of the march to Russia." The leaflet winds up by saying "Workers, our reply to this barbaric intervention has to be a general strike!" and after a few words on the spirit of revolution, exhortations not to be afraid, and some usual tall talk ends, "Woe unto those who will be in the way of progress. Let solidarity live! The Rebels."

It seems too plain to be denied that the suggestion to workers in the ammunition factories that they are producing bullets to murder their dearest, and the further advocacy of a general strike, both in the second leaflet, do urge curtailment of production of things necessary to the prosecution of the war within the meaning of the Act. But to make the conduct criminal that statute requires that it should be "with intent by such curtailment to cripple or hinder the United States in the prosecution of the war." It seems to me that no such intent is proved.

It seems to me that this statute must be taken to use its words in a strict and accurate sense. They would be absurd in any other. A patriot might think that we were wasting money on aeroplanes, or making more cannon of a certain kind than we needed, and might advocate curtailment with success, yet, even if it turned out that the curtailment hindered and was thought by other minds to have been obviously likely to hinder the United States in the prosecution of the war, no one would hold such conduct a crime. I admit that my illustration does not answer all that might be said, but it is enough to show what I think, and to let me pass to a more important aspect of the case. I refer to the First Amendment to the Constitution, that Congress shall make no law abridging the freedom of speech.

I never have seen any reason to doubt that the questions of law that alone were before this Court in the cases of *Schenck*, *Frohwerk*, and *Debs* were rightly decided. **[Imminent danger test]** I do not doubt for a moment that by the same reasoning that would justify punishing persuasion to murder, the United States constitutionally may punish speech that produces or is intended to produce a clear and imminent danger that it will bring about forthwith certain substantive evils that the United States constitutionally may seek to prevent. The power undoubtedly is greater in time of war than in time of peace, because war opens dangers that do not exist at other times.

But as against dangers peculiar to war, as against others, the principle of the right to free speech is always the same. It is only the present danger of immediate evil or an intent to bring it about that warrants Congress in setting a limit to the expression of opinion where private rights are not concerned. Congress certainly cannot forbid all effort to change the mind of the country. Now nobody can suppose that the surreptitious publishing of a silly leaflet by an unknown man, without more, would present any immediate danger that its opinions would hinder the success of the government arms or have any appreciable tendency to do so.

In this case, sentences of twenty years' imprisonment have been imposed for the publishing of two leaflets that I believe the defendants had as much right to publish as the Government has to publish the Constitution of the United States now vainly invoked by them. Even if I am technically wrong and enough can be squeezed from these poor and puny anonymities to turn the color of legal litmus paper, I will add, even if what I think the necessary intent were shown; the most nominal punishment seems to me all that possibly could be inflicted, unless the defendants are to be made to suffer not for what the indictment alleges, but for the creed that they avow—a creed that I believe to be the creed of ignorance and immaturity when honestly held, as I see no reason to doubt that it was held here, but which, although made the subject of examination at the trial, no one has a right even to consider in dealing with the charges before the Court.

Persecution for the expression of opinions seems to me perfectly logical. If you have no doubt of your premises or your power and want a certain result with all your heart, you naturally express your wishes in law, and sweep away all opposition. To allow opposition by speech seems to indicate that you think the speech impotent, as when a man says that he has squared the circle, or that you do not care whole heartedly for the result, or that you doubt either your power or your premises. But when men have realized that time has upset many fighting faiths, they may come to believe even more than they believe the very foundations of their own conduct that the ultimate good desired is better reached by free trade in ideas—that the best test of truth is the power of the thought to get itself accepted in the competition of the market, and that truth is the only ground upon which their wishes safely can be carried out. That, at any rate, is the theory of our Constitution. It is an experiment, as all life is an experiment. Every year, if not every day, we have to wager our salvation upon some prophecy based upon imperfect knowledge. While that experiment is part of our system, I think that we should be eternally vigilant against attempts to check the expression of opinions that we loathe and believe to be fraught with death, unless they so imminently threaten immediate interference with the lawful and pressing purposes of the law that an immediate check is required to save the country. I wholly disagree with the argument of the Government that the First Amendment left the common law as to seditious libel in force. History seems to me against the notion. I had conceived that the United States, through many years, had shown its repentance for the Sedition Act of 1798 by repaying fines that it imposed. Only the emergency that makes it immediately dangerous to leave the correction of evil counsels to time warrants making any exception to the sweeping command, "Congress shall make no law… abridging the freedom of speech." Of course, I am speaking only of expressions of opinion and exhortations, which were all that were uttered here, but I regret that I cannot put into more impressive words my belief that, in their conviction upon this indictment, the defendants were deprived of their rights under the Constitution of the United States.

Points to Consider

1. What happened to Abrams and his fellow defendants?

After this landmark case, Abrams and his fellow defendants began serving their terms in prison. In 1921, just months after the defeat of the anarchist-supported rebellion against the Bolsheviks, defendants Jacob Abrams, Mollie Steimer, Samuel Lipman, and Hyman Lachowsky were deported to Russia.

If their fates looked bleak in the United States, they became far more grim in Russia. Lipman died during Stalin's purge of political enemies, while Lachowsky was killed by Nazis after his hometown of Minsk was overtaken by German troops. After being first deported by the Bolsheviks to Germany, fleeing Nazi Germany to France, and then spending seven weeks in a concentration camp, Steimer joined Abrams in Mexico City, where he worked on a Yiddish-language newspaper. Abrams eventually died of throat cancer while Steimer lived out the rest of her days in Mexico City until her death at the age of 83.

2. "In times of war."

How significant is it that the facts of this case occurred during wartime? Even if one concedes that dissent should be tolerated during wartime, is Holmes' test too extreme in that it requires a clear and imminent danger? If wartime does matter, and if it should change the way we think about First Amendment freedoms, how can one be sure if the nation is really at war? While World War II amounted to "wartime," does the same hold true for the ongoing wars in the Middle East? What about "the war on terrorism"?

3. Truth & the marketplace of ideas.

Holmes suggested truth will win out in the marketplace of ideas. How certain can we be of that? Does the recent focus on "fake news" suggest otherwise? In this regard, consider the following comment from Cass Sunstein's *Democracy and the Problem of Free Speech* (1993):

In all his writings on free speech, Holmes pays little attention to the appropriate conditions under which free trade in ideas will ensure truth, a gap that is probably attributable to his skepticism about whether truth, as an independent value, is at issue at all. Thus Holmes concludes one of his other great free speech opinions [*Gitlow v. New York*] with the remarkable suggestion that if, "in the long run, the beliefs expressed in proletarian dictatorship are destined to be accepted by the dominant forces of the community, the only meaning of free speech is that they should be given their chance and have their way."

4. Consider these notable pro & con arguments for Holmes' dissent.

PRAISE: In retrospect, Holmes' dissent came to be seen as one of the great pillars of First Amendment law: "[W]ithin the legal community today, the *Abrams* dissent of Holmes stands as one of the central organizing pronouncements for our contemporary vision of free speech." Lee Bollinger, *The Tolerant Society* (1986).

In *Honorable Justice: The Life of Oliver Wendell Holmes* (1989), author Sheldon M. Novick noted that Holmes' dissent, "is at the root of modern First Amendment protections. It has also been called one of the foundation stones of modern liberalism."

In his article, "Reading Holmes Through the Lens of Schauer: The Abrams Dissent," in the *Notre Dame Law Review* (1997), Vincent Blasi, a premier First Amendment scholar, deemed Holmes' dissent "canonical." He went on to say the opinion "may be the single most influential judicial opinion ever written on" the subject of freedom of speech.

CRITICISM: Despite his friendship with Holmes, Dean of Northwestern University Law School John H. Wigmore published a law review article highly critical of Holmes's *Abrams* dissent. Professor Wigmore, who served in the Reserve Corps of the Judge Advocate General's Office during World War I, argued that the petitioners' circulars calling for a curtailment of munitions production in 1918 constituted a "present danger" to the fighting forces. He wrote in "Abrams v. U.S.: Freedom of Speech and Freedom of Thuggery in War-Time and in Peace-Time" for the *Illinois Law Review*:

> By March, 1917, intelligent America had realized what was at stake in the European contest. A ruthless military caste had inspired the Germans to dominate the world by force, at any cost to life, treasure, honor, and decency....The whole spirit and conduct of the German cause, from

start to finish, was the egoistic brutal will to bruise, smash, and destroy every other interest, however worthy in itself, which interfered in the slightest with the most trifling will of the German.

During that perilous period, the U.S. government rallied its forces and sped up the production of munitions. Wigmore noted that the military's supply of munitions did not meet their needs. He argued:

> Abrams and this band of alien parasites, and a hundred other such bands, were doing all in their power to curtail this production and cripple our fighting men. Every load of rifles less meant more hopelessness for the cause of world-morality and world-safety....[W]hen the fate of the civilized world hung in the balance, how could [Justice Holmes] interpret law and conduct in such a way as to let loose men who were doing their hardest to paralyze the supreme war efforts of our country?"

Moreover, he took issue with the dissent's purported concern for "Truth":

> This apotheosis of truth, however, shows a blindness to the deadly fact that meantime the "power of the thought" of these circulars might well "get itself accepted in the competition of the market," by munitions workers, so as to lose the war; in which case, the academic victory which Truth, "the ultimate good," might later secure in the market, would be too "ultimate" to have any practical value for a defeated America.... This Opinion, if it had made the law as the majority opinion, would have ended by our letting soldiers die helpless in France, through our anxiety to protect the distribution of a leaflet whose sole purpose was to cut off the soldiers' munitions and supplies. How would this advance the cause of Truth?

When a nation is at war, Wigmore added, "all principles of normal internal order may be suspended. As property may be taken and corporal service may be conscripted, so liberty of speech may be limited or suppressed, so far as deemed needful for the successful conduct of the war."

As for peacetime, Wigmore thought otherwise. When war is not occurring, the case becomes "different. Here, the 'free trade in ideas' may be left to signify unlicensed ventilation of the most extreme views, sane or insane, on any subject whatsoever."

DENNIS V. UNITED STATES: THE SCRAPPER, THE BELIEVER, AND THE THINKER

The Cold War generated unprecedented First Amendment activity for the Supreme Court....As a result of the Cold War, it handed down sixty such decisions. For roughly a decade, this was the dominant issue on the Court's docket....The key decision, the one that shaped the debate, was Dennis v. United States.

—Geoffrey R. Stone, Perilous Times: Free Speech in Wartime from the Sedition Act of 1798 to the War on Terrorism (2004)

They were three very different men: Communist activist Eugene Dennis was a scrapper; trial judge Harold Medina a believer; and appellate judge Learned Hand a thinker. The destinies of these three came together in *Dennis v. United States* (1951). A case about words—words that inspired and inflamed; words that turned people toward a cause and against one another.

Communism and capitalism. Such words and what they symbolized could not coexist. For some, it was honorable to defend the latter and seditious to defend the former. Dennis championed communism, Medina valued capitalism, and Hand tried to divine a way where the teachings of communists could be tolerated by capitalists. But could that be done? Or was the message preached by Marxist missionaries simply too dangerous?

Communism's "goal is the overthrow of our government." That's how J. Edgar Hoover, the director of the FBI, put it in late March of 1947, when he testified before the House Un-American Activities Committee. By Hoover's measure, to be a Communist was to be a "fifth-column" soldier, a secret enemy agent working inside the nation's borders to sabotage the American way of life and law.

Making matters for American communists more contentious, the People's Republic of China was formally established on October 1, 1949. Shortly thereafter, China and the Soviet Union signed the Treaty of Friendship, Alliance, and Mutual Assistance. The two Communist superpowers shared a common hatred of the United States that fueled American fears of nuclear warfare and the triumph of communism during the Cold War.

It was against that backdrop that Eugene Dennis and his Communist cohorts would be judged. Dennis and his co-defendants were not prosecuted for advocating the overthrow of the government, or for attempting to overthrow the government, or even for conspiring to overthrow the government. They were prosecuted for *conspiring to advocate* the overthrow of the government. The legal question, then, was the demonstrable link between their acts and the "clear and present" danger they posed to the security of the nation.

In July of 1948, the FBI arrested twelve top-ranking leaders of the Communist Party of America and charged them with violating the Alien Registration Act of 1940. One of those arrested was Dennis, the ideological scrapper who would fight back.

Character Profiles

Devout as he was to communist ideals, Eugene Dennis pleaded full fidelity to America. "We Communists are second to none in our devotion to our people and to our country," he said in his opening trial statement. America's real enemies, he had declared in 1947, were the "Fascist-minded" types like those on the House Un-American Activities Committee who would not tolerate views contrary to their own. Dennis had previously been held in contempt of Congress in 1947 for failing to respond to a subpoena issued by the House Un-American Activities Committee. When given a choice between paying a $100 fine and spending a year in jail or returning to Congress and testify, he chose the fine and incarceration. The ruddy-faced, gray-haired general secretary of the Communist Party of America was a man who not only welcomed confrontation—he invited it. Aided and abetted by his co-defendants, Eugene Dennis confronted the system that he was certain would convict them *unless* their First Amendment claims could save them.

Judge Harold Raymond Medina, a newly appointed federal district court judge, had no idea what he was in for when Dennis and his buddies strutted into his courtroom. The trial turned Judge Medina's courtroom into a theater stage, replete with real-world drama beyond all imagination.

For Judge Learned Hand, a respected appellate judge on the United States Court of Appeals for the Second Circuit, the drama was of a different order. In life and law, the barrel-chested, square-faced, and stiff-haired Hand was a perfectionist. While Judge Hand possessed liberal instincts, his approach to judicial decision-making was decidedly restrained. So when the *Dennis* case came before him, it was more a legal riddle to be solved than a political controversy to be settled—a riddle that first consumed him in 1917, when he was charged with overseeing *Masses Publishing Co. v. Patten*.

Dennis found its way to the United States Supreme Court, where it was finally settled in 1951. Perhaps "settled" is not the right word, however, for little in the case was ever entirely settled. In Justice Hugo Black's mind, it would take "calmer times, when present pressures, passions and fears subside" to resolve the great First Amendment principle raised by the case. *Dennis* stands as one of the most controversial precedents in the history of American law. In time, the *Dennis* holding was ignored, though it was never expressly overruled.

It was an astonishing First Amendment controversy—played out in Eugene Dennis' life, in Harold Medina's courtroom, in Learned Hand's mind, and ultimately in the Supreme Court. No case, in fact, better exemplifies the long and convoluted history of the most famous (perhaps infamous) doctrine in American free speech law: the clear and present danger test.

The "Curse" of Communism

The law that triggered the arrest of Dennis and his comrades was the Alien Registration Act, also known as the Smith Act, a measure first proposed in 1939 by Congressman Howard Worth Smith. The Smith Act made it a crime, punishable by a $10,000 fine and ten years in jail, to advocate, teach, advise, or abet the forceful overthrow of the government or to knowingly belong to a group that did so. The law also prohibited the publication or distribution of printed matter that advocated the violent overthrow of the government. The Smith Act was the first peacetime federal sedition law since the Alien and Sedition Acts of 1798. It was patterned after the New York Criminal Anarchy Act of 1902, the same law that gave rise to the prosecution of Benjamin Gitlow in the case of *Gitlow v. New York* (1925).

When the unrepentant Dennis and his communist cohorts went on trial on January 17, 1949, history was against them. For one, there was a series of bad First Amendment precedents from the Supreme Court dating back to 1919 concerning free speech and subversive advocacy. There was also the Smith Act Trial of 1941, in which eighteen members of the Socialist Workers Party were convicted under the Smith Act and served up to sixteen months in prison.

The defendants' lawyers complained bitterly about "an atmosphere of martial law." Their clients, they argued, were being subjected to a "police trial." Less generous charges called it "another Scottsboro case" and a "Hitler trial." They were complaining about what was transpiring outside the classic facade and colonnaded entrance of the United States courthouse located in New York City's Foley Square—the site of their historic trial.

That day, uniformed police and plainclothes detectives numbered 400 strong inside and outside the courthouse. Some marched in double-file, while others sat high on mounted horses overseeing every move. In explaining the need for these numbers, Assistant Chief Inspector Frank Fristensky, Jr., stated: "the *Daily Worker* [a Communist Party paper] has been building this thing up for days. We are in charge of protecting life and property, keeping the streets clear for unobstructed use of pedestrians and to keep vehicular traffic moving."

True to the Assistant Chief's will, the streets were kept clear, traffic flowed, and order was maintained. Meanwhile, some 500 protesters, exercising their First

Amendment right to peaceably assemble, marched up and down the courthouse sidewalk, albeit without chanting or displaying placards. There were no incidents to speak of, and Judge Medina proceeded cautiously through the crowd and to his chambers without any real threat to his safety.

When the trial got underway, defense counsel argued that the "armed camp, martial law and police trial" atmosphere prejudiced their clients' trial and intimidated the jurors. Medina replied that he had seen no such evidence as he passed through the police lines. The defense lawyers then complained that the judge was biased; a transcript of his remarks at a pretrial hearing was offered as proof. That motion was also denied.

Judge Medina made it clear that he intended to run things as "a trial, not a spectacle." While that was his intention, it was not the result. As his patience was tested, his volatile temper sometimes won out as the proceedings veered out of control. By the time the trial ended after about 275 days, it had turned contentious beyond belief. The trial transcripts are massive, speckled with five million words. The jury found all the defendants guilty.

When the case was reviewed by Judge Learned Hand of the United States Court of Appeals for the Second Circuit in 1950, it took another 20,000 words to explain the court's rationale for upholding the convictions. The story remained remarkable when it reached the Supreme Court the following year. There was no majority opinion, only a majority judgment; five of the nine justices wrote opinions totaling 32,175 words. Precedents were ignored and the law of the First Amendment recast.

Supreme Court Ruling

On June 4, 1951, the justices filed into the courtroom to announce the judgment in *Dennis v. United States*. In the end, the conference vote, 6–2 against the defendants, proved to be the final vote.

Try as he might, Chief Justice Fred Vinson could not get four other justices to sign on to his opinion. Thus, he was left with announcing a plurality opinion, one joined by Justices Harold Burton, Stanley Reed, and Sherman Minton. Justices Felix Frankfurter and Robert Jackson wrote separate opinions, joining in the judgment. And Justices William O. Douglas and Hugo Black each wrote in dissent. Justice Tom Clark did not participate.

The central question Vinson's plurality opinion had to address was the controlling law. Would he apply the *Schenck v. United States* (1919) "clear and present danger" test, or Holmes' revision of it in *Abrams v. United States* (1919)? Or even Justice Brandeis' formula from his concurrence in *Whitney v. California* (1927):

To justify suppression of free speech there must be reasonable ground to
fear that *serious evil* will result if free speech is practiced. There must be
reasonable ground to believe that the danger apprehended is *imminent*.
There must be reasonable ground to believe that the evil to be prevented
is a *serious* one....[E]ven advocacy of violation, however reprehensible
morally, is not a justification for denying free speech where the advocacy falls short of incitement and there is nothing to indicate that the
advocacy would be *immediately acted on*. The wide difference between
advocacy and incitement, between preparation and attempt, between
assembling and conspiracy, must be borne in mind. *In order to support a
finding of clear and present danger, it must be shown either that immediate
serious violence was to be expected or was advocated, or that the past conduct furnished reason to believe that such advocacy was then contemplated*
[emphasis added].

Mindful of the Holmes and Brandeis formulas, Vinson declared that "there is
little doubt that subsequent opinions have inclined toward the Holmes-Brandeis
rationale." In the end, however, Vinson's plurality opinion did not follow Holmes'
and Brandeis' more liberal formulas. Instead, Vinson reached back in time and
gave new meaning to an old test:

Chief Judge Learned Hand, writing for the majority below, interpreted
the phrase as follows: "In each case [courts] must ask whether the gravity of the 'evil,' discounted by its improbability, justifies such invasion
of free speech as is necessary to avoid the danger." We adopt this statement of the rule. As articulated by Chief Judge Hand, it is as succinct
and inclusive as any other we might devise at this time. It takes into
consideration those factors which we deem relevant, and relates their
significances. More we cannot expect from words.

Just like that, the clear and present danger test, in its most liberal form, had
been discounted. Vinson had ruled that the danger no longer had to be obvious or
"clear." Likewise, it need not even be "present"—it was enough if it could later
evolve. Meanwhile, the "direct incitement to violence" component of Hand's
Masses opinion was ignored altogether.

The result was a test that butchered the best of Hand's, Brandeis', and Holmes'
formulas. As Gerald Gunther observed, "it was viewed by many as a debacle for
the First Amendment." The new test resembled the old one in name only. "The
words actually employed take all the starch out of the clear and present danger

test," Professor Thomas Emerson quipped. For Vinson, all that mattered was the seriousness of the evil. Here, for example, Vinson felt that the "evil" was plain to see; it was the intended demise of capitalism, by revolution if necessary! A grave evil by any American measure.

If the Vinson plurality opinion was an affront to the First Amendment, Justice Felix Frankfurter's 34-page concurring opinion with its balancing test was hardly better. The First Amendment as Frankfurter construed it required that the interests of the state be balanced against those of the individual in order to determine if Congress might abridge freedom of speech. "But how are competing interests to be assessed?" he asked. His answer: "Primary responsibility for adjusting the interests which compete in the situation before us of necessity belongs to the Congress." Thus, unless Congress acted in a completely arbitrary way, its judgment was final even if there was some measure of bona fide doubt. Since the Smith Act was passed in 1940, and since Dennis and his co-defendants were indicted in 1948, it must be assumed that the "balance" Congress struck was a sufficient constitutional calculation to carry on almost ad infinitum.

For Justice Hugo Black, all of this was constitutional heresy. In his eyes, the Smith Act was plainly unconstitutional, the defendants' actions were within the purview of the First Amendment, the clear and present danger test required a reversal of the defendants' convictions, and Frankfurter's balancing test was an affront to the First Amendment. "Such a doctrine," he wrote, "waters down the First Amendment so that it amounts to little more than an admonition to Congress."

Black was addressing a future generation of judges. Black held out hope "that in calmer times, when present pressures, passions and fears subside, this or some later Court will restore the First Amendment liberties to the high preferred place where they belong in a free society."

The Dennis ruling and the communist "hysteria" it countenanced also outraged the Court's most maverick justice, William O. Douglas. Ten months later, he expressed that outrage in an article he wrote for the *Progressive* magazine titled "Frightened America." It boldly stated: "The Communist threat inside the country has been magnified and exalted far beyond its realities. Irresponsible talk by irresponsible people," he continued, "has fanned the flames of fear. Accusations have been loosely made. Character assassinations have become common. Suspicion has taken the place of good will. Once we could debate with impunity along a wide range of inquiry. Once we could safely explore to the edges of a problem, challenge orthodoxy without qualms, and run the gamut of ideas in search of solutions to perplexing problems." But those days, he argued, were past. "Now there is suspicion. Innocent acts become telltale marks of disloyalty....Suspicion grows until only the orthodox idea is the safe one....Good and honest men are pilloried....Fear runs rampant."

Aftermath

The *Dennis* case was sent back to the trial court over which Federal District Court Judge Sylvester J. Ryan presided. Eugene Dennis received a $10,000 fine and five years in prison. He was then cuffed, shackled, and carted off to the Atlanta Penitentiary—the same prison that housed mafia mobster Al Capone. Dennis served three years and nine months of his sentence (July 1951 to March 1955), having received time off for good behavior. In June of 1960, Eugene Dennis checked into Mount Sinai Hospital in New York to undergo an operation for lung cancer. He lived but another eight months, dying on January 31, 1961. He was 56 years old.

Meanwhile, Judge Harold Medina basked in the glow of his national celebrity. The majority will was clearly on his side—more than 50,000 congratulatory letters came his way from all around the world. He was out and about, speaking on the "spiritual quality of justice." Whenever he spoke, he wove God and the greater good into his discussion of the *Dennis* trial. "I do not know why," he said in May of 1953, "a judge should be ashamed to seek guidance and strength from Almighty God. According to my way of looking at things, that is precisely what a judge should do." Immediately thereafter, he referred to the "trial of the Communists." With religious fervor, he declared: "In some way, which will always remain a mystery to me, the spark had been fired and a great spiritual force had been released, and I was feeling it. I was the man who felt the impact of that force."

Though the Court had the opportunity to embrace the more speech-protective tests of Justices Holmes and Brandeis, a majority declined to do so and went instead with the more restrictive test first announced by Judge Hand: "whether the gravity of the 'evil,' discounted by its improbability, justifies such invasion of free speech as is necessary to avoid the danger."

As we will see in the next case, *Brandenburg v. Ohio* (1969), the *Dennis* test was functionally overruled.

THE CASE OF THE KKK PREACHING REVENGE AGAINST BLACK AND JEWISH PEOPLE

At a rally held in the summer of 1964, Clarence Brandenburg, a Ku Klux Klan member, proclaimed the supremacy of the white race in front of local TV reporters: "We're not a revengent [*sic*] organization...but if our President, our Congress, our Supreme Court, continues to suppress the white, Caucasian race, it's possible that there might have to be some revengeance [*sic*] taken." Brandenburg continued: "Personally, I believe the nigger should be returned to Africa, the Jew returned to Israel."

While Brandenburg did not carry a gun, some of the other hooded men carried firearms. They gathered around a large wooden cross, which they burned. No one was present other than the participants and the TV crews.

Brandenburg was convicted under an Ohio Criminal Syndicalism statute for "advocat[ing]...the duty, necessity, or propriety of crime, sabotage, violence, or unlawful methods of terrorism as a means of accomplishing industrial or political reform" and for "voluntarily assembl[ing] with any society, group, or assemblage of persons formed to teach or advocate the doctrines of criminal syndicalism." He challenged the criminal syndicalism statute on First and Fourteenth Amendment grounds.

OPINION

Brandenburg v. Ohio

(Abridged.)

395 U.S. 444 (1969)
Vote: 9–0

PER CURIAM opinion

The Ohio Criminal Syndicalism Statute was enacted in 1919. From 1917 to 1920, identical or quite similar laws were adopted by 20 States and two territories. In 1927, this Court sustained the constitutionality of California's Criminal Syndicalism Act, the text of which is quite similar to that of the laws of Ohio. See *Whitney v. California* (1927). The Court upheld the statute on the ground that, without more, "advocating" violent means to effect political and economic change involves such danger to the security of the State that the State may outlaw it. But *Whitney* has been thoroughly discredited by [our] later decisions. See *Dennis v. United States* (1951).

[**Imminence test**] These later decisions have fashioned the principle that the constitutional guarantees of free speech and free press do not permit a State to forbid or proscribe advocacy of the use of force or of law violation except where such advocacy is directed to inciting or producing imminent lawless action and is likely to incite or produce such action. As we said in *Noto v. United States* (1961), "the mere abstract teaching...of the moral propriety or even moral necessity for a resort to force and violence, is not the same as preparing a group for violent action and steeling it to such action." A statute which fails to draw this distinction impermissibly intrudes upon the freedoms guaranteed by the First and Fourteenth Amendments. It sweeps within its condemnation speech which our Constitution has immunized from governmental control.

[**Ruling**] Measured by this test, Ohio's Criminal Syndicalism Act cannot be sustained. The Act punishes persons who "advocate or teach the duty, necessity, or propriety" of violence "as a means of accomplishing industrial or political reform"; or who publish or circulate or display any book or paper containing such advocacy; or who "justify" the commission of violent acts "with intent to exemplify, spread or advocate the propriety of the doctrines of criminal syndicalism"; or who "voluntarily assemble" with a group formed "to teach or advocate the doctrines of criminal syndicalism." Neither the indictment nor the trial judge's instructions to the jury in any way refined the statute's bald definition of the crime in terms of mere advocacy not distinguished from incitement to imminent lawless action.

Accordingly, we are here confronted with a statute which, by its own words and as applied, purports to punish mere advocacy and to forbid, on pain of criminal punishment, assembly with others merely to advocate the described type of action. Such a statute falls within the condemnation of the First and Fourteenth Amendments. The contrary teaching of *Whitney v. California* cannot be supported, and that decision is therefore overruled.

JUSTICE BLACK, concurring.

I agree with the views expressed by Justice Douglas in his concurring opinion in this case that the "clear and present danger" doctrine should have no place in the interpretation of the First Amendment. I join the Court's opinion, which, as I understand it, simply cites *Dennis v. United States* (1951), but does not indicate any agreement on the Court's part with the "clear and present danger" doctrine on which *Dennis* purported to rely.

JUSTICE DOUGLAS, concurring.

While I join the opinion of the Court, I desire to enter a caveat.

The "clear and present danger" test was adumbrated by Mr. Justice Holmes in a case arising during World War I—a war "declared" by the Congress, not by the Chief Executive. The case was *Schenck v. United States* (1919), where the defendant was charged with attempts to cause insubordination in the military and obstruction of enlistment. The pamphlets that were distributed urged resistance to the draft, denounced conscription, and impugned the motives of those backing the war effort. The First Amendment was tendered as a defense. Mr. Justice Holmes in rejecting that defense said:

> [*Schenck* **clear and present danger test**] "The question in every case is whether the words used are used in such circumstances and are of such a nature as to create a clear and present danger that they will bring about the substantive evils that Congress has a right to prevent. It is a question of proximity and degree."

In the 1919 Term, the Court applied the *Schenck* doctrine to affirm the convictions of other dissidents in World War I. *Abrams v. United States* was one instance. Mr. Justice Holmes, with whom Mr. Justice Brandeis concurred, dissented. While adhering to *Schenck*, he did not think that on the facts a case for overriding the First Amendment had been made out:

> [**Holmes's *Abrams* test**] "It is only the present danger of immediate evil or an intent to bring it about that warrants Congress in setting a limit to the expression of opinion where private rights are not concerned. Congress certainly cannot forbid all effort to change the mind of the country."

There were several such World War I cases that put the gloss of "clear and present danger" on the First Amendment. Whether the war power—the greatest leveler of them all—is adequate to sustain that doctrine is debatable. The dissents in *Abrams* and other cases show how easily "clear and present danger" is manipulated. Though I doubt if the "clear and present danger" test is congenial to the First Amendment in time of a declared war, I am certain it is not reconcilable with the First Amendment in days of peace.

The Court quite properly overrules *Whitney v. California*, which involved advocacy of ideas which the majority of the Court deemed unsound and dangerous.

Mr. Justice Holmes, though never formally abandoning the "clear and present danger" test, moved closer to the First Amendment ideal when he said in dissent in *Gitlow v. New York* (1925):

> "Every idea is an incitement. It offers itself for belief and if believed it is acted on unless some other belief outweighs it or some failure of energy stifles the movement at its birth. The only difference between the expression of an opinion and an incitement in the narrower sense is the speaker's enthusiasm for the result. Eloquence may set fire to reason. But whatever may be thought of the redundant discourse before us it had no chance of starting a present conflagration. If in the long run the beliefs expressed in proletarian dictatorship are destined to be accepted by the dominant forces of the community, the only meaning of free speech is that they should be given their chance and have their way."

We have never been faithful to the philosophy of that dissent.

In *Dennis v. United States*, we opened wide the door, distorting the "clear and present danger" test beyond recognition. In that case, the prosecution dubbed an agreement to teach the Marxist creed a "conspiracy." The case was submitted to a jury on a charge that the jury could not convict unless it found that the defendants "intended to overthrow the Government 'as speedily as circumstances would permit.'"

[*Dennis* test] The Court sustained convictions under that charge, construing it to mean a determination of "whether the gravity of the evil, discounted by its improbability, justifies such invasion of free speech as is necessary to avoid the danger." Judge Learned Hand, who wrote for the Court of Appeals in affirming the judgment in *Dennis*, coined the "not improbable" test, which this Court adopted and which Judge Hand preferred over the "clear and present danger" test. Indeed, in his book, *The Bill of Rights* (1958), in referring to Holmes' creation of the "clear and present danger" test, he said, "I cannot help thinking that for once Homer nodded." My own view is quite different. I see no place in the regime of the First Amendment for any "clear and present danger" test, whether strict and tight as some would make it, or free-wheeling as the Court in *Dennis* rephrased it.

When one reads the opinions closely and sees when and how the "clear and present danger" test has been applied, great misgivings are aroused. First, the threats were often loud but always puny and made serious only by judges so wedded to the status quo that critical analysis made them nervous. Second, the test was so twisted and perverted in *Dennis* as to make the trial of those teachers of Marxism an all-out political trial which was part and parcel of the cold war that has eroded substantial parts of the First Amendment.

Action is often a method of expression and within the protection of the First Amendment.

Suppose one tears up his own copy of the Constitution in eloquent protest to a decision of this Court. May he be indicted?

Suppose one rips his own Bible to shreds to celebrate his departure from one "faith" and his embrace of atheism. May he be indicted?

The line between what is permissible and not subject to control and what may be made impermissible and subject to regulation is the line between ideas and overt acts.

The example usually given by those who would punish speech is the case of one who falsely shouts fire in a crowded theatre.

This is, however, a classic case where speech is brigaded with action. They are indeed inseparable and a prosecution can be launched for the overt acts actually caused. Apart from rare instances of that kind, speech is, I think, immune from prosecution. Certainly there is no constitutional line between advocacy of abstract ideas as in *Yates* and advocacy of political action. The quality of advocacy turns on the depth of the conviction; and government has no power to invade that sanctuary of belief and conscience.

Points to Consider

1. Author of the per curium opinion.

According to the First Amendment Encyclopedia, "the Court's unsigned, *per curiam* opinion was presumably drafted by Justice Abe Fortas, who had resigned by the time the final decision was handed down."

2. Wartime.

Note that unlike *Schenck v. United States*, *Abrams v. United States*, and *Dennis v. United States*, *Brandenburg* was not a wartime case. As such, might it be argued that the earlier tests employed in *Schenck* or *Dennis* still control when the facts occur outside a wartime context?

3. Five tests.

Compare the following First Amendment tests discussed thus far. Notice that all of these tests are couched in terms of the potential harms that free speech may cause. As such, they do not focus on the value of the speech to be protected.

- The *Shaffer* bad tendency test: "[W]hether the natural and probable tendency and effect of the words…are such as are calculated to produce the result condemned by the statute."
- The *Schenck* clear and present danger test: "[W]hether the words used are used in such circumstances and are of such a nature as to create a clear and present danger that they will bring about the substantive evils that Congress has a right to prevent."
- The *Abrams* test: "It is only the present danger of immediate evil or an intent to bring it about that warrants Congress in setting a limit to the expression of opinion where private rights are not concerned. Congress certainly cannot forbid all effort to change the mind of the country."
- The *Dennis* gravity of the evil test: "[W]hether the gravity of the evil, discounted by its improbability, justifies such invasion of free speech as is necessary to avoid the danger."
- The *Brandenburg* imminent lawless action test: "[W]here such advocacy is directed to inciting or producing imminent lawless action and is likely to incite or produce such action."

4. The lawyers.

The lawyers who represented Clarence Brandenburg were all ACLU attorneys: Allen Brown, Melvin L. Wulf, Eleanor Holmes Norton (an African American and DC congresswoman), and Bernard A. Berkman.

5. Guns and speech.

Is it significant that some of those who participated in the KKK rally were armed with guns? After the 2017 Charlottesville "Unite the Right" riots, the ACLU stated that it would stop taking cases in which hate groups demonstrate with firearms.

6. *Applying the* Brandenburg *test.*

In *Hess v. Indiana* (1973) the Supreme Court heard a case involving an antiwar protest at Indiana University. Some 100–150 protesters marched in the streets whereupon the police attempted to clear the streets. In the midst of this, Gregory Hess yelled, "We'll take the fucking street later," or, "We'll take the fucking street again." He was convicted of disorderly conduct. By a 6–3 vote, and in *a per curiam* opinion, the Court reversed his conviction.

7. *The limits of the* Brandenburg *rule.*

The 4th Circuit's 1997 decision in *Rice v. Paladin Enterprises* held that the publisher of a "hit man" murder manual could be held liable for civil damages after it was used to commit three murders. The court stated that the "First Amendment does not provide publishers a defense as a matter of law to charges of aiding and abetting a crime through the publication and distribution of instructions on how to [commit] illegal [acts]."

8.

Hostile Expression:
Fighting Words & True Threats

DOES THE FIRST AMENDMENT protect someone's speech if it is hostile, offensive, and ugly? Answer: It depends.

In August 2017, in Charlottesville, Virginia, some marchers and protesters affiliated with the so-called "Unite the Right" movement allegedly shouted highly offensive chants that included "go the fuck back to Africa," "one people, one nation, end immigration," and a litany of slurs that we're sure you can fill in for yourself. They proudly brandished Confederate flags and other symbols associated with doctrines of white supremacy. One protestor even drove his car into the crowd, killing counter-protester Heather Heyer and injuring nineteen others. Some counter-protestors responded with violence and vitriol of their own. Overall, the rally was filled with hatred and violence.

In the wake of the rally, eyes turned to the First Amendment and people began to ask why the First Amendment protects racist, homophobic, and profane speech and where the line between offensive speech and real threats or provocation of violence should be drawn.

The United States is considered a free speech outlier in that it affords constitutional protection to a great deal of hateful speech. However, we sometimes prohibit hateful speech if it falls into one of three narrow, unprotected categories: fighting words, true threats, or incitement to imminent lawless action.

In the First Amendment family, these three categories of speech are cousins. Incitement usually involves a person speaking to a large group of people, exhorting them to engage in unlawful conduct; fighting words involve profane, face-to-face personal insults; and true threats generally involve a clear statement indicating an unequivocal intent to cause serious bodily harm to another. Since we discussed incitement in depth in Chapter 7, this chapter focuses on fighting words and true threats.

FIGHTING WORDS

The Supreme Court defined fighting words in *Chaplinsky v. New Hampshire* (1942) as "words which by their very utterance inflict injury or cause an immediate breach of the peace." While this doctrine is all but dead at the Supreme Court level, it is far from dead in the lower courts. Consider the following examples:

1. A teenager yells a racial slur at another teen outside of a skating rink.
2. A woman yells, "What the fuck are you arresting my son for? What are you doing?" at a police officer and then screams, "You fucking crooked ass cop," and, "You're a bitch," at another officer.
3. A woman, upset that a store has closed, unleashes a torrent of profanity at a store manager.
4. A man tells a police officer, "I'm tired of this God damned police sticking their nose in shit that doesn't even involve them."
5. A man yells at a police officer that he is a "white racist motherfucker" and that he wishes the officer's mother would die.

In the five listed examples, courts found the speech to be fighting words in numbers 1, 2, and 5. Two other courts found the speech not to be fighting words in numbers 3 and 4.

THE FIRST FIGHTING WORDS CASE

As a Jehovah's Witness, Walter Chaplinsky felt it was his religious duty to go out in the streets and distribute literature while preaching that all other faiths were "rackets." On April 6, 1940, a particularly large crowd formed around him, offended by Chaplinsky's preaching. As the crowd grew aggressive, Chaplinsky was taken by an officer to the police headquarters. While with the officer, he ran into a marshal who had previously been at the scene and had warned Chaplinsky of a riot. Chaplinsky told the marshal: "You are a God damned racketeer," and, "a damned Fascist and the whole government of Rochester are Fascists or agents of Fascists." Chaplinsky was arrested and convicted under a New Hampshire statute making it unlawful to "address any offensive, derisive or annoying word to any other person who is lawfully in any street or other public place."

The following decision establishing the fighting words doctrine remains one of the most important free speech decisions in Supreme Court history.

OPINION

Chaplinsky v. New Hampshire

(Abridged.)

315 U.S. 568 (1942)
Vote: 9–0

JUSTICE MURPHY delivered the opinion of the Court.

[**Facts**] Appellant Walter Chaplinsky, a member of the sect known as Jehovah's Witnesses, was convicted in the municipal court of Rochester, New Hampshire, for violation of the Public Laws of New Hampshire:

> "No person shall address any offensive, derisive or annoying word to any other person who is lawfully in any street or other public place, nor call him by any offensive or derisive name, nor make any noise or exclamation in his presence and hearing with intent to deride, offend or annoy him, or to prevent him from pursuing his lawful business or occupation."

The complaint charged that appellant,

> "with force and arms, in a certain public place in said city of Rochester, to wit, on the public sidewalk on the easterly side of Wakefield Street, near unto the entrance of the City Hall, did unlawfully repeat, the words following, addressed to the complainant, that is to say, 'You are a God damned racketeer' and 'a damned Fascist and the whole government of Rochester are Fascists or agents of Fascists' the same being offensive, derisive and annoying words and names"

There is no substantial dispute over the facts. Chaplinsky was distributing the literature of his sect on the streets of Rochester on a busy Saturday afternoon. Members of the local citizenry complained to the City Marshal, Bowering, that

Chaplinsky was denouncing all religion as a "racket." Bowering told them that Chaplinsky was lawfully engaged, and then warned Chaplinsky that the crowd was getting restless. Some time later a disturbance occurred and the traffic officer on duty at the busy intersection started with Chaplinsky for the police station, but did not inform him that he was under arrest or that he was going to be arrested. On the way they encountered Marshal Bowering who had been advised that a riot was under way and was therefore hurrying to the scene. Bowering repeated his earlier warning to Chaplinsky who then addressed to Bowering the words set forth in the complaint.

Chaplinsky's version of the affair was slightly different. He testified that when he met Bowering, he asked him to arrest the ones responsible for the disturbance. In reply, Bowering cursed him and told him to come along. Appellant admitted that he said the words charged in the complaint with the exception of the name of the Deity.

Appellant assails the statute as a violation of all three freedoms, speech, press and worship, but only an attack on the basis of free speech is warranted. The spoken, not the written, word is involved. And we cannot conceive that cursing a public officer is the exercise of religion in any sense of the term. But even if the activities of the appellant which preceded the incident could be viewed as religious in character, and therefore entitled to the protection of the Fourteenth Amendment, they would not cloak him with immunity from the legal consequences for concomitant acts committed in violation of a valid criminal statute. We turn, therefore, to an examination of the statute itself.

[**Unprotected categories**] It is well understood that the right of free speech is not absolute at all times and under all circumstances. There are certain well-defined and narrowly limited classes of speech, the prevention and punishment of which has never been thought to raise any Constitutional problem. These include the lewd and obscene, the profane, the libelous, and the insulting or "fighting" words—those which by their very utterance inflict injury or tend to incite an immediate breach of the peace. It has been well observed that such utterances are no essential part of any exposition of ideas, and are of such slight social value as a step to truth that any benefit that may be derived from them is clearly outweighed by the social interest in order and morality. "Resort to epithets or personal abuse is not in any proper sense communication of information or opinion safeguarded by the Constitution, and its punishment as a criminal act would raise no question under that instrument." *Cantwell v. Connecticut* (1940).

[**Narrowing construction**] The state statute here challenged comes to us by the highest court of New Hampshire. It has two provisions—the first relates to words or names addressed to another in a public place; the second refers to noises and exclamations.

On the authority of its earlier decisions, the state court declared that the statute's purpose was to preserve the public peace, no words being "forbidden except such as have a direct tendency to cause acts of violence by the person to whom, individually, the remark is addressed."

It was further said:

> "The statute, as construed, does no more than prohibit the face-to-face words plainly likely to cause a breach of the peace by the addressee, words whose speaking constitute a breach of the peace by the speaker-including 'classical fighting words,' words in current use less 'classical' but equally likely to cause violence, and other disorderly words, including profanity, obscenity and threats."

[**Ruling**] We cannot say that the application of the statute to the facts disclosed by the record substantially or unreasonably impinges upon the privilege of free speech. Argument is unnecessary to demonstrate that the appellations "damn racketeer" and "damn Fascist" are epithets likely to provoke the average person to retaliation, and thereby cause a breach of the peace.

Our function is fulfilled by a determination that the challenged statute, on its face and as applied, does not contravene the Fourteenth Amendment.

Affirmed.

Points to Consider

1. Was the law overbroad?

The New Hampshire law under which officials charged Walter Chaplinsky with violating read: "No person shall address any offensive, derisive or annoying word to any other person who is lawfully in any street or other public place." This law is unconstitutionally overbroad by today's standards.

However, notice that the Supreme Court accepted the interpretation of the New Hampshire Supreme Court that the law applied only to fighting words. This is called a narrowing or limiting construction—when the court interprets a law narrowly instead of striking it down.

2. Was Chaplinsky actually the victim?

Walter Chaplinsky gave a very different account of what happened than Marshall Bowering, the officer who arrested him. Chaplinsky claimed that the group that formed around him became violent and was permitted by the police to attack him—even stating that one member of the crowd tried to impale him with a flag pole.

3. Unprotected categories.

The *Chaplinsky* decision contains a passage that serves as the basis for the idea that there are certain unprotected categories of speech. Justice Frank Murphy wrote for the Court:

> There are certain well-defined and narrowly limited classes of speech, the prevention and punishment of which has never been thought to raise any Constitutional problem. These include the lewd and obscene, the profane, the libelous, and the insulting or "fighting" words—those which, by their very utterance, inflict injury or tend to incite an immediate breach of the peace.

This passage forms the basis for the idea that certain categories of speech are not protected. Note that the Court also listed obscenity, profanity, and libel in addition to fighting words. Today, profanity is usually protected speech for adults.

4. Jehovah's Witnesses and the First Amendment.

Walter Chaplinsky belonged to the Jehovah's Witnesses, a group whose run-ins with numerous city officials has certainly impacted the development of First Amendment jurisprudence. Justice Harlan Fiske Stone once wrote, "The Jehovah's Witnesses ought to have an endowment in view of the aid which they give in solving the legal problems of civil liberties."

The attorney who argued on behalf of Walter Chaplinsky was Hayden Covington, who argued more than forty cases before the U.S. Supreme Court. The vast majority of his cases involved Jehovah's Witnesses. He also was well known for representing legendary boxer Muhammad Ali in his attempt to show he avoided draft induction for religious reasons.

"FUCK THE DRAFT"

Perhaps the most significant limitation to the fighting words doctrine occurred nearly thirty years after the Supreme Court addressed Walter Chaplinsky cursing at Marshall Bowering.

When Paul Robert Cohen strolled into the Los Angeles County Courthouse bearing the words "Fuck the Draft" on his jacket in protest of the draft and the Vietnam War, there was little chance he would know how much trouble his attire would cause him. These three words and the resulting Supreme Court opinion forever changed the landscape of the fighting words doctrine, limiting it to face-to-face, personal insults.

OPINION

Cohen v. California

(Abridged.)

403 U.S. 15 (1971)
Vote: 5–4

JUSTICE HARLAN delivered the opinion of the Court.

This case may seem at first blush too inconsequential to find its way into our books, but the issue it presents is of no small constitutional significance.

[**Criminal law**] Appellant Paul Robert Cohen was convicted in the Los Angeles Municipal Court of violating that part of California Penal Code which prohibits "maliciously and willfully disturb[ing] the peace or quiet of any neighborhood or person...by...offensive conduct...." He was given 30 days' imprisonment.

[**Facts**] The facts upon which his conviction rests are detailed in the opinion of the Court of Appeal of California, Second Appellate District, as follows:

> "On April 26, 1968, the defendant was observed in the Los Angeles County Courthouse in the corridor outside of division 20 of the municipal court wearing a jacket bearing the words 'Fuck the Draft' which were plainly visible. There were women and children present in the corridor. The defendant was arrested. The defendant testified that he wore the jacket knowing that the words were on the jacket as a means

of informing the public of the depth of his feelings against the Vietnam War and the draft."

"The defendant did not engage in, nor threaten to engage in, nor did anyone as the result of his conduct in fact commit or threaten to commit any act of violence. The defendant did not make any loud or unusual noise, nor was there any evidence that he uttered any sound prior to his arrest."

In affirming the conviction, the Court of Appeal held that "offensive conduct" means "behavior which has a tendency to provoke others to acts of violence or to in turn disturb the peace," and that the State had proved this element.

[Speech v. conduct] The conviction quite clearly rests upon the asserted offensiveness of the words Cohen used to convey his message to the public. The only "conduct" which the State sought to punish is the fact of communication. Thus, we deal here with a conviction resting solely upon "speech."

Appellant's conviction, then, rests squarely upon his exercise of the "freedom of speech" protected from arbitrary governmental interference by the Constitution and can be justified, if at all, only as a valid regulation of the manner in which he exercised that freedom, not as a permissible prohibition on the substantive message it conveys. This does not end the inquiry, of course, for the First and Fourteenth Amendments have never been thought to give absolute protection to every individual to speak whenever or wherever he pleases, or to use any form of address in any circumstances that he chooses.

In the first place, Cohen was tried under a statute applicable throughout the entire State. Any attempt to support this conviction on the ground that the statute seeks to preserve an appropriately decorous atmosphere in the courthouse where Cohen was arrested must fail in the absence of any language in the statute that would have put appellant on notice that certain kinds of otherwise permissible speech or conduct would nevertheless, under California law, not be tolerated in certain places.

[Profanity alone is not obscene] In the second place, as it comes to us, this case cannot be said to fall within those relatively few categories of instances where prior decisions have established the power of government to deal more comprehensively with certain forms of individual expression simply upon a showing that such a form was employed. This is not, for example, an obscenity case. Whatever else may be necessary to give rise to the States' broader power to prohibit obscene expression, such expression must be, in some significant way, erotic.

[**Not fighting words**] This Court has also held that the States are free to ban the simple use, without a demonstration of additional justifying circumstances, of so-called "fighting words," those personally abusive epithets which, when addressed to the ordinary citizen, are, as a matter of common knowledge, inherently likely to provoke violent reaction. While the four-letter word displayed by Cohen in relation to the draft is not uncommonly employed in a personally provocative fashion, in this instance it was clearly not "directed to the person of the hearer." No individual actually or likely to be present could reasonably have regarded the words on appellant's jacket as a direct personal insult. Nor do we have here an instance of the exercise of the State's police power to prevent a speaker from intentionally provoking a given group to hostile reaction.

Finally, in arguments before this Court, much has been made of the claim that Cohen's distasteful mode of expression was thrust upon unwilling or unsuspecting viewers, and that the State might therefore legitimately act as it did in order to protect the sensitive from otherwise unavoidable exposure to appellant's crude form of protest. Of course, the mere presumed presence of unwitting listeners or viewers does not serve automatically to justify curtailing all speech capable of giving offense.

[**Issue**] Against this background, the issue flushed by this case stands out in bold relief. It is whether California can excise, as "offensive conduct," one particular scurrilous epithet from the public discourse, either upon the theory of the court below that its use is inherently likely to cause violent reaction or upon a more general assertion that the States, acting as guardians of public morality, may properly remove this offensive word from the public vocabulary.

Equally important to our conclusion is the constitutional backdrop against which our decision must be made. The constitutional right of free expression is powerful medicine in a society as diverse and populous as ours. It is designed and intended to remove governmental restraints from the arena of public discussion, putting the decision as to what views shall be voiced largely into the hands of each of us, in the hope that use of such freedom will ultimately produce a more capable citizenry and more perfect polity and in the belief that no other approach would comport with the premise of individual dignity and choice upon which our political system rests.

How is one to distinguish this from any other offensive word? Surely the State has no right to cleanse public debate to the point where it is grammatically palatable to the most squeamish among us. Yet no readily ascertainable general principle exists for stopping short of that result were we to affirm the judgment below. [**Memorable line**] For, while the particular four-letter word being litigated here is perhaps more distasteful than most others of its genre, it is nevertheless often true that one man's vulgarity is another's lyric. Indeed, we think it is largely because governmental officials cannot make principled distinctions in this area that the Constitution leaves matters of taste and style so largely to the individual.

[**Warning about suppression of ideas**] Finally, and in the same vein, we cannot indulge the facile assumption that one can forbid particular words without also running a substantial risk of suppressing ideas in the process. Indeed, governments might soon seize upon the censorship of particular words as a convenient guise for banning the expression of unpopular views. We have been able, as noted above, to discern little social benefit that might result from running the risk of opening the door to such grave results.

[**Ruling**] It is, in sum, our judgment that, absent a more particularized and compelling reason for its actions, the State may not, consistently with the First and Fourteenth Amendments, make the simple public display here involved of this single four-letter expletive a criminal offense. Because that is the only arguably sustainable rationale for the conviction here at issue, the judgment below must be reversed.

JUSTICE BLACKMUN, dissenting.

Cohen's absurd and immature antic, in my view, was mainly conduct and little speech. Further, the case appears to me to be well within the sphere of *Chaplinsky v. New Hampshire* (1942), where Mr. Justice Murphy, a known champion of First Amendment freedoms, wrote for a unanimous bench.

Points to Consider

1. What ever happened to Paul Robert Cohen?

Cohen moved away from California and took a different name. For many years, he was ashamed to be associated with the case. "There are so many misconceptions about the case and about me," he said. "I didn't even see the wording on the jacket until the morning before I was headed to court to testify on behalf of an acquaintance. I was and am a patriotic person." However, in later years, Cohen took pride in his involvement in the case, viewing it as a victory for individual freedom.

2. "One man's vulgarity is another's lyric."

Perhaps the most memorable phrase in Justice Harlan's opinion is, "[O]ne man's vulgarity is another's lyric." The underlying principle is that what offends one person does not necessarily offend another. In 2016, a Canadian judge even quoted the phrase in finding a man not guilty of criminal harassment for messages on Twitter.

Cohen's attorney, UCLA law professor Melville B. Nimmer, realized he needed to get the justices more accustomed to the language on Cohen's jacket. After being told by Chief Justice Warren Burger not to say, "fuck," Nimmer continued to use the word in his oral argument.

3. Not directed at a specific person.

The primary importance of the *Cohen* case is that it limits fighting words to direct, face-to-face personal insults. Justice Harlan reasoned that the profane words on the jacket were not fighting words because they were not directed at a specific person.

If Cohen had taken his jacket and waved it in the direction of a specific person, then the result could, arguably, have been different.

4. Speech v. conduct.

In Justice Harry Blackmun's dissenting opinion, he wrote that Cohen's "immature" act of wearing the jacket with the profane language was "mainly conduct and little speech." This brings to mind what is sometimes called the speech-conduct dichotomy. In other words, if something is entitled to free speech protection, it is called speech. However, if something is not considered expressive enough for free speech protection, it is called conduct.

5. Profane language is not obscene.

The state argued that the profanity on Cohen's jacket was obscene. Justice Harlan explained that a profane word like "fuck" is not inherently erotic or sexually related; thus, it is not obscenity—a narrow category of expression reserved for the hardest of hard-core pornography. Profanity and obscenity are markedly different.

6. Cursing the police.

Many fighting words cases involve individuals who curse at the police. In *Gooding v. Wilson* (1972), the Court addressed a case involving an African-American draft protestor, Johnny C. Wilson, who yelled at a white police officer: "White son of a bitch, I'll kill you, I'll choke you to death."

The police arrested Wilson for violating a Georgia law that prohibited "opprobrious words or abusive language, tending to cause a breach of the peace." The Court ruled that the Georgia statute was unconstitutionally overbroad. The Court explained that the dictionary definitions of the word "opprobrious" applied to much more speech than fighting words.

7. A different case for juveniles.

Juvenile defendants often don't fare as well as adults when they utter profane or racist statements at others. Courts are more likely to find that their comments constitute fighting words. Is this because courts are less protective of juvenile rights?

TRUE THREATS

True threats distinguish themselves from fighting words and incitement to immediate lawlessness because they usually involve a clear statement indicating an unequivocal intent to cause serious bodily harm to another. While it may sound like true threats should be the most easily identified category out of the three, the courts have struggled throughout the years to distinguish what actually constitutes a true threat.

The First True Threat Case

The Supreme Court first addressed true threats in *Watts v. United States* (1969), a case involving a young African-American man who was protesting the Vietnam War. Robert Watts attended an antiwar rally in Washington, D.C., where he declared:

> They always holler at us to get an education. And now I have already received my draft classification as 1-A and I have got to report for my physical this Monday coming. I am not going. If they ever make me carry a rifle the first man I want to get in my sights is L.B.J.

An Army Corps Intelligence officer overheard the remark, leading to Watts' arrest for threatening the president.

Watts' attorneys challenged the constitutionality of the statute that Watts was charged with violating. The law specifically prohibits making threats against the president, vice president, and other successors to the presidency. The Court held that the law was constitutional, writing:

Certainly the statute under which petitioner was convicted is constitutional on its face. The Nation undoubtedly has a valid, even an overwhelming, interest in protecting the safety of its Chief Executive and in allowing him to perform his duties without interference from threats of physical violence.

The Supreme Court did not define true threats in *Watts*. However, the Court did offer a definition years later in a case involving a challenge to Virginia's cross-burning law.

THE TALE OF TWO CROSS BURNINGS

Barry Black, a Ku Klux Klan leader, burned a cross at a Klan rally in a yard, with the permission of the homeowner (despite unease from neighbors). In a separate incident, two men who were not Klan members, Richard Elliott and Jonathan O'Mara, burned a cross in the yard of a black neighbor to "get back" at the neighbor for complaining about Elliott's and O'Mara's use of a backyard as a shooting range. Did the history of violence surrounding cross burnings make the act a true threat? Did the intentions of those burning the crosses matter? In our next case, *Virginia v. Black* (2003), the Supreme Court took a side-by-side look at the two cross burnings and attempted to answer those questions.

OPINION

Virginia v. Black

(Abridged.)

538 U.S. 343 (2003)
Vote: 6–3

JUSTICE O'CONNOR announced the judgment of the Court.

[Issue] In this case we consider whether the Commonwealth of Virginia's statute banning cross burning with "an intent to intimidate a person or group of persons" violates the First Amendment. We conclude that while a State, consistent with the First Amendment, may ban cross burning carried out with the intent to intimidate, the provision in the Virginia statute treating any cross burning as prima facie evidence of intent to intimidate renders the statute unconstitutional in its current form.

Respondents Barry Black, Richard Elliott, and Jonathan O'Mara were convicted separately of violating Virginia's cross-burning statute. That statute provides:

> [**Criminal law**] "It shall be unlawful for any person or persons, with the intent of intimidating any person or group of persons, to burn, or cause to be burned, a cross on the property of another, a highway or other public place. Any person who shall violate any provision of this section shall be guilty of a Class 6 felony.
>
> "Any such burning of a cross shall be prima facie evidence of an intent to intimidate a person or group of persons."

[**Facts: Barry Black case**] On August 22, 1998, Barry Black led a Ku Klux Klan rally in Carroll County, Virginia. Twenty-five to thirty people attended this gathering, which occurred on private property with the permission of the owner, who was in attendance.

When the sheriff of Carroll County learned that a Klan rally was occurring in his county, he went to observe it from the side of the road. During the approximately one hour that the sheriff was present, about 40 to 50 cars passed the site, a "few" of which stopped to ask the sheriff what was happening on the property. Eight to ten houses were located in the vicinity of the rally. Rebecca Sechrist, who was related to the owner of the property where the rally took place, "sat and watched to see wha[t] [was] going on" from the lawn of her in-laws' house.

During the rally, Sechrist heard Klan members speak about "what they were" and "what they believed in." The speakers "talked real bad about the blacks and the Mexicans." One speaker told the assembled gathering that "he would love to take a .30/.30 and just random[ly] shoot the blacks." The speakers also talked about "President Clinton and Hillary Clinton," and about how their tax money "goes to…the black people." Sechrist testified that this language made her "very… scared."

At the conclusion of the rally, the crowd circled around a 25- to 30-foot cross. The cross was between 300 and 350 yards away from the road. According to the sheriff, the cross "then all of a sudden…went up in a flame." As the cross burned, the

Klan played Amazing Grace over the loudspeakers. Sechrist stated that the cross burning made her feel "awful" and "terrible."

When the sheriff observed the cross burning, he informed his deputy that they needed to "find out who's responsible and explain to them that they cannot do this in the State of Virginia." The sheriff then went down the driveway, entered the rally, and asked "who was responsible for burning the cross." Black responded, "I guess I am because I'm the head of the rally." The sheriff then told Black, "[T] here's a law in the State of Virginia that you cannot burn a cross and I'll have to place you under arrest for this."

Black was charged with burning a cross with the intent of intimidating a person or group of persons, in violation of state law. At his trial, the jury was instructed that "intent to intimidate means the motivation to intentionally put a person or a group of persons in fear of bodily harm. Such fear must arise from the willful conduct of the accused rather than from some mere temperamental timidity of the victim." The trial court also instructed the jury that "the burning of a cross by itself is sufficient evidence from which you may infer the required intent." When Black objected to this last instruction on First Amendment grounds, the prosecutor responded that the instruction was "taken straight out of the [Virginia] Model Instructions." The jury found Black guilty, and fined him $2,500. The Court of Appeals of Virginia affirmed Black's conviction.

[**Facts: Elliott and O'Mara case**] On May 2, 1998, respondents Richard Elliott and Jonathan O'Mara, as well as a third individual, attempted to burn a cross on the yard of James Jubilee. Jubilee, an African-American, was Elliott's next-door neighbor in Virginia Beach, Virginia. Four months prior to the incident, Jubilee and his family had moved from California to Virginia Beach. Before the cross burning, Jubilee spoke to Elliott's mother to inquire about shots being fired from behind the Elliott home. Elliott's mother explained to Jubilee that her son shot firearms as a hobby, and that he used the backyard as a firing range.

On the night of May 2, respondents drove a truck onto Jubilee's property, planted a cross, and set it on fire. Their apparent motive was to "get back" at Jubilee for complaining about the shooting in the backyard. Respondents were not affiliated with the Klan. The next morning, as Jubilee was pulling his car out of the drive-way, he noticed the partially burned cross approximately 20 feet from his house. After seeing the cross, Jubilee was "very nervous" because he "didn't know what would be the next phase," and because "a cross burned in your yard...tells you that it's just the first round."

Elliott and O'Mara were charged with attempted cross burning and conspiracy to commit cross burning. O'Mara pleaded guilty to both counts, reserving the right to challenge the constitutionality of the cross-burning statute. The judge sentenced O'Mara to 90 days in jail and fined him $2,500. The judge also suspended 45 days of the sentence and $1,000 of the fine.

At Elliott's trial, the judge originally ruled that the jury would be instructed "that the burning of a cross by itself is sufficient evidence from which you may infer the required intent." At trial, however, the court instructed the jury that the Commonwealth must prove that "the defendant intended to commit cross burning," that "the defendant did a direct act toward the commission of the cross burning," and that "the defendant had the intent of intimidating any person or group of persons." The court did not instruct the jury on the meaning of the word "intimidate," nor on the prima facie evidence provision of the statute. The jury found Elliott guilty of attempted cross burning and acquitted him of conspiracy to commit cross burning. It sentenced Elliott to 90 days in jail and a $2,500 fine. The Court of Appeals of Virginia affirmed the convictions of both Elliott and O'Mara.

Each respondent appealed to the Supreme Court of Virginia, arguing that the statute is facially unconstitutional. The Supreme Court of Virginia consolidated all three cases, and held that the statute is unconstitutional on its face. It held that the Virginia cross-burning statute "is analytically indistinguishable from the ordinance found unconstitutional in *R.A.V. v. St. Paul* (1992)." The Virginia statute, the court held, discriminates on the basis of content since it "selectively chooses only cross burning because of its distinctive message." The court also held that the prima facie evidence provision renders the statute overbroad because "[t]he enhanced probability of prosecution under the statute chills the expression of protected speech."

[History of cross burning] Burning a cross in the United States is inextricably intertwined with the history of the Ku Klux Klan.

The first Ku Klux Klan began in Pulaski, Tennessee, in the spring of 1866. The Klan fought Reconstruction and the corresponding drive to allow freed blacks to participate in the political process. Soon the Klan imposed "a veritable reign of terror" throughout the South. The Klan employed tactics such as whipping, threatening to burn people at the stake, and murder. By the end of Reconstruction in 1877, the first Klan no longer existed.

The genesis of the second Klan began in 1905, with the publication of Thomas Dixon's *The Clansmen: An Historical Romance of the Ku Klux Klan*. Dixon's book was a sympathetic portrait of the first Klan, depicting the Klan as a group of heroes "saving" the South from blacks and the "horrors" of Reconstruction. When D.W. Griffith turned Dixon's book into the movie *The Birth of a Nation* in 1915, the association between cross burning and the Klan became indelible.

From the inception of the second Klan, cross burnings have been used to communicate both threats of violence and messages of shared ideology. The first initiation ceremony occurred on Stone Mountain near Atlanta, Georgia. While a 40-foot cross burned on the mountain, the Klan members took their oaths of loyalty. The first known cross burning in the country had occurred a little over one month before the Klan initiation, when a Georgia mob celebrated the lynching of Leo Frank by burning a "gigantic cross" on Stone Mountain that was "visible throughout" Atlanta.

The decision of this Court in *Brown v. Board of Education* (1954), along with the civil rights movement of the 1950's and 1960's, sparked another outbreak of Klan violence. These acts of violence included bombings, beatings, shootings, stabbings, and mutilations. Members of the Klan burned crosses on the lawns of those associated with the civil rights movement, assaulted the Freedom Riders, bombed churches, and murdered blacks as well as whites whom the Klan viewed as sympathetic toward the civil rights movement.

And while cross burning sometimes carries no intimidating message, at other times the intimidating message is the *only* message conveyed. For example, when a cross burning is directed at a particular person not affiliated with the Klan, the burning cross often serves as a message of intimidation, designed to inspire in the victim a fear of bodily harm. Moreover, the history of violence associated with the Klan shows that the possibility of injury or death is not just hypothetical. Indeed, as the cases of respondents Elliott and O'Mara indicate, individuals without Klan affiliation who wish to threaten or menace another person sometimes use cross burning because of this association between a burning cross and violence.

In sum, while a burning cross does not inevitably convey a message of intimidation, often the cross burner intends that the recipients of the message fear for their lives.

The First Amendment, applicable to the States through the Fourteenth Amendment, provides that "Congress shall make no law...abridging the freedom of speech." The hallmark of the protection of free speech is to allow "free trade in ideas"—even ideas that the overwhelming majority of people might find distasteful or discomforting. *Abrams v. United States* (1919); see also *Texas v. Johnson* (1989) ("If there is a bedrock principle underlying the First Amendment, it is that the government may not prohibit the expression of an idea simply because society finds the idea itself offensive or disagreeable"). Thus, the First Amendment "ordinarily" denies a State "the power to prohibit dissemination of social, economic and political doctrine which a vast majority of its citizens believes to be false and fraught with evil consequence." *Whitney v. California* (1927). The First Amendment affords protection to symbolic or expressive conduct as well as to actual speech.

[**Unprotected speech**] The protections afforded by the First Amendment, however, are not absolute, and we have long recognized that the government may regulate certain categories of expression consistent with the Constitution. See, *e.g.*, *Chaplinsky v. New Hampshire* (1942) ("There are certain well-defined and narrowly limited classes of speech, the prevention and punishment of which has never been thought to raise any Constitutional problem"). The First Amendment permits "restrictions upon the content of speech in a few limited areas, which are 'of such slight social value as a step to truth that any benefit that may be derived from them is clearly outweighed by the social interest in order and morality.'" *R.A.V. v. City of St. Paul* (1992) (quoting *Chaplinsky v. New Hampshire*).

[**Incitement to imminent lawless**] Thus, for example, a State may punish those words "which by their very utterance inflict injury or tend to incite an immediate breach of the peace." *Chaplinsky v. New Hampshire, R.A.V. v. City of St. Paul* (listing limited areas where the First Amendment permits restrictions on the content of speech). [**Fighting words**] We have consequently held that fighting words—"those personally abusive epithets which, when addressed to the ordinary citizen, are, as a matter of common knowledge, inherently likely to provoke violent reaction"—are generally proscribable under the First Amendment. *Cohen v. California* (1971). Furthermore, "the constitutional guarantees of free speech and free press do not permit a State to forbid or proscribe advocacy of the use of force or of law violation except where such advocacy is directed to inciting or producing imminent lawless action and is likely to incite or produce such action." *Brandenburg v. Ohio* (1969). And the First Amendment also permits a State to ban a "true threat." *Watts v. United States* (1969).

[**True threats**] "True threats" encompass those statements where the speaker means to communicate a serious expression of an intent to commit an act of unlawful violence to a particular individual or group of individuals. The speaker need not actually intend to carry out the threat. Rather, a prohibition on true threats "protect[s] individuals from the fear of violence" and "from the disruption that fear engenders," in addition to protecting people "from the possibility that the threatened violence will occur." *R.A.V. v. City of St. Paul*. Intimidation in the constitutionally proscribable sense of the word is a type of true threat, where a speaker directs a threat to a person or group of persons with the intent of placing the victim in fear of bodily harm or death. Respondents do not contest that some cross burnings fit within this meaning of intimidating speech, and rightly so. As noted, the history of cross burning in this country shows that cross burning is often intimidating, intended to create a pervasive fear in victims that they are a target of violence.

The Supreme Court of Virginia ruled that in light of *R.A.V. v. City of St. Paul*, even if it is constitutional to ban cross burning in a content-neutral manner, the Virginia cross-burning statute is unconstitutional because it discriminates on the basis of content and viewpoint. It is true, as the Supreme Court of Virginia held, that the burning of a cross is symbolic expression. The reason why the Klan burns a cross at its rallies, or individuals place a burning cross on someone else's lawn, is that the burning cross represents the message that the speaker wishes to communicate. Individuals burn crosses as opposed to other means of communication because cross burning carries a message in an effective and dramatic manner.

The fact that cross burning is symbolic expression, however, does not resolve the constitutional question. The Supreme Court of Virginia relied upon *R.A.V. v. City of St. Paul, supra*, to conclude that once a statute discriminates on the basis of this type of content, the law is unconstitutional. We disagree.

In *R.A.V.*, we held that a local ordinance that banned certain symbolic conduct, including cross burning, when done with the knowledge that such conduct would "'arouse anger, alarm or resentment in others on the basis of race, color, creed, religion or gender'" was unconstitutional.

We held that the ordinance did not pass constitutional muster because it discriminated on the basis of content by targeting only those individuals who "provoke violence" on a basis specified in the law. The ordinance did not cover "[t]hose who wish to use 'fighting words' in connection with other ideas—to express hostility, for example, on the basis of political affiliation, union membership, or homosexuality." This content-based discrimination was unconstitutional because it allowed the city "to impose special prohibitions on those speakers who express views on disfavored subjects."

We did not hold in *R.A.V.* that the First Amendment prohibits *all* forms of content-based discrimination within a proscribable area of speech. Rather, we specifically stated that some types of content discrimination did not violate the First Amendment:

> "When the basis for the content discrimination consists entirely of the very reason the entire class of speech at issue is proscribable, no significant danger of idea or viewpoint discrimination exists. Such a reason, having been adjudged neutral enough to support exclusion of the entire class of speech from First Amendment protection, is also neutral enough to form the basis of distinction within the class."

Indeed, we noted that it would be constitutional to ban only a particular type of threat: "[T]he Federal Government can criminalize only those threats of violence that are directed against the President...since the reasons why threats of violence are outside the First Amendment...have special force when applied to the person of the President." And a State may "choose to prohibit only that obscenity which is the most patently offensive *in its prurience—i.e.*, that which involves the most lascivious displays of sexual activity." (Emphasis in original). Consequently, while the holding of *R.A.V.* does not permit a State to ban only obscenity based on "offensive *political* messages" or "only those threats against the President that mention his policy on aid to inner cities," the First Amendment permits content discrimination "based on the very reasons why the particular class of speech at issue...is proscribable."

[**Key language: "intent to intimidate"**] Similarly, Virginia's statute does not run afoul of the First Amendment insofar as it bans cross burning with intent to intimidate. Unlike the statute at issue in *R.A.V.*, the Virginia statute does not single out for opprobrium only that speech directed toward "one of the specified disfavored topics." It does not matter whether an individual burns a cross with intent to intimidate because of the victim's race, gender, or religion, or because of the victim's "political affiliation, union membership, or homosexuality."

The First Amendment permits Virginia to outlaw cross burnings done with the intent to intimidate because burning a cross is a particularly virulent form of intimidation. Instead of prohibiting all intimidating messages, Virginia may choose to regulate this subset of intimidating messages in light of cross burning's long and pernicious history as a signal of impending violence.

[**Prima facie provision unconstitutional**] The prima facie evidence provision, as interpreted by the jury instruction, renders the statute unconstitutional. Because this jury instruction is the Model Jury Instruction, and because the Supreme Court of Virginia had the opportunity to expressly disavow the jury instruction, the jury instruction's construction of the prima facie provision "is a ruling on a question of state law that is as binding on us as though the precise words had been written into" the statute. As construed by the jury instruction, the prima facie provision strips away the very reason why a State may ban cross burning with the intent to intimidate. The prima facie evidence provision permits a jury to convict in every cross-burning case in which defendants exercise their constitutional right not to put on a defense. And even where a defendant like Black presents a defense, the prima facie evidence provision makes it more likely that the jury will find an intent to intimidate regardless of the particular facts of the case. The provision permits the Commonwealth to arrest, prosecute, and convict a person based solely on the fact of cross burning itself.

The prima facie evidence provision in this statute blurs the line between these two meanings of a burning cross. As interpreted by the jury instruction, the provision chills constitutionally protected political speech because of the possibility that a State will prosecute—and potentially convict—somebody engaging only in lawful political speech at the core of what the First Amendment is designed to protect.

[**Not all cross burnings the same**] As the history of cross burning indicates, a burning cross is not always intended to intimidate. Rather, sometimes the cross burning is a statement of ideology, a symbol of group solidarity. It is a ritual used at Klan gatherings, and it is used to represent the Klan itself.

The prima facie provision makes no effort to distinguish among these different types of cross burnings. It does not distinguish between a cross burning done with the purpose of creating anger or resentment and a cross burning done with the purpose of threatening or intimidating a victim. It does not distinguish between a cross burning at a public rally or a cross burning on a neighbor's lawn.

For these reasons, the prima facie evidence provision, as interpreted through the jury instruction and as applied in Barry Black's case, is unconstitutional on its face. We recognize that the Supreme Court of Virginia has not authoritatively interpreted the meaning of the prima facie evidence provision. Unlike Justice Scalia, we refuse to speculate on whether *any* interpretation of the prima facie evidence provision would satisfy the First Amendment. Rather, all we hold is that because of the interpretation of the prima facie evidence provision given by the jury instruction, the provision makes the statute facially invalid at this point.

[Holding] With respect to Barry Black, we agree with the Supreme Court of Virginia that his conviction cannot stand, and we affirm the judgment of the Supreme Court of Virginia. With respect to Elliott and O'Mara, we vacate the judgment of the Supreme Court of Virginia, and remand the case for further proceedings.

Points to Consider

1. Not all cross burnings are the same.

A key to the Court's opinion in *Virginia v. Black* was the idea that not all cross-burnings are the same. One of the cases before them involved Klan leader Barry Black, who burned a cross on property with the permission of the private property owner. The other case involved two non-Klansmen who burned a cross in the yard of an African-American family in an act of retribution. Arguably, Black did not burn the flag with an intent to intimidate, but more as a form of group solidarity. This explains why the Supreme Court agreed with the Virginia Supreme Court that Black's conviction was invalid. It also explains why the Court invalidated the part of the Virginia cross-burning law that made any act of cross burning "prima facie" evidence of an intent to intimidate.

2. David Baugh: Barry Black's trial attorney.

David Baugh, an African-American man, represented Barry Black at trial. Many respected Baugh for his passionate defense of the First Amendment—even defending a client who advocated the doctrine of white supremacy.

In the Supreme Court, Rodney Smolla, a noted First Amendment scholar, represented Barry Black and his co-defendants.

3. Noose banning laws.

In the wake of the *Virginia v. Black* decision, several states passed laws that criminalized the display of a noose with an "intent to intimidate." The underlying rationale is that, because a noose is the actual tool used for lynching, its display can clearly convey a true threat.

4. What about threats online?

In recent years, many cases have been brought alleging that individuals posting angry messages on social media had issued true threats. One of these reached the Supreme Court. Anthony Elonis, who professed to be an amateur rapper, posted hateful messages to his ex-wife and others on Facebook. He was prosecuted for making a true threat.

Elonis' case eventually reached the Supreme Court. Many expected that the Court would clarify its true threat jurisprudence in *Elonis v. United States* (2015), but it did not. Instead, the Court reversed Elonis' conviction because the jury instructions in the initial trial did not indicate that Elonis had to have the requisite level of intent necessary to carry out a threat. Chief Justice John Roberts pointed out that the jury instructions failed to focus on Elonis' intentions and mental state, and required only that Elonis have made a statement in a context that a reasonable person would interpret as threatening.

In 2010, federal authorities arrested a Kentucky man for posting a poem entitled "Sniper." The poem depicted a sniper assassinating President Barack Obama. Federal prosecutors contended that the poem represented a threat. The defendant received 33 months in prison for making threats against the president. Crimes and matters involving the safety of the president have traditionally been considered with a special sensitivity.

5. There is still confusion!

The Court's true threat jurisprudence is still less than clear. Should courts focus on a purely objective standard or a subjective standard? Must conduct be intentional or can a person recklessly issue a true threat?

These are questions that have not been definitively answered. In 2017, Justice Sonia Sotomayor called on her colleagues to address these issues in her comments regarding a Florida case in which a man received a 15-year sentence for what appeared to be a drunken rant in a convenience store.

"States must prove more than the mere utterance of threatening words—some level of intent is required," she wrote. "The Court should also decide precisely what level of intent suffices under the First Amendment—a question we avoided two Terms ago in *Elonis*."

9.

Words That Wound:
Lies, Defamation, & Invasion of Privacy

And though all the winds of doctrine were let loose to play upon the earth, so Truth be in the field, we do injuriously by licensing and prohibiting to misdoubt her strength. Let her and Falsehood grapple; who ever knew Truth put to the worse in a free and open encounter?

—*Areopagitica, John Milton*

DEFAMATION

TELLING THE TRUTH is almost universally regarded as a fundamental good. Here in the United States, children are taught the importance of honesty from an early age through stories like the tale of George Washington and the cherry tree, and the boy who cried wolf.

But as we have seen in the preceding chapters, the First Amendment shields a great deal of speech that is far from encouraged—hateful screeds, for example, or pornography. So what about lies? Does the First Amendment protect the opposite of the truth we so clearly value? Do we share Milton's conviction that truth will always triumph over falsehood?

Falsehood comes in many flavors, of course. In this chapter, we will discuss the First Amendment implications of flatly lying about one's honors and accomplishments—the kind of basic résumé fraud put forth by blowhards in bars and boardrooms nationwide. But we'll also examine dishonesty regarding others, including elected officials and private citizens, and the First Amendment's interaction with satire, defamation, and invasion of privacy. In each case, we'll ask: Do those "wounded" by false words have recourse against the speaker?

As a lawyer might answer: "It depends."

Simply speaking, defamation is a false statement that harms the reputation of another. When written, defamatory statements are known as libel; when spoken, they are known as slander. In the United States, defamation is a tort—a civil, rather than criminal, wrong.

A defamation plaintiff must establish all of the following six elements:

1. *Identification*: The publication was "of and concerning" the plaintiff.
2. *Publication*: The defamatory statements were disseminated to a third party.
3. *Defamatory meaning*: The statements in question were defamatory.
4. *Falsity*: The statements must be false. Truth is an absolute defense to a defamation claim. Generally, the plaintiff bears the burden of proof of establishing falsity.
5. *Statements of fact*: The statements in question must be objectively verifiable as false statements of fact. This means the statements were presented as true facts, but are demonstrably false.
6. *Damages*: The false and defamatory statements must cause actual injury or special damages.

We penalize defamation in an attempt to protect a person's "good name," and defamation is an ancient offense. One of the Ten Commandments revealed to Moses barred bearing false witness against one's neighbor, and prohibitions against defamation evolved through the Middle Ages and English common law.

Given the centrality of reputation to our social, professional, and emotional identities, the fact that humans have been concerned with defamation for millennia is perhaps unsurprising. Reviewing the "social norms that underlie defamation law," scholar David S. Ardia argued that reputation provides an essential foundation for the development of human civilization:

> What makes humankind uniquely capable of creating complex social systems is our ability to assess, process, and communicate reputational information. This reputational information is distinguishable from other behavioral cues in that it allows third parties—who have had no previous involvement with the original parties—to make assessments about the characteristics (e.g., honesty, skill, kindness) of others. The ability to assess a previously unknown party's reputation helps explain how cooperation was achievable at all when human interactions moved beyond small villages where one could rely on a history of personal interactions.

In other words, as Justice Brennan put it in 1966's *Rosenblatt v. Baer*, "Society has a pervasive and strong interest in preventing and redressing attacks upon reputation."

DEFAMING PUBLIC FIGURES

What happens when our societal commitment to protecting reputational interests is in tension with our First Amendment freedom to tell the government exactly what we think of it? What happens when the good name of a government official is supposedly at stake?

In the next case—often hailed as the most important First Amendment decision ever issued—the Supreme Court answered precisely that question. Here's the full-page advertisement that sparked the case:

The civil rights movement advertisement at issue in the New York Times *case.*

OPINION

New York Times Company v. Sullivan

(Abridged.)

376 U.S. 254 (1964)
Vote: 8–0

JUSTICE BRENNAN delivered the opinion of the Court.

[**Issue**] We are required in this case to determine for the first time the extent to which the constitutional protections for speech and press limit a State's power to award damages in a libel action brought by a public official against critics of his official conduct.

[**Facts**] Respondent L.B. Sullivan is one of the three elected Commissioners of the City of Montgomery, Alabama. He testified that he was "Commissioner of Public Affairs and the duties are supervision of the Police Department, Fire Department, Department of Cemetery and Department of Scales." He brought this civil libel action against the four individual petitioners, who are Negroes and Alabama clergymen, and against petitioner the New York Times Company, a New York corporation which publishes the New York Times, a daily newspaper. A jury in the Circuit Court of Montgomery County awarded him damages of $500,000, the full amount claimed, against all the petitioners, and the Supreme Court of Alabama affirmed.

Respondent's complaint alleged that he had been libeled by statements in a full-page advertisement that was carried in the New York Times on March 29, 1960. Entitled "Heed Their Rising Voices," the advertisement began by stating that "As the whole world knows by now, thousands of Southern Negro students are engaged in widespread non-violent demonstrations in positive affirmation of the right to live in human dignity as guaranteed by the U. S. Constitution and the Bill of Rights." It went on to charge that "in their efforts to uphold these guarantees, they are being met by an unprecedented wave of terror by those who would deny and negate that document which the whole world looks upon as setting the pattern for modern freedom...." Succeeding paragraphs purported to illustrate the "wave of terror" by describing certain alleged events. The text concluded with an appeal for funds for three purposes: support of the student movement, "the struggle for the right-to-vote," and the legal defense of Dr. Martin Luther King, Jr., leader of the movement, against a perjury indictment then pending in Montgomery.

[Libel claim] Of the 10 paragraphs of text in the advertisement, the third and a portion of the sixth were the basis of respondent's claim of libel. They read as follows:

Third paragraph:

> "In Montgomery, Alabama, after students sang 'My Country, 'Tis of Thee' on the State Capitol steps, their leaders were expelled from school, and truckloads of police armed with shotguns and tear-gas ringed the Alabama State College Campus. When the entire student body protested to state authorities by refusing to re-register, their dining hall was padlocked in an attempt to starve them into submission."

Sixth paragraph:

> "Again and again the Southern violators have answered Dr. King's peaceful protests with intimidation and violence. They have bombed his home almost killing his wife and child. They have assaulted his person. They have arrested him seven times—for 'speeding,' 'loitering' and similar 'offenses.' And now they have charged him with 'perjury'—a *felony* under which they could imprison him for *ten years*...."

Although neither of these statements mentions respondent by name, he contended that the word "police" in the third paragraph referred to him as the Montgomery Commissioner who supervised the Police Department, so that he was being accused of "ringing" the campus with police. He further claimed that the paragraph would be read as imputing to the police, and hence to him, the padlocking of the dining hall in order to starve the students into submission. As to the sixth paragraph, he contended that since arrests are ordinarily made by the police, the statement "They have arrested [Dr. King] seven times" would be read as referring to him; he further contended that the "They" who did the arresting would be equated with the "They" who committed the other described acts and with the "Southern violators." Thus, he argued, the paragraph would be read as accusing the Montgomery police, and hence him, of answering Dr. King's protests with "intimidation and violence," bombing his home, assaulting his person, and charging him with perjury. Respondent and six other Montgomery residents testified that they read some or all of the statements as referring to him in his capacity as Commissioner.

[**Truth of statements**] It is uncontroverted that some of the statements contained in the paragraphs were not accurate descriptions of events which occurred in Montgomery. Although Negro students staged a demonstration on the State Capitol steps, they sang the National Anthem and not "My Country, 'Tis of Thee." Although nine students were expelled by the State Board of Education, this was not for leading the demonstration at the Capitol, but for demanding service at a lunch counter in the Montgomery County Courthouse on another day. Not the entire student body, but most of it, had protested the expulsion, not by refusing to register, but by boycotting classes on a single day; virtually all the students did register for the ensuing semester. The campus dining hall was not padlocked on any occasion, and the only students who may have been barred from eating there were the few who had neither signed a preregistration application nor requested temporary meal tickets. Although the police were deployed near the campus in large numbers on three occasions, they did not at any time "ring" the campus, and they were not called to the campus in connection with the demonstration on the State Capitol steps, as the third paragraph implied. Dr. King had not been arrested seven times, but only four; and although he claimed to have been assaulted some years earlier in connection with his arrest for loitering outside a courtroom, one of the officers who made the arrest denied that there was such an assault.

On the premise that the charges in the sixth paragraph could be read as referring to him, respondent was allowed to prove that he had not participated in the events described. Although Dr. King's home had in fact been bombed twice when his wife and child were there, both of these occasions antedated respondent's tenure as Commissioner, and the police were not only not implicated in the bombings, but had made every effort to apprehend those who were. Three of Dr. King's four arrests took place before respondent became Commissioner. Although Dr. King had in fact been indicted (he was subsequently acquitted) on two counts of perjury, each of which carried a possible five-year sentence, respondent had nothing to do with procuring the indictment.

[**Harm suffered**] Respondent made no effort to prove that he suffered actual pecuniary loss as a result of the alleged libel. One of his witnesses, a former employer, testified that if he had believed the statements, he doubted whether he "would want to be associated with anybody who would be a party to such things that are stated in that ad," and that he would not re-employ respondent if he believed "that he allowed the Police Department to do the things that the paper say he did." But neither this witness nor any of the others testified that he had actually believed the statements in their supposed reference to respondent.

[**Trial judge's ruling**] The judge rejected petitioners' contention that his rulings abridged the freedoms of speech and of the press that are guaranteed by the First and Fourteenth Amendments.

[**Appeal to the Supreme Court of Alabama**] In affirming the judgment, the Supreme Court of Alabama sustained the trial judge's rulings and instructions in all respects. It rejected petitioners' constitutional contentions with the brief statements that "The First Amendment of the U. S. Constitution does not protect libelous publications" and "The Fourteenth Amendment is directed against State action and not private action."

[**U.S. Supreme Court's review**] Because of the importance of the constitutional issues involved, we granted the separate petitions for certiorari of the individual petitioners and of the Times. We reverse the judgment. We hold that the rule of law applied by the Alabama courts is constitutionally deficient for failure to provide the safeguards for freedom of speech and of the press that are required by the First and Fourteenth Amendments in a libel action brought by a public official against critics of his official conduct.

[**Libel**] In deciding the question now, we are compelled by neither precedent nor policy to give any more weight to the epithet "libel" than we have to other "mere labels" of state law. Like insurrection, contempt, advocacy of unlawful acts, breach of the peace, obscenity, solicitation of legal business, and the various other formulae for the repression of expression that have been challenged in this court, libel can claim no talismanic immunity from constitutional limitations. It must be measured by standards that satisfy the First Amendment.

The general proposition that freedom of expression upon public questions is secured by the First Amendment has long been settled by our decisions. The constitutional safeguard, we have said, "was fashioned to assure unfettered interchange of ideas for the bringing about of political and social changes desired by the people." *Roth v. United States* (1957).

[**Competing interests**] Thus we consider this case against the background of a profound national commitment to the principle that debate on public issues should be uninhibited, robust, and wide-open, and that it may well include vehement, caustic, and sometimes unpleasantly sharp attacks on government and public officials. The present advertisement, as an expression of grievance and protest on one of the major public issues of our time, would seem clearly to qualify for the constitutional protection. The question is whether it forfeits that protection by the falsity of some of its factual statements and by its alleged defamation of respondent.

Authoritative interpretations of the First Amendment guarantees have consistently refused to recognize an exception for any test of truth—whether administered by judges, juries, or administrative officials—and especially one that puts the burden of proving truth on the speaker. The constitutional protection does not turn upon "the truth, popularity, or social utility of the ideas and beliefs which are offered." *NAACP v. Button* (1963). As Madison said, "Some degree of abuse is inseparable from the proper use of every thing; and in no instance is this more true than in that of the press." *Elliot's Debates on the Federal Constitution* (1876).

Injury to official reputation affords no more warrant for repressing speech that would otherwise be free than does factual error. Where judicial officers are involved, this Court has held that concern for the dignity and reputation of the courts does not justify the punishment as criminal contempt of criticism of the judge or his decision. *Bridges v. California* (1941). If judges are to be treated as "men of fortitude, able to thrive in a hardy climate," *Craig v. Harney* (1947), surely the same must be true of other government officials, such as elected city commissioners. Criticism of their official conduct does not lose its constitutional protection merely because it is effective criticism and hence diminishes their official reputations.

A rule compelling the critic of official conduct to guarantee the truth of all his factual assertions—and to do so on pain of libel judgments virtually unlimited in amount—leads to a comparable "self-censorship." Allowance of the defense of truth, with the burden of proving it on the defendant, does not mean that only false speech will be deterred. Even courts accepting this defense as an adequate safeguard have recognized the difficulties of adducing legal proofs that the alleged libel was true in all its factual particulars. Under such a rule, would-be critics of official conduct may be deterred from voicing their criticism, even though it is believed to be true and even though it is in fact true, because of doubt whether it can be proved in court or fear of the expense of having to do so. They tend to make only statements which "steer far wider of the unlawful zone." *Speiser v.*

Randall (1958). The rule thus dampens the vigor and limits the variety of public debate. It is inconsistent with the First and Fourteenth Amendments.

[**Defamation legal test**] The constitutional guarantees require, we think, a federal rule that prohibits a public official from recovering damages for a defamatory falsehood relating to his official conduct unless he proves that the statement was made with "actual malice"—that is, with knowledge that it was false or with reckless disregard of whether it was false or not.

[**Application of test**] Applying these standards, we consider that the proof presented to show actual malice lacks the convincing clarity which the constitutional standard demands, and hence that it would not constitutionally sustain the judgment for respondent under the proper rule of law.

[**Criticism of government as "personal criticism"**] We also think the evidence was constitutionally defective in another respect: it was incapable of supporting the jury's finding that the allegedly libelous statements were made "of and concerning" respondent.

For good reason, "no court of last resort in this country has ever held, or even suggested, that prosecutions for libel on government have any place in the American system of jurisprudence." *City of Chicago v. Tribune Co.* (1923). The present proposition would sidestep this obstacle by transmuting criticism of government, however impersonal it may seem on its face, into personal criticism, and hence potential libel, of the officials of whom the government is composed. There is no legal alchemy by which a State may thus create the cause of action that would otherwise be denied for a publication which, as respondent himself said of the advertisement, "reflects not only on me but on the other Commissioners and the community." Raising as it does the possibility that a good-faith critic of government will be penalized for his criticism, the proposition relied on by the Alabama courts strikes at the very center of the constitutionally protected area of free expression. [**Ruling**] We hold that such a proposition may not constitutionally be utilized to establish that an otherwise impersonal attack on governmental operations was a libel of an official responsible for those operations. Since it was relied on exclusively here, and there was no other evidence to connect the statements with respondent, the evidence was constitutionally insufficient to support a finding that the statements referred to respondent.

The judgment of the Supreme Court of Alabama is reversed and the case is remanded to that court for further proceedings not inconsistent with this opinion.

Points to Consider

1. The aftermath.

The Court's ruling impacted not just the *New York Times*, but newspapers nationwide. For publications engaged in the daily work of covering the movement for equality and racial justice, the financial stakes were massive. The trial jury's award of $500,000 to plaintiff L.B. Sullivan (the full amount requested by the complaint) would have been the equivalent of over $4 million in 2018.

Sullivan's libel suit wasn't the only one filed against the *Times* over this advertisement, either; there were five other libel claims brought by Alabama officials, seeking a total of $3 million in damages—over $24.5 million today. As Professor Mary-Rose Papandrea notes, other papers faced similar suits filed by officials in segregated states who wanted to stop journalists from covering civil rights activism: "By 1964, the press was facing almost $300 million in potential libel damages." Again, adjusting for inflation, that's an over $2.4 *billion* risk for reporting on the Civil Rights Movement—and because losing a libel case could bankrupt a paper, these lawsuits effectively constituted an attempt at censorship by other means.

2. Sullivan *as a landmark decision for civil rights.*

Had the threat of financially ruinous libel lawsuits remained viable, officials like Sullivan might well have scared newspapers into silence—effectively allowing violent reprisals against brave civil rights demonstrators to continue. Without national attention to the injustice and inequality of the Jim Crow South, the civil rights movement might have taken a much different path. These high stakes were apparent to the Supreme Court justices, who might well have ruled differently had the possibility of continued racial injustice not been presented squarely before them.

3. The Court's rule.

A public official cannot recover damages for allegedly defamatory statements concerning his conduct "unless he proves that the statement was made with 'actual malice'—that is, with knowledge that it was false or with reckless disregard of whether it was false or not." That's a high bar to meet—and because the First Amendment backstopped the Court's analysis, it's effectively a national standard.

4. What does "actual malice" look like in practice?

In 1989's *Harte-Hanks Communications v. Connaughton*, the Court found that a newspaper's failure to interview a key witness or listen to tapes containing relevant information—despite otherwise diligent reporting—was "utterly bewildering" and strongly suggested a "deliberate decision not to acquire knowledge of facts that might confirm the probable falsity" of the paper's story. "Although failure to investigate will not alone support a finding of actual malice, the purposeful avoidance of the truth is in a different category," wrote the Court.

5. What about public figures—people who, while not holding government office, are nevertheless well known?

In the combined cases of *Curtis Publishing Co. v. Butts* (1967) and *Associated Press v. Walker* (1967), the Court considered two state libel cases that raised this question. *Butts* involved a *Saturday Evening Post* article that accused Wally Butts, former head coach of the University of Georgia's football team, of throwing a game against the University of Alabama. In *Walker*, Edwin A. Walker, a private citizen, was reported by the Associated Press to have led a violent crowd in a charge against federal marshals who were attempting to uphold a court decree to desegregate the University of Mississippi.

The Court determined that because both men enjoyed "sufficient continuing public interest and had sufficient access to the means of counterargument to be able 'to expose through discussion the falsehood and fallacies' of the defamatory statements," they were the functional equivalent of the government officials in *Sullivan*. In his concurring opinion, Chief Justice Warren extended the "actual malice" standard to "public figures," writing: "Evenly applied to cases involving 'public men'—whether they be 'public officials' or 'public figures'—[the standard] will afford the necessary insulation for the fundamental interests which the First Amendment was designed to protect."

Recently, courts have had to grapple with defamation charges against public figures such as comedian John Oliver and conspiracy theorist Alex Jones.

DEFAMATION AND PRIVATE INDIVIDUALS

That's the law for public figures. What about private citizens? In a case pitting attorney Elmer Gertz (famous for representing author Henry Miller and Jack Ruby, who killed Lee Harvey Oswald) against Robert Welch (founder of the conservative John Birch Society), the Supreme Court would consider whether to apply the "actual malice" standard to the rest of us.

OPINION

Gertʑ v. Robert Welch, Inc.

(Abridged.)

418 U.S. 323 (1974)
Vote: 7–2

JUSTICE POWELL delivered the opinion of the Court.

[**Issue**] This Court has struggled for nearly a decade to define the proper accommodation between the law of defamation and the freedoms of speech and press protected by the First Amendment. With this decision we return to that effort. We granted certiorari to reconsider the extent of a publisher's constitutional privilege against liability for defamation of a private citizen.

[**Facts**] In 1968 a Chicago policeman named Nuccio shot and killed a youth named Nelson. The state authorities prosecuted Nuccio for the homicide and ultimately obtained a conviction for murder in the second degree. The Nelson family retained petitioner Elmer Gertz, a reputable attorney, to represent them in civil litigation against Nuccio.

Respondent publishes American Opinion, a monthly outlet for the views of the John Birch Society. Early in the 1960's the magazine began to warn of a nationwide conspiracy to discredit local law enforcement agencies and create in their stead a national police force capable of supporting a Communist dictatorship. As part of the continuing effort to alert the public to this assumed danger, the managing editor of American Opinion commissioned an article on the murder trial of Officer Nuccio. In March 1969 respondent published the resulting article under the title "FRAME-UP: Richard Nuccio And The War On Police." The article purports to demonstrate that the testimony against Nuccio at his criminal trial was false and that his prosecution was part of the Communist campaign against the police.

In his capacity as counsel for the Nelson family in the civil litigation, petitioner attended the coroner's inquest into the boy's death and initiated actions for damages, but he neither discussed Officer Nuccio with the press nor played any part in the criminal proceeding. Notwithstanding petitioner's remote connection with the prosecution of Nuccio, respondent's magazine portrayed him as an architect of the "frame-up." According to the article, the police file on petitioner took "a big, Irish cop to lift." The article stated that petitioner had been an official of the "Marxist League for Industrial Democracy, originally known as the Intercollegiate Socialist Society, which has advocated the violent seizure of our government." It labeled Gertz a "Leninist" and a "Communist-fronter." It also stated that Gertz had been an officer of the National Lawyers Guild, described as a Communist organization that "probably did more than any other outfit to plan the Communist attack on the Chicago police during the 1968 Democratic Convention."

These statements contained serious inaccuracies. The implication that petitioner had a criminal record was false. Petitioner had been a member and officer of the National Lawyers Guild some 15 years earlier, but there was no evidence that he or that organization had taken any part in planning the 1968 demonstrations in Chicago. There was also no basis for the charge that petitioner was a "Leninist" or a "Communist-fronter." And he had never been a member of the "Marxist League for Industrial Democracy" or the "Intercollegiate Socialist Society."

The managing editor of American Opinion made no effort to verify or substantiate the charges against petitioner. Instead, he appended an editorial introduction stating that the author had "conducted extensive research into the Richard Nuccio Case." And he included in the article a photograph of petitioner and wrote the caption that appeared under it: "Elmer Gertz of Red Guild harrasses Nuccio." Respondent placed the issue of American Opinion containing the article on sale at newsstands throughout the country and distributed reprints of the article on the streets of Chicago.

Petitioner filed a diversity action for libel in the United States District Court for the Northern District of Illinois.

[**Defendants' response**] After answering the complaint, respondent filed a pretrial motion for summary judgment, claiming a constitutional privilege against liability for defamation. It asserted that petitioner was a public official or a public figure and that the article concerned an issue of public interest and concern. For these reasons, respondent argued, it was entitled to invoke the privilege enunciated in *New York Times Co. v. Sullivan* (1964). Under this rule respondent would escape liability unless petitioner could prove publication of defamatory falsehood "with 'actual malice'—that is, with knowledge that it was false or with reckless disregard of whether it was false or not." Respondent claimed that petitioner could not make such a showing and submitted a supporting affidavit by the magazine's managing editor. The editor denied any knowledge of the falsity of the statements concerning petitioner and stated that he had relied on the author's reputation and on his prior experience with the accuracy and authenticity of the author's contributions to American Opinion.

[**District court ruling**] The jury awarded $50,000 to petitioner. Following the jury verdict and on further reflection, the District Court concluded that the *New York Times* standard should govern this case even though petitioner was not a public official or public figure. It accepted respondent's contention that that privilege protected discussion of any public issue without regard to the status of a person defamed therein. Accordingly, the court entered judgment for respondent notwithstanding the jury's verdict.

[**Appeal**] Petitioner appealed to contest the applicability of the *New York Times* standard to this case. Although the Court of Appeals for the Seventh Circuit doubted the correctness of the District Court's determination that petitioner was not a public figure, it did not overturn that finding. It agreed with the District Court that respondent could assert the constitutional privilege because the article concerned a matter of public interest...

[**U.S. Supreme Court's review**] For the reasons stated below, we reverse.

[**Issue**] The principal issue in this case is whether a newspaper or broadcaster that publishes defamatory falsehoods about an individual who is neither a public official nor a public figure may claim a constitutional privilege against liability for the injury inflicted by those statements.

[**Analysis**] Under the First Amendment, there is no such thing as a false idea. However pernicious an opinion may seem, we depend for its correction not on the conscience of judges and juries but on the competition of other ideas. But there is no constitutional value in false statements of fact. Neither the intentional lie nor the careless error materially advances society's interest in "uninhibited, robust, and wide-open" debate on public issues. *New York Times Co. v. Sullivan.* They belong to that category of utterances which "are no essential part of any exposition of ideas, and are of such slight social value as a step to truth that any benefit that may be derived from them is clearly outweighed by the social interest in order and morality." *Chaplinsky v. New Hampshire* (1942).

Although the erroneous statement of fact is not worthy of constitutional protection, it is nevertheless inevitable in free debate. Our decisions recognize that a rule of strict liability that compels a publisher or broadcaster to guarantee the accuracy of his factual assertions may lead to intolerable self-censorship. Allowing the media to avoid liability only by proving the truth of all injurious statements does not accord adequate protection to First Amendment liberties. The First Amendment requires that we protect some falsehood in order to protect speech that matters.

The need to avoid self-censorship by the news media is, however, not the only societal value at issue. If it were, this Court would have embraced long ago the view that publishers and broadcasters enjoy an unconditional and indefeasible immunity from liability for defamation.

The legitimate state interest underlying the law of libel is the compensation of individuals for the harm inflicted on them by defamatory falsehood.

Some tension necessarily exists between the need for a vigorous and uninhibited press and the legitimate interest in redressing wrongful injury.

[**Public figures**] The *New York Times* standard defines the level of constitutional protection appropriate to the context of defamation of a public person. Those who, by reason of the notoriety of their achievements or the vigor and success with which they seek the public's attention, are properly classed as public figures and those who hold governmental office may recover for injury to reputation only on clear and convincing proof that the defamatory falsehood was made with knowledge of its falsity or with reckless disregard for the truth. This standard administers an extremely powerful antidote to the inducement to media self-censorship of the common-law rule of strict liability for libel and slander. And it exacts a correspondingly high price from the victims of defamatory falsehood.

[**Private individuals**] For the reasons stated below, we conclude that the state interest in compensating injury to the reputation of private individuals requires that a different rule should obtain with respect to them.

[**Susceptibility to injury**] We have no difficulty in distinguishing among defamation plaintiffs. The first remedy of any victim of defamation is self-help—using available opportunities to contradict the lie or correct the error and thereby to minimize its adverse impact on reputation. Public officials and public figures usually enjoy significantly greater access to the channels of effective communication and hence have a more realistic opportunity to counteract false statements than private individuals normally enjoy. Private individuals are therefore more vulnerable to injury, and the state interest in protecting them is correspondingly greater.

[**Public figures assent to scrutiny**] More important than the likelihood that private individuals will lack effective opportunities for rebuttal, there is a compelling normative consideration underlying the distinction between public and private defamation plaintiffs. An individual who decides to seek governmental office must accept certain necessary consequences of that involvement in public affairs. He runs the risk of closer public scrutiny than might otherwise be the case. And society's interest in the officers of government is not strictly limited to the formal discharge of official duties. As the Court pointed out in *Garrison v. Louisiana* (1964), the public's interest extends to "anything which might touch on an official's fitness for office....Few personal attributes are more germane to fitness for office than dishonesty, malfeasance, or improper motivation, even though these characteristics may also affect the official's private character."

Those classed as public figures stand in a similar position. Hypothetically, it may be possible for someone to become a public figure through no purposeful action of his own, but the instances of truly involuntary public figures must be exceedingly rare. For the most part those who attain this status have assumed roles of especial prominence in the affairs of society. Some occupy positions of such persuasive power and influence that they are deemed public figures for all purposes. More commonly, those classed as public figures have thrust themselves to the forefront of particular public controversies in order to influence the resolution of the issues involved. In either event, they invite attention and comment.

[**Private individuals**] No such assumption is justified with respect to a private individual. He has not accepted public office or assumed an "influential role in ordering society." *Curtis Publishing Co. v. Butts* (1967). He has relinquished no part of his interest in the protection of his own good name, and consequently he has a more compelling call on the courts for redress of injury inflicted by defamatory falsehood. Thus, private individuals are not only more vulnerable to injury than public officials and public figures; they are also more deserving of recovery.

For these reasons, we conclude that the States should retain substantial latitude in their efforts to enforce a legal remedy for defamatory falsehood injurious to the reputation of a private individual.

[Holding] We hold that, so long as they do not impose liability without fault, the States may define for themselves the appropriate standard of liability for a publisher or broadcaster of defamatory falsehood injurious to a private individual. This approach provides a more equitable boundary between the competing concerns involved here. It recognizes the strength of the legitimate state interest in compensating private individuals for wrongful injury to reputation, yet shields the press and broadcast media from the rigors of strict liability for defamation.

[Damages] But this countervailing state interest extends no further than compensation for actual injury. We hold that the States may not permit recovery of presumed or punitive damages, at least when liability is not based on a showing of knowledge of falsity or reckless disregard for the truth.

The private defamation plaintiff who establishes liability under a less demanding standard than that stated by *New York Times* may recover only such damages as are sufficient to compensate him for actual injury.

[Application of holding to facts] Petitioner has served as an officer of local civic groups and of various professional organizations, and he has published several books and articles on legal subjects. Although petitioner was consequently well known in some circles, he had achieved no general fame or notoriety in the community. None of the prospective jurors called at the trial had ever heard of petitioner prior to this litigation, and respondent offered no proof that this response was atypical of the local population. We would not lightly assume that a citizen's participation in community and professional affairs rendered him a public figure for all purposes. Absent clear evidence of general fame or notoriety in the community, and pervasive involvement in the affairs of society, an individual should not be deemed a public personality for all aspects of his life. It is preferable to reduce the public-figure question to a more meaningful context by looking to the nature and extent of an individual's participation in the particular controversy giving rise to the defamation.

In this context it is plain that petitioner was not a public figure. He played a minimal role at the coroner's inquest, and his participation related solely to his representation of a private client. He took no part in the criminal prosecution of Officer Nuccio. Moreover, he never discussed either the criminal or civil litigation with the press and was never quoted as having done so. He plainly did not thrust himself into the vortex of this public issue, nor did he engage the public's attention in an attempt to influence its outcome. We are persuaded that the trial court did not err in refusing to characterize petitioner as a public figure for the purpose of this litigation.

[**Ruling**] We therefore conclude that the *New York Times* standard is inapplicable to this case and that the trial court erred in entering judgment for respondent. Because the jury was allowed to impose liability without fault and was permitted to presume damages without proof of injury, a new trial is necessary. We reverse and remand for further proceedings in accord with this opinion.

Points to Consider

1. The Gertz *framework.*

This framework places central importance on *who* is speaking or publishing the statement at issue. As Ronald Collins and Sam Chaltain explained in *We Must Not Be Afraid to Be Free: Stories of Free Expression in America*, "the primary First Amendment focus was now on the *status of the person* rather than the *nature of the issue*." Is this fair?

2. The Gertz–Welch legal battle did not end there.

As Collins and Chaltain noted, the Court's ruling in *Gertz* did not end the legal battle between Elmer Gertz and Robert Welch. Indeed, the case stretched on for *fourteen years*. When the "long winter of litigation" finally ended, Welch paid Gertz $400,000 in damages and an additional $81,808.08 in legal fees. For Welch, that was the high price of besmirching a private citizen's good name.

3. What about private speech about private people?

When private individuals bring suit against each other for statements regarding private matters, the *Sullivan* framework is inapplicable. In 1985's *Dun & Bradstreet, Inc. v. Greenmoss Builders, Inc.*, the Court held that because "speech on matters of purely private concern is of less First Amendment concern," courts may award "presumed and punitive damages" to private individuals—"even absent a showing of 'actual malice.'"

WHEN A PORN MAGAZINE SATIRIZES A TELEVANGELIST

Thus far, we've covered statements that, while perhaps false, cause harm precisely because they may be taken as true by their audience. But what about that kind of false statement that—by design—is absurdly over-the-top? What about satire?

Whether deployed for comedic or political purposes, whether found in Jonathan Swift's "A Modest Proposal" or memes on Twitter, satire is often barbed, caustic, brutal, and biting—and deliberately so. Accordingly, satire can leave the ego bruised, and the reputation of its target in tatters. So does satire merit First Amendment protection? In our next case, the Supreme Court reviews the boundaries of satire in the context of the torts of libel, the invasion of privacy, and the intentional infliction of emotional distress. Here's the fake advertisement for Campari liqueur published in *Hustler Magazine*—purporting to feature an interview with televangelist Jerry Falwell—that sparked the case:

Jerry Falwell talks about his first time.*

FALWELL: My first time was in an outhouse outside Lynchburg, Virginia.

INTERVIEWER: Wasn't it a little cramped?

FALWELL: Not after I kicked the goat out.

INTERVIEWER: I see. You must tell me all about it.

FALWELL: I never really expected to make it with Mom, but then after she showed all the other guys in town such a good time, I figured, "What the hell!"

INTERVIEWER: But your mom? Isn't that a bit odd?

FALWELL: I don't think so. Looks don't mean that much to me in a woman.

INTERVIEWER: Go on.

FALWELL: Well, we were drunk off our God-fearing asses on Campari, ginger ale and soda—that's called a Fire and Brimstone—at the time. And Mom looked better than a Baptist whore with a $100 donation.

INTERVIEWER: Campari in the crapper with Mom . . . how interesting. Well, how was it?

FALWELL: The Campari was great, but Mom passed out before I could come.

INTERVIEWER: Did you ever try it again?

FALWELL: Sure . . .

lots of times. But not in the outhouse. Between Mom and the shit, the flies were too much to bear.

INTERVIEWER: We meant the Campari.

FALWELL: Oh, yeah. I always get sloshed before I go out to the pulpit. You don't think I could lay down all that bullshit sober, do you?

Campari, like all liquor, was made to mix you up. It's a light, 48-proof, refreshing spirit, just mild enough to make you drink too much before you know you're schnockered. For your first time, mix it with orange juice. Or maybe some white wine. Then you won't remember anything the next morning. **Campari. The mixable that smarts.**

CAMPARI You'll never forget your first time.

AD PARODY—NOT TO BE TAKEN SERIOUSLY

The Jerry Falwell parody ad at issue in Hustler.

OPINION

Hustler Magazine, Inc., et al. v. Falwell

(Abridged.)

485 U.S. 46 (1988)
Vote: 8–0

CHIEF JUSTICE REHNQUIST delivered the opinion of the Court.

Petitioner Hustler Magazine, Inc., is a magazine of nationwide circulation. Respondent Jerry Falwell, a nationally known minister who has been active as a commentator on politics and public affairs, sued petitioner and its publisher, petitioner Larry Flynt, to recover damages for invasion of privacy, libel, and intentional infliction of emotional distress. The District Court directed a verdict against respondent on the privacy claim, and submitted the other two claims to a jury. The jury found for petitioners on the defamation claim, but found for respondent on the claim for intentional infliction of emotional distress and awarded damages. **[Issue]** We now consider whether this award is consistent with the First and Fourteenth Amendments of the United States Constitution.

[Facts] The inside front cover of the November 1983 issue of Hustler Magazine featured a "parody" of an advertisement for Campari Liqueur that contained the name and picture of respondent and was entitled "Jerry Falwell talks about his first time." This parody was modeled after actual Campari ads that included interviews with various celebrities about their "first times." Although it was apparent by the end of each interview that this meant the first time they sampled Campari, the ads clearly played on the sexual double entendre of the general subject of "first times." Copying the form and layout of these Campari ads, Hustler's editors chose respondent as the featured celebrity and drafted an alleged "interview" with him in which he states that his "first time" was during a drunken incestuous rendezvous with his mother in an outhouse. The Hustler parody portrays respondent and his mother as drunk and immoral, and suggests that respondent is a hypocrite who preaches only when he is drunk. In small print at the bottom of the page, the ad contains the disclaimer, "ad parody—not to be taken seriously." The magazine's table of contents also lists the ad as "Fiction; Ad and Personality Parody."

[**Complaint filed**] Soon after the November issue of Hustler became available to the public, respondent brought this diversity action in the United States District Court for the Western District of Virginia against Hustler Magazine, Inc., Larry C. Flynt, and Flynt Distributing Co., Inc. Respondent stated in his complaint that publication of the ad parody in Hustler entitled him to recover damages for libel, invasion of privacy, and intentional infliction of emotional distress. At the close of the evidence, the District Court granted a directed verdict for petitioners on the invasion of privacy claim. The jury then found against respondent on the libel claim, specifically finding that the ad parody could not "reasonably be understood as describing actual facts about [respondent] or actual events in which [he] participated." The jury ruled for respondent on the intentional infliction of emotional distress claim, however, and stated that he should be awarded $100,000 in compensatory damages, as well as $50,000 each in punitive damages from petitioners.

On appeal, the United States Court of Appeals for the Fourth Circuit affirmed the judgment against petitioners.

This case presents us with a novel question involving First Amendment limitations upon a State's authority to protect its citizens from the intentional infliction of emotional distress. [**Issue restated**] We must decide whether a public figure may recover damages for emotional harm caused by the publication of an ad parody offensive to him, and doubtless gross and repugnant in the eyes of most. Respondent would have us find that a State's interest in protecting public figures from emotional distress is sufficient to deny First Amendment protection to speech that is patently offensive and is intended to inflict emotional injury, even when that speech could not reasonably have been interpreted as stating actual facts about the public figure involved. This we decline to do.

[**Analysis**] At the heart of the First Amendment is the recognition of the fundamental importance of the free flow of ideas and opinions on matters of public interest and concern. "[T]he freedom to speak one's mind is not only an aspect of individual liberty—and thus a good unto itself—but also is essential to the common quest for truth and the vitality of society as a whole." *Bose Corp. v. Consumers Union of United States* (1984). We have therefore been particularly vigilant to ensure that individual expressions of ideas remain free from governmentally imposed sanctions. The First Amendment recognizes no such thing as a "false" idea.

The sort of robust political debate encouraged by the First Amendment is bound to produce speech that is critical of those who hold public office or those public figures who are "intimately involved in the resolution of important public questions or, by reason of their fame, shape events in areas of concern to society at large." *Curtis Publishing Co. v. Butts* (1967) Justice Frankfurter put it succinctly in *Baumgartner v. United States* (1944), when he said that "[o]ne of the prerogatives of American citizenship is the right to criticize public men and measures." Such criticism, inevitably, will not always be reasoned or moderate; public figures as well as public officials will be subject to "vehement, caustic, and sometimes unpleasantly sharp attacks," *New York Times Co. v. Sullivan* (1964). "[T]he candidate who vaunts his spotless record and sterling integrity cannot convincingly cry 'Foul!' when an opponent or an industrious reporter attempts to demonstrate the contrary." *Monitor Patriot Co. v. Roy* (1971).

[*Sullivan* and *Gertz* explained] Of course, this does not mean that *any* speech about a public figure is immune from sanction in the form of damages. Since *New York Times Co.*, we have consistently ruled that a public figure may hold a speaker liable for the damage to reputation caused by publication of a defamatory falsehood, but only if the statement was made "with knowledge that it was false or with reckless disregard of whether it was false or not." False statements of fact are particularly valueless; they interfere with the truth-seeking function of the marketplace of ideas, and they cause damage to an individual's reputation that cannot easily be repaired by counterspeech, however persuasive or effective. See *Gertz v. Robert Welch, Inc.* (1974) But even though falsehoods have little value in and of themselves, they are "nevertheless inevitable in free debate," and a rule that would impose strict liability on a publisher for false factual assertions would have an undoubted "chilling" effect on speech relating to public figures that does have constitutional value. "Freedoms of expression require 'breathing space.'" *Philadelphia Newspapers, Inc. v. Hepps* (1986). This breathing space is provided by a constitutional rule that allows public figures to recover for libel or defamation only when they can prove *both* that the statement was false and that the statement was made with the requisite level of culpability.

Respondent argues, however, that a different standard should apply in this case because here the State seeks to prevent not reputational damage, but the severe emotional distress suffered by the person who is the subject of an offensive publication. In respondent's view, and in the view of the Court of Appeals, so long as the utterance was intended to inflict emotional distress, was outrageous, and did in fact inflict serious emotional distress, it is of no constitutional import whether the statement was a fact or an opinion, or whether it was true or false. It is the intent to cause injury that is the gravamen of the tort, and the State's interest in preventing emotional harm simply outweighs whatever interest a speaker may have in speech of this type.

Generally speaking, the law does not regard the intent to inflict emotional distress as one which should receive much solicitude, and it is quite understandable that most, if not all, jurisdictions have chosen to make it civilly culpable where the conduct in question is sufficiently "outrageous." But in the world of debate about public affairs, many things done with motives that are less than admirable are protected by the First Amendment.

Thus, while such a bad motive may be deemed controlling for purposes of tort liability in other areas of the law, we think the First Amendment prohibits such a result in the area of public debate about public figures.

[**Political satire**] Were we to hold otherwise, there can be little doubt that political cartoonists and satirists would be subjected to damages awards without any showing that their work falsely defamed its subject. The appeal of the political cartoon or caricature is often based on exploitation of unfortunate physical traits or politically embarrassing events—an exploitation often calculated to injure the feelings of the subject of the portrayal. The art of the cartoonist is often not reasoned or evenhanded, but slashing and one-sided.

Several famous examples of this type of intentionally injurious speech were drawn by Thomas Nast, probably the greatest American cartoonist to date, who was associated for many years during the post-Civil War era with Harper's Weekly. In the pages of that publication Nast conducted a graphic vendetta against William M. "Boss" Tweed and his corrupt associates in New York City's "Tweed Ring." It has been described by one historian of the subject as "a sustained attack which in its passion and effectiveness stands alone in the history of American graphic art." M. Keller, *The Art and Politics of Thomas Nast* (1968).

Despite their sometimes caustic nature, from the early cartoon portraying George Washington as an ass down to the present day, graphic depictions and satirical cartoons have played a prominent role in public and political debate. Lincoln's tall, gangling posture, Teddy Roosevelt's glasses and teeth, and Franklin D. Roosevelt's jutting jaw and cigarette holder have been memorialized by political cartoons with an effect that could not have been obtained by the photographer or the portrait artist. From the viewpoint of history it is clear that our political discourse would have been considerably poorer without them.

[**"Outrageous" nature of satire**] Respondent contends, however, that the caricature in question here was so "outrageous" as to distinguish it from more traditional political cartoons. There is no doubt that the caricature of respondent and his mother published in Hustler is at best a distant cousin of the political cartoons described above, and a rather poor relation at that. If it were possible by laying down a principled standard to separate the one from the other, public discourse would probably suffer little or no harm. But we doubt that there is any such standard, and we are quite sure that the pejorative description "outrageous" does not supply one. "Outrageousness" in the area of political and social discourse has an inherent subjectiveness about it which would allow a jury to impose liability on the basis of the jurors' tastes or views, or perhaps on the basis of their dislike of a particular expression. An "outrageousness" standard thus runs afoul of our long-standing refusal to allow damages to be awarded because the speech in question may have an adverse emotional impact on the audience.

[**Holding**] We conclude that public figures and public officials may not recover for the tort of intentional infliction of emotional distress by reason of publications such as the one here at issue without showing in addition that the publication contains a false statement of fact which was made with "actual malice," *i.e.*, with knowledge that the statement was false or with reckless disregard as to whether or not it was true. This is not merely a "blind application" of the *New York Times* standard, it reflects our considered judgment that such a standard is necessary to give adequate "breathing space" to the freedoms protected by the First Amendment.

[**Falwell as public figure**] Here it is clear that respondent Falwell is a "public figure" for purposes of First Amendment law. The jury found against respondent on his libel claim when it decided that the Hustler ad parody could not "reasonably be understood as describing actual facts about [respondent] or actual events in which [he] participated." The Court of Appeals interpreted the jury's finding to be that the ad parody "was not reasonably believable," and, in accordance with our custom, we accept this finding. Respondent is thus relegated to his claim for damages awarded by the jury for the intentional infliction of emotional distress by "outrageous" conduct. But, for reasons heretofore stated, this claim cannot, consistently with the First Amendment, form a basis for the award of damages when the conduct in question is the publication of a caricature such as the ad parody involved here. The judgment of the Court of Appeals is accordingly

Reversed.

Points to Consider

1. An unexpected friendship.

After appearing together on CNN's Larry King show in 1997, *Hustler* publisher Larry Flynt and Jerry Falwell kindled a friendship, even going on a college tour where they debated First Amendment issues. In a 2007 opinion piece for the *Los Angeles Times*, Flynt described their friendship:

> In the years that followed and up until his death, he'd come to see me every time he was in California. We'd have interesting philosophical conversations. We'd exchange personal Christmas cards. He'd show me pictures of his grandchildren....
>
> The truth is, the reverend and I had a lot in common. He was from Virginia, and I was from Kentucky. His father had been a bootlegger, and I had been one too in my twenties before I went into the Navy.

2. Reception of the Falwell *decision.*

The Court's opinion in *Falwell* was not universally lauded. To some, the opinion represented "a startling act of moral indifference" in which the Court "made public figures appallingly vulnerable to emotional injury, thereby violating basic expectations for moral decency."

3. Privacy and matters of public concern.

In *Barnicki v. Vopper* (2001), the Supreme Court addressed a different variation on the question of private speech and matters of public concern. An unidentified third party intercepted a cell phone conversation between two teachers' union leaders about negotiations with the school board, and leaked it to local media. The union leaders filed suit against Vopper (the local radio host who broadcast it) and others, arguing "that each of the defendants 'knew or had reason to know' that the recording of the private phone conversation had been obtained by means of an illegal interception."

The Court accepted plaintiffs' contention that "the interception was intentional, and therefore unlawful, and that, at a minimum, respondents 'had reason to know' that it was unlawful." But that didn't end the First Amendment analysis. Finding that "it would be quite remarkable to hold that speech by a law-abiding possessor of information can be suppressed in order to deter conduct by a non-law-abiding third party," the Court declined to impose "sanctions on the publication of truthful information of public concern." Reasoning that "privacy concerns give way when balanced against the interest in publishing matters of public importance" and that "[o]ne of the costs associated with participation in public affairs is an attendant loss of privacy," the Court found for the defendants.

Do you think the Court reached the right result? Or should privacy concerns have been prioritized over the media's ability to publish the intercepted conversation? How would you feel if someone illegally intercepted one of your own phone calls, then transcribed and published it for the world to read? What does privacy mean to you?

THE STOLEN VALOR CASE

The Congressional Medal of Honor is the most prestigious military award a member of the armed forces can receive. What happens when a civilian falsely claims to have received one? Can Congress outlaw false claims of valor? Is outlawing a specific lie a proper government interest? The Supreme Court grappled with these questions in the next case.

OPINION

United States v. Alvarez

(Abridged.)

567 U.S. 709 (2012)
Vote: 5–3

JUSTICE KENNEDY announced the judgment of the Court and delivered the opinion.

[**Facts**] Lying was his habit. Xavier Alvarez, the respondent here, lied when he said that he played hockey for the Detroit Red Wings and that he once married a starlet from Mexico. But when he lied in announcing he held the Congressional Medal of Honor, respondent ventured onto new ground; for that lie violates a federal criminal statute, the Stolen Valor Act of 2005. 18 U.S.C. §704.

In 2007, respondent attended his first public meeting as a board member of the Three Valley Water District Board. The board is a governmental entity with headquarters in Claremont, California. He introduced himself as follows: "I'm a retired marine of 25 years. I retired in the year 2001. Back in 1987, I was awarded the Congressional Medal of Honor. I got wounded many times by the same guy." None of this was true. For all the record shows, respondent's statements were but a pathetic attempt to gain respect that eluded him. The statements do not seem to have been made to secure employment or financial benefits or admission to privileges reserved for those who had earned the Medal.

[**Lower courts' decisions**] Respondent was indicted under the Stolen Valor Act for lying about the Congressional Medal of Honor at the meeting. The United States District Court for the Central District of California rejected his claim that the statute is invalid under the First Amendment. Respondent pleaded guilty to one count, reserving the right to appeal on his First Amendment claim. The United States Court of Appeals for the Ninth Circuit, in a decision by a divided panel, found the Act invalid under the First Amendment and reversed the conviction. With further opinions on the issue, and over a dissent by seven judges, rehearing en banc was denied. This Court granted certiorari.

This is the second case in two Terms requiring the Court to consider speech that can disparage, or attempt to steal, honor that belongs to those who fought for this Nation in battle. See *Snyder v. Phelps* (2011) (hateful protests directed at the funeral of a serviceman who died in Iraq). Here the statement that the speaker held the Medal was an intended, undoubted lie.

It is right and proper that Congress, over a century ago, established an award so the Nation can hold in its highest respect and esteem those who, in the course of carrying out the "supreme and noble duty of contributing to the defense of the rights and honor of the nation," have acted with extraordinary honor. And it should be uncontested that this is a legitimate Government objective, indeed a most valued national aspiration and purpose. This does not end the inquiry, however. Fundamental constitutional principles require that laws enacted to honor the brave must be consistent with the precepts of the Constitution for which they fought.

The Government contends the criminal prohibition is a proper means to further its purpose in creating and awarding the Medal. When content-based speech regulation is in question, however, exacting scrutiny is required. Statutes suppressing or restricting speech must be judged by the sometimes inconvenient principles of the First Amendment. By this measure, the statutory provisions under which respondent was convicted must be held invalid, and his conviction must be set aside.

[**Analysis**] Respondent's claim to hold the Congressional Medal of Honor was false. There is no room to argue about interpretation or shades of meaning. On this premise, respondent violated 18 U.S.C. §704(b); and, because the lie concerned the Congressional Medal of Honor, he was subject to an enhanced penalty under subsection (c). Those statutory provisions are as follows:

> "(b) False Claims About Receipt of Military Decorations or Medals.— Whoever falsely represents himself or herself, verbally or in writing, to have been awarded any decoration or medal authorized by Congress for the Armed Forces of the United States…shall be fined under this title, imprisoned not more than six months, or both.

> "(c) Enhanced Penalty for Offenses Involving Congressional Medal of Honor.—

> "(1) In General.—If a decoration or medal involved in an offense under subsection (a) or (b) is a Congressional Medal of Honor, in lieu of the punishment provided in that subsection, the offender shall be fined under this title, imprisoned not more than 1 year, or both."

Respondent challenges the statute as a content-based suppression of pure speech, speech not falling within any of the few categories of expression where content-based regulation is permissible. The Government defends the statute as necessary to preserve the integrity and purpose of the Medal, an integrity and purpose it contends are compromised and frustrated by the false statements the statute prohibits. It argues that false statements "have no First Amendment value in themselves," and thus "are protected only to the extent needed to avoid chilling fully protected speech." Although the statute covers respondent's speech, the Government argues that it leaves breathing room for protected speech, for example, speech which might criticize the idea of the Medal or the importance of the military. The Government's arguments cannot suffice to save the statute.

In light of the substantial and expansive threats to free expression posed by content-based restrictions, this Court has rejected as "startling and dangerous" a "free-floating test for First Amendment coverage...[based on] an ad hoc balancing of relative social costs and benefits." *United States v. Stevens* (2010). Instead, content-based restrictions on speech have been permitted, as a general matter, only when confined to the few "historic and traditional categories [of expression] long familiar to the bar." *Simon & Schuster, Inc. v. Members of N.Y. State Crime Victims Bd.* (1991). These categories have a historical foundation in the Court's free speech tradition. The vast realm of free speech and thought always protected in our tradition can still thrive, and even be furthered, by adherence to those categories and rules.

Absent from those few categories where the law allows content-based regulation of speech is any general exception to the First Amendment for false statements. This comports with the common understanding that some false statements are inevitable if there is to be an open and vigorous expression of views in public and private conversation, expression the First Amendment seeks to guarantee.

The Government disagrees with this proposition. It cites language from some of this Court's precedents to support its contention that false statements have no value and hence no First Amendment protection. These isolated statements in some earlier decisions do not support the Government's submission that false statements, as a general rule, are beyond constitutional protection. That conclusion would take the quoted language far from its proper context. For instance, the Court has stated "[f]alse statements of fact are particularly valueless [because] they interfere with the truth-seeking function of the marketplace of ideas," *Hustler Magazine, Inc. v. Falwell* (1988), and that false statements "are not protected by the First Amendment in the same manner as truthful statements," *Brown v. Hartlage* (1982).

These quotations all derive from cases discussing defamation, fraud, or some other legally cognizable harm associated with a false statement, such as an invasion of privacy or the costs of vexatious litigation. In those decisions the falsity of the speech at issue was not irrelevant to our analysis, but neither was it determinative. The Court has never endorsed the categorical rule the Government advances: that false statements receive no First Amendment protection. Our prior decisions have not confronted a measure, like the Stolen Valor Act, that targets falsity and nothing more.

Even when considering some instances of defamation and fraud, moreover, the Court has been careful to instruct that falsity alone may not suffice to bring the speech outside the First Amendment. The statement must be a knowing or reckless falsehood.

The Government thus seeks to use this principle for a new purpose. It seeks to convert a rule that limits liability even in defamation cases where the law permits recovery for tortious wrongs into a rule that expands liability in a different, far greater realm of discourse and expression. That inverts the rationale for the exception. The requirements of a knowing falsehood or reckless disregard for the truth as the condition for recovery in certain defamation cases exists to allow more speech, not less. A rule designed to tolerate certain speech ought not blossom to become a rationale for a rule restricting it.

The Government then gives three examples of regulations on false speech that courts generally have found permissible: first, the criminal prohibition of a false statement made to a Government official; second, laws punishing perjury; and third, prohibitions on the false representation that one is speaking as a Government official or on behalf of the Government. These restrictions, however, do not establish a principle that all proscriptions of false statements are exempt from exacting First Amendment scrutiny.

[**Distinguishing false statements to government officials**] The federal statute prohibiting false statements to Government officials punishes "whoever, in any matter within the jurisdiction of the executive, legislative, or judicial branch of the Government...makes any materially false, fictitious, or fraudulent statement or representation." The law's prohibition on false statements made to Government officials, in communications concerning official matters, does not lead to the broader proposition that false statements are unprotected when made to any person, at any time, in any context.

[**Distinguishing perjury**] The same point can be made about what the Court has confirmed is the "unquestioned constitutionality of perjury statutes," both the federal statute and its state-law equivalents. *United States v. Grayson* (1978) It is not simply because perjured statements are false that they lack First Amendment protection. Perjured testimony "is at war with justice" because it can cause a court to render a "judgment not resting on truth." *In re Michael* (1945). Unlike speech in other contexts, testimony under oath has the formality and gravity necessary to remind the witness that his or her statements will be the basis for official governmental action, action that often affects the rights and liberties of others. Sworn testimony is quite distinct from lies not spoken under oath and simply intended to puff up oneself.

[Distinguishing impersonating the government] Statutes that prohibit falsely representing that one is speaking on behalf of the Government, or that prohibit impersonating a Government officer, also protect the integrity of Government processes, quite apart from merely restricting false speech. Title 18 U.S.C. §912, for example, prohibits impersonating an officer or employee of the United States. Even if that statute may not require proving an "actual financial or property loss" resulting from the deception, the statute is itself confined to "maintain[ing] the general good repute and dignity of...government...service itself." *United States v. Lepowitch* (1943) The same can be said for prohibitions on the unauthorized use of the names of federal agencies such as the Federal Bureau of Investigation in a manner calculated to convey that the communication is approved or using words such as "Federal" or "United States" in the collection of private debts in order to convey that the communication has official authorization. These examples, to the extent that they implicate fraud or speech integral to criminal conduct, are inapplicable here.

As our law and tradition show, then, there are instances in which the falsity of speech bears upon whether it is protected. Some false speech may be prohibited even if analogous true speech could not be. This opinion does not imply that any of these targeted prohibitions are somehow vulnerable. But it also rejects the notion that false speech should be in a general category that is presumptively unprotected.

The Government has not demonstrated that false statements generally should constitute a new category of unprotected speech on this basis.

[Impact of statute] The probable, and adverse, effect of the Act on freedom of expression illustrates, in a fundamental way, the reasons for the law's distrust of content-based speech prohibitions.

The Act by its plain terms applies to a false statement made at any time, in any place, to any person. It can be assumed that it would not apply to, say, a theatrical performance. Still, the sweeping, quite unprecedented reach of the statute puts it in conflict with the First Amendment. Here the lie was made in a public meeting, but the statute would apply with equal force to personal, whispered conversations within a home. The statute seeks to control and suppress all false statements on this one subject in almost limitless times and settings. And it does so entirely without regard to whether the lie was made for the purpose of material gain.

Permitting the government to decree this speech to be a criminal offense, whether shouted from the rooftops or made in a barely audible whisper, would endorse government authority to compile a list of subjects about which false statements are punishable. That governmental power has no clear limiting principle. Our constitutional tradition stands against the idea that we need Oceania's Ministry of Truth. See G. Orwell, *Nineteen Eighty-Four* (1949) (Centennial ed. 2003). Were this law to be sustained, there could be an endless list of subjects the National Government or the States could single out. Where false claims are made to effect a fraud or secure moneys or other valuable considerations, say, offers of employment, it is well established that the Government may restrict speech without affronting the First Amendment. But the Stolen Valor Act is not so limited in its reach. Were the Court to hold that the interest in truthful discourse alone is sufficient to sustain a ban on speech, absent any evidence that the speech was used to gain a material advantage, it would give government a broad censorial power unprecedented in this Court's cases or in our constitutional tradition. The mere potential for the exercise of that power casts a chill, a chill the First Amendment cannot permit if free speech, thought, and discourse are to remain a foundation of our freedom.

Although the objectives the Government seeks to further by the statute are not without significance, the Court must, and now does, find the Act does not satisfy exacting scrutiny.

The First Amendment requires that the Government's chosen restriction on the speech at issue be "actually necessary" to achieve its interest. There must be a direct causal link between the restriction imposed and the injury to be prevented. The link between the Government's interest in protecting the integrity of the military honors system and the Act's restriction on the false claims of liars like respondent has not been shown. Although appearing to concede that "an isolated misrepresentation by itself would not tarnish the meaning of military honors," the Government asserts it is "common sense that false representations have the tendency to dilute the value and meaning of military awards." It must be acknowledged that when a pretender claims the Medal to be his own, the lie might harm the Government by demeaning the high purpose of the award, diminishing the honor it confirms, and creating the appearance that the Medal is awarded more often than is true. Furthermore, the lie may offend the true holders of the Medal.

From one perspective it insults their bravery and high principles when falsehood puts them in the unworthy company of a pretender.

[**Impact of counterspeech**] The Government has not shown, and cannot show, why counterspeech would not suffice to achieve its interest. The facts of this case indicate that the dynamics of free speech, of counterspeech, of refutation, can overcome the lie. Respondent lied at a public meeting. Even before the FBI began investigating him for his false statements "Alvarez was perceived as a phony[.]" Once the lie was made public, he was ridiculed online, and a fellow board member called for his resignation. There is good reason to believe that a similar fate would befall other false claimants.

The remedy for speech that is false is speech that is true. This is the ordinary course in a free society. The response to the unreasoned is the rational; to the uninformed, the enlightened; to the straight-out lie, the simple truth. The theory of our Constitution is "that the best test of truth is the power of the thought to get itself accepted in the competition of the market." *Abrams v. United States* (1919), The First Amendment itself ensures the right to respond to speech we do not like, and for good reason. Freedom of speech and thought flows not from the beneficence of the state but from the inalienable rights of the person. And suppression of speech by the government can make exposure of falsity more difficult, not less so. Society has the right and civic duty to engage in open, dynamic, rational discourse. These ends are not well served when the government seeks to orchestrate public discussion through content-based mandates.

[**Ruling**] It is a fair assumption that any true holders of the Medal who had heard of Alvarez's false claims would have been fully vindicated by the community's expression of outrage, showing as it did the Nation's high regard for the Medal. The same can be said for the Government's interest. The American people do not need the assistance of a government prosecution to express their high regard for the special place that military heroes hold in our tradition. Only a weak society needs government protection or intervention before it pursues its resolve to preserve the truth. Truth needs neither handcuffs nor a badge for its vindication.

The Nation well knows that one of the costs of the First Amendment is that it protects the speech we detest as well as the speech we embrace. Though few might find respondent's statements anything but contemptible, his right to make those statements is protected by the Constitution's guarantee of freedom of speech and expression. The Stolen Valor Act infringes upon speech protected by the First Amendment.

The judgment of the Court of Appeals is affirmed.

Points to Consider

1. Alvarez's criminal record.

For what it's worth, Alvarez was convicted of misappropriation of public funds, grand theft, and insurance fraud in 2009. He spent three years in prison.

2. The dissent.

Justices Alito, Scalia, and Thomas issued a scathing dissent, arguing that the majority's "radical interpretation of the First Amendment is not supported by any precedent of this Court." The trio continued: "The lies covered by the Stolen Valor Act have no intrinsic value and thus merit no First Amendment protection unless their prohibition would chill other expression that falls within the Amendment's scope." The dissent scoffs at the majority's concerns about overbreadth: "The speech punished by the Act is not only verifiably false and entirely lacking in intrinsic value, but it also fails to serve any instrumental purpose that the First Amendment might protect. Tellingly, when asked at oral argument what truthful speech the Stolen Valor Act might chill, even respondent's counsel conceded that the answer is none."

Which side has the better argument, in your opinion?

3. Reception of the Alvarez *decision.*

The majority's decision proved controversial amongst the public and Congress, as well. In 2013, Congress passed and President Obama signed the Stolen Valor Act of 2013:

> Whoever, with intent to obtain money, property, or other tangible benefit, fraudulently holds oneself out to be a recipient of a decoration or medal described in subsection (c)(2) or (d) shall be fined under this title, imprisoned not more than one year, or both.

Does that fix the problem identified by the majority? What's the difference between this law and the one struck down in *Alvarez*?

10.

We Live by Symbols: Speaking without Words

SPEECH, CONDUCT, AND SYMBOLIC EXPRESSION

> *O say can you see, by the dawn's early light,*
> *What so proudly we hail'd at the twilight's last gleaming,*
> *Whose broad stripes and bright stars through the perilous fight*
> *O'er the ramparts we watch'd were so gallantly streaming?*
> *And the rocket's red glare, the bombs bursting in air,*
> *Gave proof through the night that our flag was still there,*
> *O say does that star-spangled banner yet wave*
> *O'er the land of the free and the home of the brave?*
> —*Francis Scott Key, "The Star-Spangled Banner"*

SYMBOLS ARE IMPORTANT. Our shared understanding of symbolic meaning allows us to communicate in both simple and sophisticated ways. Babies discover early on that a smile carries meaning. Emojis contain a multitude of meanings, depending on context. Veterans may be moved to tears at the sight of a carefully folded American flag. Sports fans and gang members may be spurred to action by the sight of "their" colors. Political movements rally behind symbols—a rainbow, a raised fist. Symbols may change in meaning over time: the pink triangle that marked queer people for death in Nazi Germany was reclaimed decades later by the queer community and used as a call to action against AIDS.

Francis Scott Key was inspired to write the lyrics to what would become our national anthem after catching a glimpse of our young nation's flag still flying at dawn over Fort McHenry after a long night of British shelling in the War of 1812.

To Key's tired eyes, the flag served as a symbol of perseverance and patriotism. A century and a half later, as the United States fought overseas in Vietnam, one could find the American flag spangled with a different symbol, communicating a different message: a peace sign placed on the flag in protest of the war.

Symbols are powerful because they permit us to speak without words. But are symbols "speech" for First Amendment purposes? Think again of flags and the sentiments they invoke. Is waving a flag simply an action one takes, like riding a bicycle, or a form of protected expression, like speaking aloud? What about *burning* a flag—or a draft card? When does physical conduct become sufficiently "symbolic" to earn constitutional protection as speech?

THE RED FLAG CASE

The Supreme Court began answering such questions in 1931's *Stromberg v. California*, a case involving a 19-year-old woman named Yetta Stromberg, who was a counselor at a Communist summer camp for children in Yucaipa, California. As described in a 1930 ACLU pamphlet about the case, the children attending the camp would stand at attention every morning while a homemade Soviet flag was raised and recite the following pledge: "*I pledge allegiance to the worker's red flag, and to the cause for which it stands; one aim throughout our lives, freedom for the working class.*" In 1929, members of the American Legion conducted a raid on the camp, led by the district attorney of San Bernardino County. Six women and one man were arrested, including Stromberg, and charged with violating a 1919 California state law prohibiting the display of red flags if they were used: "as a sign, symbol or emblem of opposition to organized government"; "as an invitation or stimulus to anarchistic action"; or "as an aid to propaganda that is of a seditious character."

At trial, Stromberg was found guilty, but the court did not state which part of the statute she had violated. She appealed on First Amendment grounds.

OPINION

Stromberg v. California

(Abridged.)

283 U.S. 359 (1931)
Vote: 7–2

CHIEF JUSTICE HUGHES delivered the opinion of the Court.

[Charge and lower court decision] The appellant was convicted in the Superior Court of San Bernardino County, California, for violation of the Penal Code of that State. That section provides:

> "Any person who displays a red flag, banner or badge or any flag, badge, banner, or device of any color or form whatever in any public place or in any meeting place or public assembly, or from or on any house, building or window as a sign, symbol or emblem of opposition to organized government or as an invitation or stimulus to anarchistic action or as an aid to propaganda that is of a seditious character is guilty of a felony."

The information, in its first count, charged that the appellant and other defendants, at the time and place set forth, "did willfully, unlawfully and feloniously display a red flag and banner in a public place and in a meeting place as a sign, symbol and emblem of opposition to organized government and as an invitation and stimulus to anarchistic action and as an aid to propaganda that is and was of a seditious character."

[Facts] This Court granted an order permitting the appellant to prosecute the appeal *in forma pauperis* and, for the purpose of shortening the record, a stipulation of facts has been presented on behalf of the appellant and the Attorney General of the State. It appears that the appellant, a young woman of nineteen, a citizen of the United States by birth, was one of the supervisors of a summer camp for children, between ten and fifteen years of age, in the foothills of the San Bernardino mountains. Appellant led the children in their daily study, teaching them history and economics. "Among other things, the children were taught class consciousness, the solidarity of the workers, and the theory that the workers of the world are of one blood and brothers all." Appellant was a member of the Young Communist League, an international organization affiliated with the Communist Party. The charge against her concerned a daily ceremony at the camp, in which the appellant supervised and directed the children in raising a red flag, "a camp-made reproduction of the flag of Soviet Russia, which was also the flag of the Communist Party in the United States." In connection with the flag-raising, there was a ritual at which the children stood at salute and recited a pledge of allegiance "to the worker's red flag, and to the cause for which it stands; one aim throughout our lives, freedom for the working class." The stipulation further shows that "a library was maintained at the camp containing a large number of books, papers and pamphlets, including much radical communist propaganda, specimens of which are quoted in the opinion of the state court." These quotations abundantly demonstrated that the books and pamphlets contained incitements to violence and to "armed uprisings," teaching "the indispensability of a desperate, bloody, destructive war as the immediate task of the coming action." Appellant admitted ownership of a number of the books, some of which bore her name. It appears from the stipulation that none of these books or pamphlets were used in the teaching at the camp. With respect to the conduct of the appellant, the stipulation contains the following statement: "She" (the appellant) "testified, however, that none of the literature in the library, and particularly none of the exhibits containing radical communist propaganda, was in any way brought to the attention of any child or of any other person, and that no word of violence or anarchism or sedition was employed in her teaching of the children. There was no evidence to the contrary."

[**Analysis**] We are unable to agree with the lower court's disposition of the case. The verdict against the appellant was a general one. It did not specify the ground upon which it rested.

We are thus brought to the question whether any one of the three clauses, as construed by the state court, is upon its face repugnant to the Federal Constitution so that it could not constitute a lawful foundation for a criminal prosecution. The principles to be applied have been clearly set forth in our former decisions. It has been determined that the conception of liberty under the due process clause of the Fourteenth Amendment embraces the right of free speech. The right is not an absolute one, and the State in the exercise of its police power may punish the abuse of this freedom. There is no question but that the State may thus provide for the punishment of those who indulge in utterances which incite to violence and crime and threaten the overthrow of organized government by unlawful means. There is no constitutional immunity for such conduct abhorrent to our institutions. We have no reason to doubt the validity of the second and third clauses of the statute as construed by the state court to relate to such incitements to violence.

[**Flag as symbols of opposition**] The question is thus narrowed to that of the validity of the first clause, that is, with respect to the display of the flag "as a sign, symbol or emblem of opposition to organized government," and the construction which the state court has placed upon this clause removes every element of doubt. The state court recognized the indefiniteness and ambiguity of the clause. The court considered that it might be construed as embracing conduct which the State could not constitutionally prohibit. Thus it was said that the clause "might be construed to include the peaceful and orderly opposition to a government as organized and controlled by one political party by those of another political party equally high minded and patriotic, which did not agree with the one in power. It might also be construed to include peaceful and orderly opposition to government by legal means and within constitutional limitations." The maintenance of the opportunity for free political discussion to the end that government may be responsive to the will of the people and that changes may be obtained by lawful means, an opportunity essential to the security of the Republic, is a fundamental principle of our constitutional system. [**Ruling**] A statute which, upon its face, and as authoritatively construed, is so vague and indefinite as to permit the punishment of the fair use of this opportunity is repugnant to the guaranty of liberty contained in the Fourteenth Amendment. The first clause of the statute being invalid upon its face, the conviction of the appellant, which so far as the record discloses may have rested upon that clause exclusively, must be set aside.

As, for this reason, the case must be remanded for further proceedings not inconsistent with this opinion, and other facts may be adduced in such proceedings, it is not necessary to deal with the questions which have been argued at the bar as to the constitutional validity of the second and third clauses of the statute, not simply upon their face, but as applied in the instant case; that is, to consider the conclusions of fact warranted by the evidence, either as shown by the original record filed with the Court on the present appeal, or as disclosed by the stipulation, as to the import of which the parties do not agree.

Judgment reversed.

Points to Consider

1. The aftermath.

According to her great-niece Judy Branfman, Yetta Stromberg was hounded by the FBI for decades following the Court's decision in her favor and blacklisted from teaching in public schools. Branfman is producing a documentary, *The Land of Orange Groves and Jails*, about her great-aunt's life.

2. A 1919 California law was the key to the case.

The Court concludes that a California statute prohibiting "opposition to organized government" was "vague and indefinite," and thus unconstitutional. Would it have even been possible for the state of California to craft a more precise statute? What would a more exacting statute look like?

If you're having a hard time writing one, ask yourself why. You may be running into the same difficulties the Court here identifies—namely, the First Amendment problems inherent in prohibiting symbolic expression. Should the display of a flag to send a political message always be protected? What about Confederate flags? If not, under what circumstances might the state lawfully limit such a display?

3. Kneeling during the national anthem.

One of the most controversial acts of symbolic speech in the past few years has been the decision of former NFL quarterback Colin Kaepernick and other athletes to "take a knee" during the national anthem in protest of racial inequality and police violence.

Student athletes at public institutions across the country began following Kaepernick's example and brought this controversy out of the business of professional sports and into the realm of the First Amendment. Cheerleaders at Kennesaw State University took a knee during the anthem prior to football games and were taken off the field for doing so. Under pressure from the Lawyers' Committee for Civil Rights Under Law and others, the university relented. In fact, Kennesaw State's president resigned in the months afterward, in part as a result of his role in the university's response to the cheerleaders' protest. However, after the majority of the protesting cheerleaders failed to make the squad the following year. One such cheerleader filed a lawsuit accusing university officials, a local sheriff, and a state representative of violating her civil rights.

One public high school senior went to federal court to successfully defend his First Amendment right to take a knee. In *V.A. v. San Pasqual Valley Unified School District* (2017), a federal district court issued an injunction preventing a school district from adopting a policy designed to prevent students like V.A. (the student's initials) from protesting during the national anthem. Observing that "certain actions, though not spoken, are considered speech and protected by the First Amendment," the court held that "kneeling during the National Anthem is speech." The court reasoned that symbolic protests like V.A.'s were unlikely to disrupt or interfere with school activities; thus, they were protected by the First Amendment, and the school district was prohibited from enforcing the policy.

Do you think the court was right in *V.A.*? How does the precedent discussed throughout this chapter shape your opinion?

THE DRAFT CARD BURNING CASE

To determine if expressive conduct should be protected under the First Amendment, courts sometimes apply the *Spence* test (also known as the *Spence-Johnson* test. The *Spence* test originated from the U.S. Supreme Court's decision in *Spence v. Washington* (1974), which examined the punishment of a college student for using tape to add peace symbols to an American flag and hanging it outside his dorm window, in protest of the Kent State shootings. The Court found that student Harold Spence clearly intended to convey a form of political speech with his treatment of the American flag. This test requires both of the following:

1. The person engaging in the expressive content intended to convey a particularized message.
2. The message being conveyed would reasonably be understood by onlookers.

Courts do not apply the *Spence* test if they find that the government has not targeted the actual underlying message, but the conduct itself. In those instances, the use another test, developed in the draft card-burning case *United States v. O'Brien* (1968).

David Paul O'Brien burned his draft card on the steps of a South Boston courthouse to protest the draft and the Vietnam War. Prosecutors charged him with violating a federal law prohibiting the burning of draft cards. O'Brien argued that he had a First Amendment right to protest by burning the draft card, but the Supreme Court disagreed by a 5–4 vote.

Read the opinion highlights and ponder the following questions: How can one objectively determine when expressive conduct crosses the line and becomes harmful to significant government interests? Can conduct like burning a draft card really be separated from its message?

OPINION

United States v. O'Brien

(Abridged.)

391 U.S. 367 (1968)
Vote: 7–1

CHIEF JUSTICE WARREN delivered the opinion of the Court.

[Facts] On the morning of March 31, 1966, David Paul O'Brien and three companions burned their Selective Service registration certificates on the steps of the

South Boston Courthouse. A sizable crowd, including several agents of the Federal Bureau of Investigation, witnessed the event. Immediately after the burning, members of the crowd began attacking O'Brien and his companions. An FBI agent ushered O'Brien to safety inside the courthouse. After he was advised of his right to counsel and to silence, O'Brien stated to FBI agents that he had burned his registration certificate because of his beliefs, knowing that he was violating federal law. He produced the charred remains of the certificate, which, with his consent, were photographed.

For this act, O'Brien was indicted, tried, convicted, and sentenced in the United States District Court for the District of Massachusetts. He did not contest the fact that he had burned the certificate. He stated in argument to the jury that he burned the certificate publicly to influence others to adopt his antiwar beliefs, as he put it, "so that other people would reevaluate their positions with Selective Service, with the armed forces, and reevaluate their place in the culture of today, to hopefully consider my position."

[**Law violated**] The indictment upon which he was tried charged that he "willfully and knowingly did mutilate, destroy, and change by burning...[his] Registration Certificate (Selective Service System Form No. 2); in violation of [50 U.S.C.App. § 462]." The code is part of the Universal Military Training and Service Act of 1948. One of six numbered subdivisions of the code, was amended by Congress in 1965, (adding the words italicized below), so that, at the time O'Brien burned his certificate, an offense was committed by any person, "who forges, alters, *knowingly destroys, knowingly mutilates,* or in any manner changes any such certificate...."

[**District court rejects First Amendment defense**] The District Court rejected O'Brien's speech arguments, holding that the statute on its face did not abridge First Amendment rights, that the court was not competent to inquire into the motives of Congress in enacting the 1965 Amendment, and that the Amendment was a reasonable exercise of the power of Congress to raise armies.

[**First Circuit strikes down law**] On appeal, the Court of Appeals for the First Circuit held the 1965 Amendment unconstitutional as a law abridging freedom of speech.

[**Supreme Court upholds law**] We hold that the 1965 Amendment is constitutional both as enacted and as applied. We therefore vacate the judgment of the

Court of Appeals and reinstate the judgment and sentence of the District Court without reaching the issue raised by O'Brien.

[**Registering with Selective Service**] When a male reaches the age of 18, he is required by the Universal Military Training and Service Act to register with a local draft board. He is assigned a Selective Service number, and within five days he is issued a registration certificate. Subsequently, and based on a questionnaire completed by the registrant, he is assigned a classification denoting his eligibility for induction, and "[a]s soon as practicable" thereafter he is issued a Notice of Classification.

Both the registration and classification certificates bear notices that the registrant must notify his local board in writing of every change in address, physical condition, and occupational, marital, family, dependency, and military status, and of any other fact which might change his classification. Both also contain a notice that the registrant's Selective Service number should appear on all communications to his local board.

[**Congressional intent**] Congress demonstrated its concern that certificates issued by the Selective Service System might be abused well before the 1965 Amendment here challenged. The 1948 Act itself prohibited many different abuses involving "any registration certificate,…or any other certificate issued pursuant to or prescribed by the provisions of this title, or rules or regulations promulgated hereunder.…"

By the 1965 Amendment, Congress added to the 1948 Act the provision here at issue, subjecting to criminal liability not only one who "forges, alters, or in any manner changes" but also one who "knowingly destroys, [or] knowingly mutilates" a certificate.

[**Speech analysis**] We note at the outset that the 1965 Amendment plainly does not abridge free speech on its face, and we do not understand O'Brien to argue otherwise. O'Brien nonetheless argues that the 1965 Amendment is unconstitutional in its application to him, and is unconstitutional as enacted because what he calls the "purpose" of Congress was "to suppress freedom of speech." We consider these arguments separately.

[**Symbolic speech**] O'Brien first argues that the 1965 Amendment is unconstitutional as applied to him because his act of burning his registration certificate was protected "symbolic speech" within the First Amendment. His argument is that the freedom of expression which the First Amendment guarantees includes all modes of "communication of ideas by conduct," and that his conduct is within this definition because he did it in "demonstration against the war and against the draft."

We cannot accept the view that an apparently limitless variety of conduct can be labeled "speech" whenever the person engaging in the conduct intends thereby to express an idea. However, even on the assumption that the alleged communicative element in O'Brien's conduct is sufficient to bring into play the First Amendment, it does not necessarily follow that the destruction of a registration certificate is constitutionally protected activity. This Court has held that when "speech" and "nonspeech" elements are combined in the same course of conduct, a sufficiently important governmental interest in regulating the nonspeech element can justify incidental limitations on First Amendment freedoms. To characterize the quality of the governmental interest which must appear, the Court has employed a variety of descriptive terms: compelling; substantial; subordinating; paramount; cogent; strong. [Legal test] Whatever imprecision inheres in these terms, we think it clear that a government regulation is sufficiently justified [1] if it is within the constitutional power of the Government; [2] if it furthers an important or substantial governmental interest; [3] if the governmental interest is unrelated to the suppression of free expression; and [4] if the incidental restriction on alleged First Amendment freedoms is no greater than is essential to the furtherance of that interest. We find that the 1965 Amendment to the Universal Military Training and Service Act meets all of these requirements, and consequently that O'Brien can be constitutionally convicted for violating it.

The issuance of certificates indicating the registration and eligibility classification of individuals is a legitimate and substantial administrative aid in the functioning of this system. And legislation to insure the continuing availability of issued certificates serves a legitimate and substantial purpose in the system's administration.

O'Brien's argument to the contrary is necessarily premised upon his unrealistic characterization of Selective Service certificates. He essentially adopts the position that such certificates are so many pieces of paper designed to notify registrants of their registration or classification, to be retained or tossed in the wastebasket according to the convenience or taste of the registrant. Once the registrant has received notification, according to this view, there is no reason for him to retain the certificates. O'Brien notes that most of the information on a registration certificate serves no notification purpose at all; the registrant hardly needs to be told his address and physical characteristics. We agree that the registration certificate contains much information of which the registrant needs no notification. This circumstance, however, does not lead to the conclusion that the certificate serves no purpose, but that, like the classification certificate, it serves purposes in addition to initial notification. Many of these purposes would be defeated by the certificates' destruction or mutilation. Among these are:

[Justifying prohibiting destruction of cards] 1. The registration certificate serves as proof that the individual described thereon has registered for the draft. The classification certificate shows the eligibility classification of a named but undescribed individual. Voluntarily displaying the two certificates is an easy and painless way for a young man to dispel a question as to whether he might be delinquent in his Selective Service obligations. Correspondingly, the availability of the certificates for such display relieves the Selective Service System of the administrative burden it would otherwise have in verifying the registration and classification of all suspected delinquents. Further, since both certificates are in the nature of "receipts" attesting that the registrant has done what the law requires, it is in the interest of the just and efficient administration of the system that they be continually available, in the event, for example, of a mix-up in the registrant's file. Additionally, in a time of national crisis, reasonable availability to each registrant of the two small cards assures a rapid and uncomplicated means for determining his fitness for immediate induction, no matter how distant in our mobile society he may be from his local board.

2. The information supplied on the certificates facilitates communication between registrants and local boards, simplifying the system and benefiting all concerned. To begin with, each certificate bears the address of the registrant's local board, an item unlikely to be committed to memory. Further, each card bears the registrant's Selective Service number, and a registrant who has his number readily available so that he can communicate it to his local board when he supplies or requests information can make simpler the board's task in locating his file. Finally, a registrant's inquiry, particularly through a local board other than his own, concerning his eligibility status is frequently answerable simply on the basis of his classification certificate; whereas, if the certificate were not reasonably available and the registrant were uncertain of his classification, the task of answering his questions would be considerably complicated.

3. Both certificates carry continual reminders that the registrant must notify his local board of any change of address, and other specified changes in his status. The smooth functioning of the system requires that local boards be continually

aware of the status and whereabouts of registrants, and the destruction of certificates deprives the system of a potentially useful notice device.

4. The regulatory scheme involving Selective Service certificates includes clearly valid prohibitions against the alteration, forgery, or similar deceptive misuse of certificates. The destruction or mutilation of certificates obviously increases the difficulty of detecting and tracing abuses such as these. Further, a mutilated certificate might itself be used for deceptive purposes.

[**Governmental interest and "noncommunicative conduct"**] We think it apparent that the continuing availability to each registrant of his Selective Service certificates substantially furthers the smooth and proper functioning of the system that Congress has established to raise armies. We think it also apparent that the Nation has a vital interest in having a system for raising armies that functions with maximum efficiency and is capable of easily and quickly responding to continually changing circumstances. For these reasons, the Government has a substantial interest in assuring the continuing availability of issued Selective Service certificates.

In conclusion, we find that because of the Government's substantial interest in assuring the continuing availability of issued Selective Service certificates, because the amendment is an appropriately narrow means of protecting this interest and condemns only the independent noncommunicative impact of conduct within its reach, and because the noncommunicative impact of O'Brien's act of burning his registration certificate frustrated the Government's interest, a sufficient governmental interest has been shown to justify O'Brien's conviction.

[**Ruling**] Since the 1965 Amendment to the Universal Military Training and Service Act is constitutional as enacted and as applied, the Court of Appeals should have affirmed the judgment of conviction entered by the District Court. Accordingly, we vacate the judgment of the Court of Appeals, and reinstate the judgment and sentence of the District Court. This disposition makes unnecessary consideration of O'Brien's claim that the Court of Appeals erred in affirming his conviction on the basis of the nonpossession regulation.

Points to Consider

1. The O'Brien *test.*
In *O'Brien*, the Court established the following test for reviewing governmental regulations that impact speech. A government regulation on speech is sufficiently justified if:

1. It is within the constitutional power of the government;
2. It furthers an important or substantial governmental interest;
3. The governmental interest is unrelated to the suppression of free expression; and
4. The incidental restriction on alleged First Amendment freedoms is no greater than is essential to the furtherance of that interest.

Does this seem protective enough of symbolic speech to you? Does it grant too much deference to the government? Not enough?

2. *The Court's reasoning.*

The Court in *O'Brien* examined the governmental interest furthered by the statute's prohibition by reviewing the administrative reasons for keeping one's draft card in good shape. Do these reasons make sense today in today's online world, where "hard copies" may not be as important as they were in the 1960s? What current action might be the equivalent of burning a draft card?

3. *Form and content.*

Justice Harlan wrote in his concurring opinion that O'Brien "manifestly could have conveyed his message in many ways other than by burning his draft card." Is this true? Even if O'Brien could have simply held up a sign or handed out a flyer, should that matter? In other words: Is choosing the form in which one's message is expressed part of the expressive act?

Think about it this way. You can tell someone you love them in a poem, in a letter, or in a quick spoken statement. The core message—that you love that person—is the same in each case. However, does the form in which you express that message change its communicative impact?

4. *Colonial symbolic speech.*

Humans are hardwired to be drawn to fire. Small wonder, then, that we've been using fire to communicate messages for millennia—whether through sending smoke signals, burning draft cards and bras, or the enduring practice of torching effigies in protest.

In his 2016 book *Revolutionary Dissent: How the Founding Generation Created the Freedom of Speech*, New York University journalism professor Stephen Solomon explores how the founding generation of Americans protested. Burning the British in effigy was a searing symbol of colonial anger. Solomon wrote that symbolic political protests helped grow the rebellion because they "expressed ideas in ways very different from the essays and letters and petitions that had dominated the debate until then":

> The Loyal Nine and others who strung the effigies of the devil and the stamp distributor did so to communicate a profound disagreement with the taxes inflicted on them by England. Their use of symbols to express opposition to the new taxes involved a completely different mode of speech, but one that was ultimately as important as the essays discussing the constitutional rights of Englishmen.
>
> Symbolic speech, in fact, possessed some power that the written and spoken word did not. The essays and speeches against the Stamp Act used complex arguments that were foreign to many people's understanding and experience, and even vigorous opponents of the tax sometimes disagreed themselves on many of the arguments they were putting forward. But symbols stripped away the complexity of intellectual arguments and offered immediate clarity....As the relationship between the colonies and England deteriorated over the issue of taxes, the patriots in Boston and throughout the colonies increasingly recognized the power of symbolic speech to excite passions and define public debate.

THE FLAG BURNING CASE

So burning your draft card does not qualify for First Amendment protection. But what about burning an American flag? Does the government have an interest in preserving the dignity of symbols of national unity? Gregory Lee Johnson got the Supreme Court to grapple with these and other questions after burning a flag in protest of the 1984 Republican National Convention.

Prior to the Court's opinion in 1989's *Texas v. Johnson*, 48 states maintained legislation prohibiting flag burnings. With this opinion, the Court reaffirmed the protection of symbolic speech throughout the nation.

OPINION

Texas v. Johnson

(Abridged.)

491 U.S. 397 (1989)
Vote: 5–4

JUSTICE BRENNAN delivered the opinion of the Court.

[**Issue**] After publicly burning an American flag as a means of political protest, Gregory Lee Johnson was convicted of desecrating a flag in violation of Texas law. This case presents the question whether his conviction is consistent with the First Amendment. We hold that it is not.

[**Facts**] While the Republican National Convention was taking place in Dallas in 1984, respondent Johnson participated in a political demonstration dubbed the "Republican War Chest Tour." As explained in literature distributed by the demonstrators and in speeches made by them, the purpose of this event was to protest the policies of the Reagan administration and of certain Dallas-based corporations. The demonstrators marched through the Dallas streets, chanting political slogans and stopping at several corporate locations to stage "die-ins" intended to dramatize the consequences of nuclear war. On several occasions they spray-painted the walls of buildings and overturned potted plants, but Johnson himself took no part in such activities. He did, however, accept an American flag handed to him by a fellow protestor who had taken it from a flagpole outside one of the targeted buildings.

The demonstration ended in front of Dallas City Hall, where Johnson unfurled the American flag, doused it with kerosene, and set it on fire. While the flag burned, the protestors chanted: "America, the red, white, and blue, we spit on you." After the demonstrators dispersed, a witness to the flag burning collected the flag's remains and buried them in his backyard. No one was physically injured or threatened with injury, though several witnesses testified that they had been seriously offended by the flag burning.

[**Charge and lower courts' decisions**] Of the approximately 100 demonstrators, Johnson alone was charged with a crime. The only criminal offense with which he was charged was the desecration of a venerated object in violation of Tex. Penal Code. After a trial, he was convicted, sentenced to one year in prison, and fined $2,000. The Court of Appeals for the Fifth District of Texas at Dallas affirmed Johnson's conviction, but the Texas Court of Criminal Appeals reversed, holding that the State could not, consistent with the First Amendment, punish Johnson for burning the flag in these circumstances.

Because it reversed Johnson's conviction on the ground that the statute was unconstitutional as applied to him, the state court did not address Johnson's argument that the statute was, on its face, unconstitutionally vague and overbroad. We granted certiorari and now affirm.

[**Application of *O'Brien* test**] Johnson was convicted of flag desecration for burning the flag rather than for uttering insulting words. This fact somewhat complicates our consideration of his conviction under the First Amendment. We must first determine whether Johnson's burning of the flag constituted expressive conduct, permitting him to invoke the First Amendment in challenging his conviction. If his conduct was expressive, we next decide whether the State's regulation is related to the suppression of free expression. If the State's regulation is not related to expression, then the less stringent standard we announced in *United States v. O'Brien* (1968) for regulations of noncommunicative conduct controls. If it is, then we are outside of *O'Brien*'s test, and we must ask whether this interest justifies Johnson's conviction under a more demanding standard. A third possibility is that the State's asserted interest is simply not implicated on these facts, and in that event the interest drops out of the picture.

[**First Amendment protections for expressive conduct**] The First Amendment literally forbids the abridgment only of "speech," but we have long recognized that its protection does not end at the spoken or written word. While we have rejected "the view that an apparently limitless variety of conduct can be labeled 'speech' whenever the person engaging in the conduct intends thereby to express an idea," *United States v. O'Brien*, we have acknowledged that conduct may be "sufficiently imbued with elements of communication to fall within the scope of the First and Fourteenth Amendments," *Spence v. Washington* (1974).

In deciding whether particular conduct possesses sufficient communicative elements to bring the First Amendment into play, we have asked whether "[a]n intent to convey a particularized message was present, and [whether] the likelihood was great that the message would be understood by those who viewed it." *Spence v. Washington*. Hence, we have recognized the expressive nature of students' wearing of black armbands to protest American military involvement in Vietnam, *Tinker v. Des Moines Independent Community School Dist.* (1969); of a sit-in by blacks in a "whites only" area to protest segregation, *Brown v. Louisiana* (1966); of the wearing of American military uniforms in a dramatic presentation criticizing American involvement in Vietnam, *Schacht v. United States* (1970); and of picketing about a wide variety of causes, see, *e.g., Food Employees v. Logan Valley Plaza, Inc.* (1968); *United States v. Grace* (1983).

[Expressive conduct involving flags] Especially pertinent to this case are our decisions recognizing the communicative nature of conduct relating to flags. Attaching a peace sign to the flag, *Spence*; refusing to salute the flag, *West Virginia Bd. of Educ. v. Barnette* (1943); and displaying a red flag, *Stromberg v. California* (1931), we have held, all may find shelter under the First Amendment. That we have had little difficulty identifying an expressive element in conduct relating to flags should not be surprising. The very purpose of a national flag is to serve as a symbol of our country; it is, one might say, "the one visible manifestation of two hundred years of nationhood." *Smith v. Goguen* (1974). Thus, we have observed:

> "[T]he flag salute is a form of utterance. Symbolism is a primitive but effective way of communicating ideas. The use of an emblem or flag to symbolize some system, idea, institution, or personality, is a short cut from mind to mind. Causes and nations, political parties, lodges and ecclesiastical groups seek to knit the loyalty of their followings to a flag or banner, a color or design." (*Barnette.*)

Pregnant with expressive content, the flag as readily signifies this Nation as does the combination of letters found in "America."

[Johnson's explanation] The State of Texas conceded for purposes of its oral argument in this case that Johnson's conduct was expressive conduct. Johnson burned an American flag as part—indeed, as the culmination—of a political demonstration that coincided with the convening of the Republican Party and its renomination of Ronald Reagan for President. The expressive, overtly political nature of this conduct was both intentional and overwhelmingly apparent. At his trial, Johnson explained his reasons for burning the flag as follows: "The American Flag was burned as Ronald Reagan was being renominated as President. And a more powerful statement of symbolic speech, whether you agree with it or not, couldn't have been made at that time. It's quite a just position [juxtaposition]. We had new patriotism and no patriotism." In these circumstances, Johnson's burning of the flag was conduct "sufficiently imbued with elements of communication," *Spence*, to implicate the First Amendment.

[Texas' interest in prohibiting flag burning] In order to decide whether *O'Brien*'s test applies here, therefore, we must decide whether Texas has asserted an interest in support of Johnson's conviction that is unrelated to the suppression of expression. If we find that an interest asserted by the State is simply not implicated on the facts before us, we need not ask whether *O'Brien*'s test applies. The

State offers two separate interests to justify this conviction: preventing breaches of the peace and preserving the flag as a symbol of nationhood and national unity. We hold that the first interest is not implicated on this record and that the second is related to the suppression of expression.

[Breaches of the peace] Texas claims that its interest in preventing breaches of the peace justifies Johnson's conviction for flag desecration. However, no disturbance of the peace actually occurred or threatened to occur because of Johnson's burning of the flag. Although the State stresses the disruptive behavior of the protestors during their march toward City Hall, it admits that "no actual breach of the peace occurred at the time of the flagburning or in response to the flagburning." The State's emphasis on the protestors' disorderly actions prior to arriving at City Hall is not only somewhat surprising given that no charges were brought on the basis of this conduct, but it also fails to show that a disturbance of the peace was a likely reaction to Johnson's conduct. The only evidence offered by the State at trial to show the reaction to Johnson's actions was the testimony of several persons who had been seriously offended by the flag burning.

The State's position, therefore, amounts to a claim that an audience that takes serious offense at particular expression is necessarily likely to disturb the peace and that the expression may be prohibited on this basis. Our precedents do not countenance such a presumption. On the contrary, they recognize that a principal "function of free speech under our system of government is to invite dispute. It may indeed best serve its high purpose when it induces a condition of unrest, creates dissatisfaction with conditions as they are, or even stirs people to anger." *Terminiello v. Chicago* (1949). It would be odd indeed to conclude *both* that "if it is the speaker's opinion that gives offense, that consequence is a reason for according it constitutional protection," *FCC v. Pacifica Foundation* (1978), *and* that the government may ban the expression of certain disagreeable ideas on the unsupported presumption that their very disagreeableness will provoke violence.

Thus, we have not permitted the government to assume that every expression of a provocative idea will incite a riot, but have instead required careful consideration of the actual circumstances surrounding such expression, asking whether the expression "is directed to inciting or producing imminent lawless action and is likely to incite or produce such action." *Brandenburg v. Ohio* (1969). To accept Texas' arguments that it need only demonstrate "the potential for a breach of the peace," and that every flag burning necessarily possesses that potential, would be to eviscerate our holding in *Brandenburg*. This we decline to do.

[**Fighting words**] Nor does Johnson's expressive conduct fall within that small class of "fighting words" that are "likely to provoke the average person to retaliation, and thereby cause a breach of the peace." *Chaplinsky v. New Hampshire* (1942). No reasonable onlooker would have regarded Johnson's generalized expression of dissatisfaction with the policies of the Federal Government as a direct personal insult or an invitation to exchange fisticuffs.

We thus conclude that the State's interest in maintaining order is not implicated on these facts. The State need not worry that our holding will disable it from preserving the peace. We do not suggest that the First Amendment forbids a State to prevent "imminent lawless action." *Brandenburg.* And, in fact, Texas already has a statute specifically prohibiting breaches of the peace, which tends to confirm that Texas need not punish this flag desecration in order to keep the peace.

[**Preserving flag as a symbol**] The State also asserts an interest in preserving the flag as a symbol of nationhood and national unity. In *Spence*, we acknowledged that the government's interest in preserving the flag's special symbolic value "is directly related to expression in the context of activity" such as affixing a peace symbol to a flag. We are equally persuaded that this interest is related to expression in the case of Johnson's burning of the flag. The State, apparently, is concerned that such conduct will lead people to believe either that the flag does not stand for nationhood and national unity, but instead reflects other, less positive concepts, or that the concepts reflected in the flag do not in fact exist, that is, that we do not enjoy unity as a Nation. These concerns blossom only when a person's treatment of the flag communicates some message, and thus are related "to the suppression of free expression" within the meaning of *O'Brien*. We are thus outside of *O'Brien*'s test altogether.

It remains to consider whether the State's interest in preserving the flag as a symbol of nationhood and national unity justifies Johnson's conviction.

As in *Spence*, "[w]e are confronted with a case of prosecution for the expression of an idea through activity," and "[a]ccordingly, we must examine with particular care the interests advanced by [petitioner] to support its prosecution." Johnson was not, we add, prosecuted for the expression of just any idea; he was prosecuted for his expression of dissatisfaction with the policies of this country, expression situated at the core of our First Amendment values.

Moreover, Johnson was prosecuted because he knew that his politically charged expression would cause "serious offense." If he had burned the flag as a means of disposing of it because it was dirty or torn, he would not have been convicted of flag desecration under this Texas law: federal law designates burning as the preferred means of disposing of a flag "when it is in such condition that it is no longer a fitting emblem for display," and Texas has no quarrel with this means of disposal. The Texas law is thus not aimed at protecting the physical integrity of the flag in all circumstances, but is designed instead to protect it only against impairments that would cause serious offense to others. Texas concedes as much: "[The statute] reaches only those severe acts of physical abuse of the flag carried out in a way likely to be offensive. The statute mandates intentional or knowing abuse, that is, the kind of mistreatment that is not innocent, but rather is intentionally designed to seriously offend other individuals."

Whether Johnson's treatment of the flag violated Texas law thus depended on the likely communicative impact of his expressive conduct. Johnson's political expression was restricted because of the content of the message he conveyed. We must therefore subject the State's asserted interest in preserving the special symbolic character of the flag to "the most exacting scrutiny." *Boos v. Barry* (1988).

Texas argues that its interest in preserving the flag as a symbol of nationhood and national unity survives this close analysis. Quoting extensively from the writings of this Court chronicling the flag's historic and symbolic role in our society, the State emphasizes the "special place" reserved for the flag in our Nation. The State's argument is not that it has an interest simply in maintaining the flag as a symbol of *something*, no matter what it symbolizes; indeed, if that were the State's position, it would be difficult to see how that interest is endangered by highly symbolic conduct such as Johnson's. Rather, the State's claim is that it has an interest in preserving the flag as a symbol of *nationhood* and *national unity*, a symbol with a determinate range of meanings. According to Texas, if one physically treats the flag in a way that would tend to cast doubt on either the idea that nationhood and national unity are the flag's referents or that national unity actually exists, the message conveyed thereby is a harmful one and therefore may be prohibited.

[**Oft-cited sentence**] If there is a bedrock principle underlying the First Amendment, it is that the government may not prohibit the expression of an idea simply because society finds the idea itself offensive or disagreeable.

We have not recognized an exception to this principle even where our flag has been involved. In *Street v. New York* (1969), we held that a State may not criminally punish a person for uttering words critical of the flag. Rejecting the argument that the conviction could be sustained on the ground that Street had "failed to show the respect for our national symbol which may properly be demanded of every citizen," we concluded that "the constitutionally guaranteed 'freedom to be intellectually…diverse or even contrary,' and the 'right to differ as to things that touch the heart of the existing order,' encompass the freedom to express publicly one's opinions about our flag, including those opinions which are defiant or contemptuous." quoting *Barnette*. Nor may the government, we have held, compel conduct that would evince respect for the flag. "To sustain the compulsory flag salute we are required to say that a Bill of Rights which guards the individual's right to speak his own mind left it open to public authorities to compel him to utter what is not in his mind."

In short, nothing in our precedents suggests that a State may foster its own view of the flag by prohibiting expressive conduct relating to it. To bring its argument outside our precedents, Texas attempts to convince us that even if its interest in preserving the flag's symbolic role does not allow it to prohibit words or some expressive conduct critical of the flag, it does permit it to forbid the outright destruction of the flag. The State's argument cannot depend here on the distinction between written or spoken words and nonverbal conduct.

Texas' focus on the precise nature of Johnson's expression, moreover, misses the point of our prior decisions: their enduring lesson, that the government may not prohibit expression simply because it disagrees with its message, is not dependent on the particular mode in which one chooses to express an idea. If we were to hold that a State may forbid flag burning wherever it is likely to endanger the flag's symbolic role, but allow it wherever burning a flag promotes that role—as where, for example, a person ceremoniously burns a dirty flag—we would be saying that when it comes to impairing the flag's physical integrity, the flag itself may be used as a symbol—as a substitute for the written or spoken word or a "short cut from mind to mind"—only in one direction. We would be permitting a State to "prescribe what shall be orthodox" by saying that one may burn the flag to convey one's attitude toward it and its referents only if one does not endanger the flag's representation of nationhood and national unity.

We never before have held that the Government may ensure that a symbol be used to express only one view of that symbol or its referents. Indeed, in *Schacht v. United States*, we invalidated a federal statute permitting an actor portraying a member of one of our Armed Forces to "'wear the uniform of that armed force if the portrayal does not tend to discredit that armed force.'" This proviso, we held, "which leaves Americans free to praise the war in Vietnam but can send persons like Schacht to prison for opposing it, cannot survive in a country which has the First Amendment."

We perceive no basis on which to hold that the principle underlying our decision in *Schacht* does not apply to this case. To conclude that the government may permit designated symbols to be used to communicate only a limited set of messages would be to enter territory having no discernible or defensible boundaries. Could the government, on this theory, prohibit the burning of state flags? Of copies of the Presidential seal? Of the Constitution? In evaluating these choices under the First Amendment, how would we decide which symbols were sufficiently special to warrant this unique status? To do so, we would be forced to consult our own political preferences, and impose them on the citizenry, in the very way that the First Amendment forbids us to do.

There is, moreover, no indication—either in the text of the Constitution or in our cases interpreting it—that a separate juridical category exists for the American flag alone. Indeed, we would not be surprised to learn that the persons who framed our Constitution and wrote the Amendment that we now construe were not known for their reverence for the Union Jack. The First Amendment does not guarantee that other concepts virtually sacred to our Nation as a whole—such as the principle that discrimination on the basis of race is odious and destructive—will go unquestioned in the marketplace of ideas. We decline, therefore, to create for the flag an exception to the joust of principles protected by the First Amendment.

It is not the State's ends, but its means, to which we object. It cannot be gainsaid that there is a special place reserved for the flag in this Nation, and thus we do not doubt that the government has a legitimate interest in making efforts to "preserv[e] the national flag as an unalloyed symbol of our country." *Spence*. We reject the suggestion, urged at oral argument by counsel for Johnson, that the government lacks "any state interest whatsoever" in regulating the manner in which the flag may be displayed. Congress has, for example, enacted precatory regulations describing the proper treatment of the flag, and we cast no doubt on the legitimacy of its interest in making such recommendations. To say that the government has an interest in encouraging proper treatment of the flag, however, is not to say that it may criminally punish a person for burning a flag as a means of political protest. "National unity as an end which officials may foster by persuasion and example is not in question. The problem is whether under our Constitution compulsion as here employed is a permissible means for its achievement." *Barnette*.

We are fortified in today's conclusion by our conviction that forbidding criminal punishment for conduct such as Johnson's will not endanger the special role played by our flag or the feelings it inspires. To paraphrase Justice Holmes, we submit that nobody can suppose that this one gesture of an unknown man will change our Nation's attitude towards its flag. Indeed, Texas' argument that the burning of an American flag "'is an act having a high likelihood to cause a breach of the peace,'" quoting *Sutherland v. DeWulf* (1971), and its statute's implicit assumption that physical mistreatment of the flag will lead to "serious offense," tend to confirm that the flag's special role is not in danger; if it were, no one would riot or take offense because a flag had been burned.

We are tempted to say, in fact, that the flag's deservedly cherished place in our community will be strengthened, not weakened, by our holding today. Our decision is a reaffirmation of the principles of freedom and inclusiveness that the flag best reflects, and of the conviction that our toleration of criticism such as Johnson's is a sign and source of our strength. Indeed, one of the proudest images of our flag, the one immortalized in our own national anthem, is of the bombardment it survived at Fort McHenry. It is the Nation's resilience, not its rigidity, that Texas sees reflected in the flag—and it is that resilience that we reassert today.

[Responding to flag burning] The way to preserve the flag's special role is not to punish those who feel differently about these matters. It is to persuade them that they are wrong. And, precisely because it is our flag that is involved, one's response to the flag burner may exploit the uniquely persuasive power of the flag itself. We can imagine no more appropriate response to burning a flag than waving one's own, no better way to counter a flag burner's message than by saluting the flag that burns, no surer means of preserving the dignity even of the flag that burned than by—as one witness here did—according its remains a respectful burial. We do not consecrate the flag by punishing its desecration, for in doing so we dilute the freedom that this cherished emblem represents.

[Ruling] Johnson was convicted for engaging in expressive conduct. The State's interest in preventing breaches of the peace does not support his conviction because Johnson's conduct did not threaten to disturb the peace. Nor does the State's interest in preserving the flag as a symbol of nationhood and national unity justify his criminal conviction for engaging in political expression. The judgment of the Texas Court of Criminal Appeals is therefore

Affirmed.

Points to Consider

1. The dissent.

Given the symbolic power of the flag—a power acknowledged at length in Justice Brennan's majority opinion—it may be unsurprising that the dissenting justices were unsparing and passionate in their criticism of the outcome. Joined by Justice Byron White and Justice Sandra Day O'Connor, Chief Justice William Rehnquist filed a dissenting opinion arguing that the flag is more than just another symbol. Could Johnson have made the same point by other means? Why and how is this case different from *O'Brien*?

> The American flag, then, throughout more than 200 years of our history, has come to be the visible symbol embodying our Nation. It does not represent the views of any particular political party, and it does not represent any particular political philosophy. The flag is not simply another "idea" or "point of view" competing for recognition in the marketplace of ideas. Millions and millions of Americans regard it with an almost mystical reverence, regardless of what sort of social, political, or philosophical beliefs they may have. I cannot agree that the First Amendment invalidates the Act of Congress, and the laws of 48 of the 50 States, which make criminal the public burning of the flag....
>
> Here it may equally well be said that the public burning of the American flag by Johnson was no essential part of any exposition of ideas, and at the same time it had a tendency to incite a breach of the peace. Johnson was free to make any verbal denunciation of the flag that he wished; indeed, he was free to burn the flag in private. He could publicly burn other symbols of the Government or effigies of political leaders. He did lead a march through the streets of Dallas, and conducted a rally in front of the Dallas City Hall. He engaged in a "die-in" to protest nuclear weapons. He shouted out various slogans during the march, including: "Reagan, Mondale which will it be? Either one means World War III"; "Ronald Reagan, killer of the hour, Perfect example of U. S.

power"; and "red, white and blue, we spit on you, you stand for plunder, you will go under." For none of these acts was he arrested or prosecuted; it was only when he proceeded to burn publicly an American flag stolen from its rightful owner that he violated the Texas statute.

The Court could not, and did not, say that Chaplinsky's utterances [referring to *Chaplinsky v. New Hampshire* (1942), discussed in Chapter 3] were not expressive phrases—they clearly and succinctly conveyed an extremely low opinion of the addressee. The same may be said of Johnson's public burning of the flag in this case; it obviously did convey Johnson's bitter dislike of his country. But his act, like Chaplinsky's provocative words, conveyed nothing that could not have been conveyed and was not conveyed just as forcefully in a dozen different ways. As with "fighting words," so with flag burning, for purposes of the First Amendment: It is "no essential part of any exposition of ideas, and [is] of such slight social value as a step to truth that any benefit that may be derived from [it] is clearly outweighed" by the public interest in avoiding a probable breach of the peace. The highest courts of several States have upheld state statutes prohibiting the public burning of the flag on the grounds that it is so inherently inflammatory that it may cause a breach of public order.

The result of the Texas statute is obviously to deny one in Johnson's frame of mind one of many means of "symbolic speech." Far from being a case of "one picture being worth a thousand words," flag burning is the equivalent of an inarticulate grunt or roar that, it seems fair to say, is most likely to be indulged in not to express any particular idea, but to antagonize others. Only five years ago we said in *City Council of Los Angeles v. Taxpayers for Vincent* (1984), that "the First Amendment does not guarantee the right to employ every conceivable method of communication at all times and in all places." The Texas statute deprived Johnson of only one rather inarticulate symbolic form of protest—a form of protest that was profoundly offensive to many—and left him with a full panoply of other symbols and every conceivable form of verbal expression to express his deep disapproval of national policy. Thus, in no way can it be said that Texas is punishing him because his hearers—or any other group of people—were profoundly opposed to the message that he sought to convey. Such opposition is no proper basis for restricting speech or expression under the First Amendment. It was Johnson's use of this particular symbol, and not the idea that he sought to convey by it or by his many other expressions, for which he was punished.

2. The congressional response.

The dissenting justices weren't the only Americans disappointed by the Court's decision. Shortly after the Court's opinion was issued, Congress passed the Flag Protection Act of 1989. The statute stated plainly that "[w]hoever knowingly mutilates, defaces, physically defiles, burns, maintains on the floor or ground, or tramples upon any flag of the United States shall be fined under this title or imprisoned for not more than one year, or both."

On the day the law took effect (October 30, 1989), flags were burned nationwide in simultaneous protest. Multiple arrests in Seattle and D.C. resulted in a consolidated case before the Supreme Court, and in *U.S. v. Eichman* (1990), a sharply split Court issued another 5–4 decision again holding flag burning to be protected speech under the First Amendment. Writing for the majority, Justice Brennan rejected the government's argument that the passage of the law represented a "national consensus" about the impropriety of flag burning, noting that "any suggestion that the Government's interest in suppressing speech becomes more weighty as popular opposition to that speech grows is foreign to the First Amendment."

The Court's twin rulings in *Eichman* and *Johnson* haven't stopped attempts to ban flag burning, however. Though Justice Brennan wrote in *Eichman* that "[p]unishing desecration of the flag dilutes the very freedom that makes this emblem so revered, and worth revering," a Flag Desecration Amendment to the Constitution was introduced in every Congress from the 104th to the 109th, falling just one Senate vote short of approval in 2006. The proposed amendment states that "Congress shall have power to prohibit the physical desecration of the flag of the United States."

3. President Trump and the flag.

President Trump has come out in support of imposing consequences for burning the flag. Shortly after being elected in November 2016, Trump tweeted: "Nobody should be allowed to burn the American flag—if they do, there must be consequences—perhaps loss of citizenship or year in jail!"

4. What ever happened to Gregory Lee Johnson?

Gregory Lee "Joey" Johnson is still burning flags in protest, including outside the Republican National Convention in 2016.

11.

Student Speech & the First Amendment

K-12 STUDENT SPEECH

> *It can hardly be argued that either students or teachers shed their constitutional rights to freedom of speech or expression at the schoolhouse gate.*
>
> —*Justice Abe Fortas in Tinker v. Des Moines Independent Community School District (1969)*

AFTER THE 2018 Parkland, Florida, shooting at Marjory Stoneman Douglas High School (MSDHS), in which a former student killed seventeen people and wounded seventeen others, high school students across the country engaged in walkouts from school and marched in the streets to protest gun violence.

When administrators at MSDHS mandated the use of clear backpacks as a security effort, many survivors of the shooting used their backpacks as a form of protest. Some filled the backpacks with highly personal items like tampons to protest the invasion of privacy the backpacks represented; others placed $1.05 price tags on them to represent what they saw as the value of their lives to Senator Marco Rubio (equal to the total donations from the National Rifle Association to Rubio divided by the number of students in Florida); while others wrote messages in support of gun control on them.

From a legal standpoint, the question becomes whether public school students have a First Amendment right to engage in a walkout or symbolic political speech. While walkouts are not protected symbolic conduct (rather, they are acts of civil disobedience), we will break down the history of and current protections for public K–12 student speech, like the MSDHS students' backpack protest, in this section.

The Pledge of Allegiance

The Supreme Court did not provide public school students any First Amendment rights until *West Virginia State Board of Education v. Barnette* in 1943. In this case, two sisters, Gathie and Marie Barnette, refused to salute the American flag and recite the Pledge of Allegiance at Slip Hill Grade School near Charleston, West Virginia. The Barnette sisters were Jehovah's Witnesses and believed that saluting the flag was prohibited under their religious beliefs. To them, the flag was a graven image.

School officials expelled the sisters for their act of defiance. West Virginia law not only permitted their expulsion, but also provided that parents could be fined or even jailed for thirty days for their children's actions.

Their father, Walter Barnette, took their case to court. At the time, the legal landscape was not favorable to him. In *Minersville School District v. Gobitis* (1940), the U.S. Supreme Court had upheld a similar Pennsylvania law. But some members of the Court realized they had made a mistake in *Gobitis*. So when the case of the Barnette sisters came across their desk, they took their chance to correct the precedent.

These events occurred against the backdrop of World War II, when patriotism at times drifted into jingoism. There were many acts of violence against Jehovah's Witnesses due to their perceived lack of patriotism for refusing to recite the pledge or salute the flag.

On Flag Day—June 14, 1943—the U.S. Supreme Court dramatically overruled *Gobitis* in its 6–3 *Barnette* decision. Writing for the majority, Justice Robert Jackson famously wrote: "If there is any fixed star in our constitutional constellation, it is that no official, high or petty, can prescribe what shall be orthodox in politics, nationalism, religion, or other matters of opinion, or force citizens to confess by word or act their faith therein."

Jackson memorably explained why it is paramount for public school officials and others to respect the free speech rights of students: "That they are educating the young for citizenship is reason for scrupulous protection of Constitutional freedoms of the individual, if we are not to strangle the free mind at its source and teach youth to discount important principles of our government as mere platitudes."

The *Barnette* case established that the First Amendment applies in public schools. It also ruled that government officials can violate the First Amendment by compelling people to engage in certain expression. Perhaps paradoxically, what it did not do was establish a test or legal standard to judge whether school officials violated the First Amendment rights of the students involved.

Many years later, Marie Barnette reflected on the case. "It has given us a sense of importance, not from a personal standpoint but from a sense of just how important the case was and what it stood for," she said. "We're proud of the fact that we stood up for our rights."

Black Armbands and a Supreme Court Victory

Nearly 25 years after *Barnette*, the Supreme Court again addressed the free speech rights of public school students in *Tinker v. Des Moines Independent Community School District* (1969). This time, the Court provided more guidance as to when student speech receives First Amendment protection.

The case involved several students, including Christopher Eckhardt and siblings John and Mary Beth Tinker, who were suspended for wearing black armbands to school to protest U.S. involvement in the Vietnam War, to support Robert Kennedy's call for a Christmas truce, and to mourn those who had died in the conflict.

School officials learned of the armband protest in advance and quickly passed a resolution prohibiting the wearing of black armbands. This ultimately led to a court battle that culminated in a stunning victory for the students.

OPINION

Tinker v. Des Moines Independent Community School District

(Abridged.)

393 U.S. 503 (1969)
Vote: 7–2

JUSTICE FORTAS delivered the opinion of the Court.

[**Facts**] Petitioner John F. Tinker, 15 years old, and petitioner Christopher Eckhardt, 16 years old, attended high schools in Des Moines, Iowa. Petitioner Mary Beth Tinker, John's sister, was a 13-year-old student in junior high school.

In December 1965, a group of adults and students in Des Moines held a meeting at the Eckhardt home. The group determined to publicize their objections to the hostilities in Vietnam and their support for a truce by wearing black armbands during the holiday season and by fasting on December 16 and New Year's Eve.

Petitioners and their parents had previously engaged in similar activities, and they decided to participate in the program.

The principals of the Des Moines schools became aware of the plan to wear arm-bands. On December 14, 1965, they met and adopted a policy that any student wearing an armband to school would be asked to remove it, and if he refused he would be suspended until he returned without the armband. Petitioners were aware of the regulation that the school authorities adopted.

On December 16, Mary Beth and Christopher wore black armbands to their schools. John Tinker wore his armband the next day. They were all sent home and suspended from school until they would come back without their armbands. They did not return to school until after the planned period for wearing armbands had expired—that is, until after New Year's Day.

This complaint was filed in the United States District Court by petitioners, through their fathers. After an evidentiary hearing, the District Court dismissed the complaint. It upheld the constitutionality of the school authorities' action on the ground that it was reasonable in order to prevent disturbance of school discipline.

On appeal, the Court of Appeals for the Eighth Circuit considered the case en banc. The court was equally divided, and the District Court's decision was accordingly affirmed, without opinion. We granted certiorari.

[**Armbands as symbolic speech**] The District Court recognized that the wearing of an armband for the purpose of expressing certain views is the type of symbolic act that is within the Free Speech Clause of the First Amendment. As we shall discuss, the wearing of armbands in the circumstances of this case was entirely divorced from actually or potentially disruptive conduct by those partic-ipating in it. It was closely akin to "pure speech" which, we have repeatedly held, is entitled to comprehensive protection under the First Amendment.

[**The "schoolhouse gate" passage**] First Amendment rights, applied in light of the special characteristics of the school environment, are available to teachers and students. It can hardly be argued that either students or teachers shed their constitutional rights to freedom of speech or expression at the schoolhouse gate.

Our problem lies in the area where students in the exercise of First Amendment rights collide with the rules of the school authorities.

The problem posed by the present case does not relate to regulation of the length of skirts or the type of clothing, to hair style, or deportment. It does not concern aggressive, disruptive action or even group demonstrations. Our problem involves direct, primary First Amendment rights akin to "pure speech."

The school officials banned and sought to punish petitioners for a silent, passive expression of opinion, unaccompanied by any disorder or disturbance on the part of petitioners. There is here no evidence whatever of petitioners' interference, actual or nascent, with the schools' work or of collision with the rights of other students to be secure and to be let alone. Accordingly, this case does not concern speech or action that intrudes upon the work of the schools or the rights of other students.

[**No disruption**] Only a few of the 18,000 students in the school system wore the black armbands. Only five students were suspended for wearing them. There is no indication that the work of the schools or any class was disrupted. Outside the classrooms, a few students made hostile remarks to the children wearing armbands, but there were no threats or acts of violence on school premises.

The District Court concluded that the action of the school authorities was reasonable because it was based upon their fear of a disturbance from the wearing of the armbands. But, in our system, undifferentiated fear or apprehension of disturbance is not enough to overcome the right to freedom of expression.

In order for the State in the person of school officials to justify prohibition of a particular expression of opinion, it must be able to show that its action was caused by something more than a mere desire to avoid the discomfort and unpleasantness that always accompany an unpopular viewpoint. Certainly where there is no finding and no showing that engaging in the forbidden conduct would "materially and substantially interfere with the requirements of appropriate discipline in the operation of the school," the prohibition cannot be sustained. *Burnside v. Byars* (1966).

In the present case, the District Court made no such finding, and our independent examination of the record fails to yield evidence that the school authorities had reason to anticipate that the wearing of the armbands would substantially interfere with the work of the school or impinge upon the rights of other students. Even an official memorandum prepared after the suspension that listed the reasons for the ban on wearing the armbands made no reference to the anticipation of such disruption.

[**Viewpoint discrimination**] It is also relevant that the school authorities did not purport to prohibit the wearing of all symbols of political or controversial significance. The record shows that students in some of the schools wore buttons relating to national political campaigns, and some even wore the Iron Cross, traditionally a symbol of Nazism. The order prohibiting the wearing of armbands did not extend to these. Instead, a particular symbol—black armbands worn to exhibit opposition to this Nation's involvement in Vietnam—was singled out for prohibition. Clearly, the prohibition of expression of one particular opinion, at least without evidence that it is necessary to avoid material and substantial interference with schoolwork or discipline, is not constitutionally permissible.

In our system, state-operated schools may not be enclaves of totalitarianism. School officials do not possess absolute authority over their students. Students in school as well as out of school, are "persons" under our Constitution.

[**Substantial disruption test**] The principal use to which the schools are dedicated is to accommodate students during prescribed hours for the purpose of certain types of activities. Among those activities is personal intercommunication among the students. This is not only an inevitable part of the process of attending school; it is also an important part of the educational process. A student's rights, therefore, do not embrace merely the classroom hours. When he is in the cafeteria, or on the playing field, or on the campus during the authorized hours, he may express his opinions, even on controversial subjects like the conflict in Vietnam, if he does so without "materially and substantially interfer[ing] with the requirements of appropriate discipline in the operation of the school" and without colliding with the rights of others. *Burnside v. Byars*. But conduct by the student, in class or out of it, which for any reason—whether it stems from time, place, or type of behavior—materially disrupts classwork or involves substantial disorder or invasion of the rights of others is, of course, not immunized by the constitutional guarantee of freedom of speech.

As we have discussed, the record does not demonstrate any facts which might reasonably have led school authorities to forecast substantial disruption of or material interference with school activities, and no disturbances or disorders on the school premises in fact occurred. They neither interrupted school activities nor sought to intrude in the school affairs or the lives of others. They caused discussion outside of the classrooms, but no interference with work and no disorder. In the circumstances, our Constitution does not permit officials of the State to deny their form of expression.

[Ruling] We express no opinion as to the form of relief which should be granted, this being a matter for the lower courts to determine. We reverse and remand for further proceedings consistent with this opinion.

Points to Consider

1. Justice Abe Fortas.

Justice Fortas served on the U.S. Supreme Court for only a short time (1965–1969), but he wrote some influential decisions, including *Tinker*. He authored another significant school law decision, *Epperson v. Arkansas* (1968), striking down an Arkansas law that prohibited the teaching of evolution. Fortas reasoned that the law violated the Establishment Clause.

He also wrote the Court's decision in *Brown v. Louisiana* (1966), which reversed the breach-of-peace convictions of several individuals who conducted a sit-in at a public library to protest segregation policies.

2. Burnside v. Byars *and the substantial disruption test.*

Justice Fortas did not create the substantial disruption test out of thin air. Instead, he borrowed it from an earlier decision rendered by the U.S. Court of Appeals for the Fifth Circuit: *Burnside v. Byars* (1966). The case involved several young African-American female students who fought for their right to wear "Freedom Buttons" to protest voter discrimination in Philadelphia, Mississippi.

In *Burnside*, Judge Walter Gewin declared that school officials "cannot infringe on their students' right to free and unrestricted expression as guaranteed to them under the First Amendment to the Constitution, where the exercise of such rights in the school buildings and schoolrooms do not materially and substantially interfere with the requirements of appropriate discipline in the operation of the school."

3. Viewpoint discrimination.

Arguably the most important First Amendment free speech principle is that government officials cannot engage in viewpoint discrimination. In *Tinker*, the school officials committed viewpoint discrimination by banning a symbol representing a specific viewpoint, while at the same time allowing students to wear other symbols, such as Iron Crosses and political campaign buttons.

4. Christopher Eckhardt.

The name Tinker will forever be associated with this groundbreaking First Amendment case, but we should not forget the forgotten litigant, Christopher

Eckhardt. He, too, passionately defended the First Amendment. Upon his death in 2013, Mary Beth Tinker said: "He spoke up for the First Amendment, but also used it in his life to promote justice. Most recently, he published a book on the rights of psychiatric patients. He was also a strong advocate for the rights of prisoners, and for gay rights."

For their part, Mary Beth and John Tinker have both remained committed defenders of free speech. Mary Beth Tinker has even organized a Tinker Tour, travelling across the country to spread the word on free expression. During the tour, she encourages young people to use their voices and exercise their First Amendment freedoms.

5. Invasion of the rights of others.

Most scholars cite *Tinker* for its substantial disruption test, which provides that school officials can restrict student expression only if they can reasonably forecast that the speech will cause a material interference with or substantial disruption of school activities.

However, Justice Fortas simply wrote that school officials can restrict student speech that impinges on or invades the rights of others; he did not define what constitutes such speech. The Supreme Court never has explained in detail what types of speech impinge upon or invade the rights of others.

Some lower courts have applied the substantial disruption test to *limit* student speech. For example, the U.S. Court of Appeals for the Ninth Circuit ruled in *Harper v. Poway Unified School District* (2006) that school officials could prohibit a student from wearing T-shirts with Bible verses from Leviticus condemning homosexuality. Quoting *Tinker*, the court reasoned that such expression invaded the rights of gay and lesbian students "to be secure and to be let alone."

Uncertainty remains as to the "invasion of the rights of others" language. The issue is important in First Amendment law, particularly as more school districts adopt anti-cyberbullying policies.

6. Online student speech.

While the *Tinker* decision explains that students do not "shed" their free speech rights at school, it permits schools to limit certain student expression. But what about off-campus student speech that might create a substantial disruption at school? Many schools have punished students for the content of social media posts that they wrote from their own homes. Most courts still apply the *Tinker* substantial disruption test to speech created entirely off campus. The U.S. Supreme Court has not yet addressed this question.

Rolling Back *Tinker*

The Supreme Court cut back the free speech protections that *Tinker* granted to high school students in three subsequent decisions: *Bethel School District v. Fraser* (1986), *Hazelwood School District v. Kuhlmeier* (1988), and *Morse v. Frederick* (2007).

Vulgar and lewd speech

Bethel School District v. Fraser (1986) involved a high school junior from Washington named Matthew Fraser, who delivered a speech before the student body at Bethel High School nominating a classmate for student vice-president. Fraser's speech used sexually loaded terms that prompted laughter, hooting, yelling, and a few graphic gestures. His speech read:

> I know a man who is firm—he's firm in his pants, he's firm in his shirt, his character is firm—but most…of all, his belief in you, the students of Bethel, is firm.
>
> Jeff Kuhlman is a man who takes his point and pounds it in. If necessary, he'll take an issue and nail it to the wall. He doesn't attack things in spurts—he drives hard, pushing and pushing until finally—he succeeds.
>
> Jeff is a man who will go to the very end—even the climax, for each and every one of you.
>
> So vote for Jeff for A.S.B. vice-president—he'll never come between you and the best our high school can be.

School officials suspended Fraser for violating a school policy prohibiting "disruptive conduct." Fraser challenged the suspension in federal court on First Amendment grounds. A federal district court ruled in favor of Fraser, a decision affirmed by the Ninth Circuit Court of Appeals. However, school officials successfully appealed to the Supreme Court.

Writing his last opinion for the Court, Chief Justice Warren Burger created a new rule, reasoning that school officials could prohibit student speech that was vulgar, lewd, or plainly offensive. He wrote that "[t]he undoubted freedom to advocate unpopular and controversial views in schools and classrooms must be balanced against the society's countervailing interest in teaching students the boundaries of socially appropriate behavior."

The Court characterized Matthew Fraser's speech as disruptive as well as vulgar and lewd, particularly to younger students in the audience. It focused on the "sexual content" of Fraser's speech and seemingly ignored the fact that Fraser was giving a political speech, nominating a fellow student for elected office.

School-sponsored speech

The Supreme Court took a bigger bite out of *Tinker* in its next student First Amendment decision, *Hazelwood School District v. Kuhlmeier* (1988). The case involved the censorship of two student-written articles for the school newspaper, *Spectrum*, at Hazelwood East High School in St. Louis, Missouri. The two articles dealt with teen pregnancy and the impact of divorce upon children.

The school principal, Robert Eugene Reynolds, believed that the articles were inappropriate and ordered them excised from the newspaper. Three student editors, Cathy Kuhlmeier, Leslie Smart, and Leanne Tippett-West, challenged the principal's action in federal court. The students lost before the federal district court but prevailed before the Eighth Circuit Court of Appeals.

Hazelwood appealed to the Supreme Court and prevailed in a 5–3 decision. The Court, in an opinion by Justice Byron White, created yet another new rule for what it termed "school-sponsored" student speech. White wrote:

> [W]e hold that educators do not offend the First Amendment by exercising editorial control over the style and content of student speech in school-sponsored expressive activities so long as their actions are reasonably related to legitimate pedagogical concerns.

This "rational basis" type of standard meant that school officials had greater control over any student speech deemed school-sponsored. In turn, many school officials began to assert greater authority over the content of student newspapers. But several states also responded by enacting so-called anti-*Hazelwood* statutes. In these states, students generally have greater free speech protections under state law than under the U.S. Constitution.

A student-rights group called New Voices U.S. seeks the passage of more state laws prohibiting press censorship at all public schools—including high schools, colleges, and universities. New Voices' anti-*Hazelwood* legislation has passed in more than a dozen states, including California, North Dakota, Vermont, and Washington.

Promoting drug use: "Bong Hits 4 Jesus"

For nearly twenty years, *Tinker, Fraser,* and *Hazelwood* represented the "Holy Trinity" of K–12 student speech law. Then, in 2007, *Morse v. Frederick* emerged on the scene.

A high school student from Alaska's Juneau-Douglas High School named Joseph Frederick conducted what he termed his ultimate free speech experiment—conduct that eventually brought him to the U.S. Supreme Court. Frederick became very interested in First Amendment issues, particularly after he faced criticism for refusing to stand and recite the Pledge of Allegiance. When questioned by school officials, he responded by referencing the *Barnette* decision.

On January 24, 2002, the Olympic Torch Relay came through a public street across from Frederick's high school. He showed up to school late and joined his classmates in watching the relay. As the torchbearers passed by, he and his friends unveiled an 8-by-14-foot banner bearing an unusual message: "Bong Hits 4 Jesus."

Principal Deborah Morse was less than pleased. She walked across the street and ordered the students to drop the banner. All complied except for Frederick. After Morse gave him a five-day suspension, he allegedly responded with a quote from Thomas Jefferson: "Speech limited is speech lost." Morse upped the suspension from five to ten days.

Morse challenged the suspension in court. He lost in federal district court but prevailed in the Ninth Circuit—much as Matthew Fraser did years earlier. On further appeal, the U.S. Supreme Court reversed the Ninth Circuit decision. Writing for the majority, Chief Justice John Roberts reasoned that public school officials can prohibit student speech that they reasonably believe promotes the illegal use of drugs. The Court also ruled that Principal Deborah Morse was entitled to qualified immunity (a legal doctrine that shields government officials from being sued for discretionary actions performed within their official capacity, unless they violate clearly established constitutional law).

THE FIRST AMENDMENT GOES TO COLLEGE

As you've now learned, the Supreme Court in *Tinker* granted substantial First Amendment rights to public grade school students—and those rights have been steadily eroded by the decisions that followed *Tinker* in recent decades.

But those rulings concern the speech rights of public K–12 students. What kind of First Amendment protection do students have when they speak their minds on the campus of a public college or university?

The quick answer is *full* protection. Public college students enjoy the same First Amendment rights on campus that they do off campus.

In 1981's *Widmar v. Vincent*, for example, the Supreme Court stated plainly that students don't check their First Amendment rights at the campus gates: "With respect to persons entitled to be there, our cases leave no doubt that the First Amendment rights of speech and association extend to the campuses of state universities." And this protection applies to student groups, as well. *Widmar* concerned the expressive activities of a campus religious student group called Cornerstone at the University of Missouri at Kansas City. The Court held that the

First Amendment's bar against viewpoint discrimination meant that the school couldn't ban Cornerstone students from meeting in university buildings that it made available to secular student groups.

The *Widmar* Court's clear commitment to student First Amendment rights was not a new development. In 1972's *Healy v. James*, the Court flatly stated that "the precedents of this Court leave no room for the view that, because of the acknowledged need for order, First Amendment protections should apply with less force on college campuses than in the community at large." In other words, an administrator's desire to keep things calm on their campus doesn't justify interference with student speech rights. "Quite to the contrary," the *Healy* Court continued quoting *Shelton v. Tucker* (1960), "[t]he vigilant protection of constitutional freedoms is nowhere more vital than in the community of American schools."

Like *Widmar*, *Healy* concerned a student group—this time, a prospective chapter of Students for a Democratic Society (SDS), a left-wing political group famous for its antiwar advocacy. The Court found that Central Connecticut State University's denial of recognition to SDS, a decision made in part because of the group's political beliefs, "failed to accord due recognition to First Amendment principles."

So if you're reading this textbook as a student at a public institution of higher education, rest assured that the First Amendment generally protects your right to speak out on campus. If you're a student at a private institution, however, the First Amendment doesn't legally bind your school because it isn't a government agency. Yet most private colleges promise their students extensive expressive rights. So be sure to review your student handbook and other institutional documents.

What's the Difference between High School and College?

Why do public college students enjoy First Amendment protections that courts have denied to public high school students? That's a good question, and the answer is multifaceted. Here's how the U.S. Court of Appeals for the Third Circuit eloquently explained the difference in *McCauley v. University of the Virgin Islands* (2010):

> [**Difference in pedagogical mission**] Public universities encourage teachers and students to launch new inquiries into our understanding of the world....
>
> Public elementary and high schools, on the other hand, are tasked with inculcating a "child [with] cultural values, [to] prepar[e] him for later professional training, and [to] help[] him to adjust normally to his environment."...Public elementary and high school education is as

much about learning how to be a good citizen as it is about multiplication tables and United States history.

[**Difference in authority**] Second, "public elementary and high school administrators," unlike their counterparts at public universities, "have the unique responsibility to act *in loco parentis*." Public university administrators, officials, and professors do not hold the same power over students....

College students today are no longer minors; they are now regarded as adults in almost every phase of community life....[E]ighteen year old students are now identified with an expansive bundle of individual and social interests and possess discrete rights not held by college students from decades past....

[**Difference in trust afforded students**] Closely related to the *in loco parentis* issue is the third observation, that public elementary and high schools must be empowered to address the "special needs of school discipline" unique to those environs....Unlike the strictly controlled, smaller environments of public elementary and high schools, where a student's course schedule, class times, lunch time, and curriculum are determined by school administrators, public universities operate in a manner that gives students great latitude....In short, public university students are given opportunities to acquit themselves as adults. Those same opportunities are not afforded to public elementary and high school students.

[**Difference in maturity**] Fourth, public elementary and high school administrators "must be able to take into account the emotional maturity of the intended audience in determining whether to disseminate student speech on potentially sensitive topics....Considerations of maturity are not nearly as important for university students, most of whom are already over the age of 18 and entrusted with a panoply of rights and responsibilities as legal adults....Moreover, research has confirmed the common sense observation that younger members of our society, children and teens, lack the maturity found in adults.

[**Difference in physical location**] Finally, university students, unlike public elementary and high school students, often reside in dormitories on campus, so they remain subject to university rules at almost all hours of the day. The concept of the "schoolhouse gate," and the idea that students may lose some aspects of their First Amendment right to freedom of speech while in school, does not translate well to an environment where the student is constantly within the confines of the schoolhouse.

The Third Circuit's explanation is comprehensive. When it comes to First Amendment rights, leaving the shelter of K–12 education and choosing a path to follow into adulthood is like earning your driver's license for navigating our American democracy. You're an adult now, empowered to make your own decisions—and at a public college, you can generally speak your mind in the same way that other adults can.

Free Speech on Campus

Of course, being on campus doesn't make balancing First Amendment rights against other important societal interests any easier. Campus free speech conflicts have often presaged or mirrored the cultural battles raging in the larger society: the anti-Communist blacklists of the Red Scare in the 1950s, the antiwar protests of the 1960s and 1970s, the struggle to adapt to a diversifying campus and workplace in the 1980s and 1990s, and the hyper-partisanship of the 2000s and 2010s.

Throughout each of these societal upheavals, however, our courts have sent a remarkably consistent message: To ensure the American public college campus fulfills its unique and important role as our most lively marketplace of ideas, the First Amendment rights of students and faculty must be protected.

So what does the judicial system's commitment to First Amendment rights mean in practice for you as a college student? Does it protect you from punishment for distributing an underground newspaper that offends administrators? In the next case, we'll meet Barbara Papish, a graduate student expelled from her public university for doing just that.

<hr />

OPINION

Papish v. Board of Curators of the University of Missouri

(Abridged.)

410 U.S. 667 (1973)
Vote: 6–3

PER CURIAM.

[Facts] Petitioner Barbara Papish, a graduate student in the University of Missouri School of Journalism, was expelled for distributing on campus a newspaper "containing forms of indecent speech" in violation of a bylaw of the Board of Curators. The newspaper, the Free Press Underground, had been sold on this state university campus for more than four years pursuant to an authorization obtained from the University Business Office. The particular newspaper issue in question was found to be unacceptable for two reasons. First, on the front cover, the publishers had reproduced a political cartoon previously printed in another newspaper depicting policemen raping the Statue of Liberty and the Goddess of Justice. The caption under the cartoon read: "…With Liberty and Justice for All." Secondly, the issue contained an article entitled "M_____f_____ Acquitted," which discussed the trial and acquittal on an assault charge of a New York City youth who was a member of an organization known as "Up Against the Wall, M_____f_____." Following a hearing, the Student Conduct Committee found that petitioner had violated the General Standards of Student Conduct, which requires students "to observe generally accepted standards of conduct" and specifically prohibits "indecent conduct or speech." Her expulsion, after affirmance first by the Chancellor of the University and then by its Board of Curators, was made effective in the middle of the spring semester.

[**Analysis**] We think *Healy v. James* (1972) makes it clear that the mere dissemination of ideas—no matter how offensive to good taste—on a state university campus may not be shut off in the name alone of "conventions of decency." Other recent precedents of this Court make it equally clear that neither the political cartoon nor the headline story involved in this case can be labeled as constitutionally obscene or otherwise unprotected. There is language in the opinions below which suggests that the University's action here could be viewed as an exercise of its legitimate authority to enforce reasonable regulations as to the time, place, and manner of speech and its dissemination. While we have repeatedly approved such regulatory authority, the facts set forth in the opinions below show clearly that petitioner was expelled because of the disapproved content of the newspaper rather than the time, place, or manner of its distribution.

[**Ruling**] Since the First Amendment leaves no room for the operation of a dual standard in the academic community with respect to the content of speech, and because the state University's action here cannot be justified as a nondiscriminatory application of reasonable rules governing conduct, the judgments of the courts below must be reversed.

Points to Consider

1. Decency.

In *Papish*, the Court cast aside the university's concerns about "decency," making plain that public institutions of higher education cannot discipline student speech due to "disapproved content."

Papish's clear holding—that public universities, as government actors, violate the First Amendment when they regulate student speech on account of viewpoint—provided a foundation for later decisions.

2. Papish *'s legacy:* Gay and Lesbian Students Association v. Gohn *(1988).*

In *Gohn*, the Eighth Circuit confronted a case involving a University of Arkansas student organization, the Gay and Lesbian Students Association (GLSA), that served as a support group for gay and lesbian students on campus. The group's funding requests for events were repeatedly denied by the student government in proceedings that evidenced obvious discrimination. Under pressure from state legislators who had threatened the university's budget if it supported the group, university leadership upheld the funding denials. The GLSA filed suit, alleging a violation of their First Amendment rights.

On appeal, the Eighth Circuit restated the central premise of *Papish*—the essentiality of viewpoint neutrality—in finding for the student group:

> The GLSA met all objective criteria for funding and received the Finance Committee's recommendation, yet was denied funds twice....It is apparent that the GLSA was denied "B" funds because of the views it espoused. Nor is there a compelling state interest justifying the Senate's denial of funds. The University provides no argument, and we can think of none. True, sodomy is illegal in Arkansas. However, the GLSA does not advocate sodomy, and, even if it did, its speech about an illegal activity would still be protected by the First Amendment. People may extol the virtues of arson or even cannibalism. They simply may not commit the acts. Thus, we reverse the District Court on the First Amendment issue. Conduct may be prohibited or regulated, within broad limits. *But government may not discriminate against people because it dislikes their ideas, not even when the ideas include advocating that certain conduct now criminal be legalized* [emphasis added].

The court noted that "[t]he University need not supply funds to student organizations; but once having decided to do so, it is bound by the First Amendment to act without regard to the content of the ideas being expressed."

3. Student rights and changing community standards.

The underground newspaper distributed by Barbara Papish contained the word "Motherfucker" and a graphic political cartoon, and *Gohn* concerned LGBTQ advocacy. Such speech may be considered relatively tame or commonplace by you and your peers today. But ask yourself: What if Papish's newspaper had contained explicitly racist or sexist speech? As you've seen in other chapters, bigoted speech, in and of itself, is protected by the First Amendment. So if the First Amendment protects student rights at public colleges just as it would the rights of adults off campus, does it also protect hateful student expression?

In the 1980s and 1990s, courts began to answer that question. As colleges nationwide finally began to welcome more diverse classes of students to their campuses, administrators sought to ensure tranquility on campus by enacting sweeping prohibitions against racist and sexist speech. However well-intentioned, these "speech codes"—university regulations prohibiting expression that would be constitutionally protected in society at large—ran headlong into the First Amendment.

Speech Codes

Discriminatory harassment

One early case that tested the interplay between the First Amendment and campus anti-harassment "speech codes" was *Doe v. University of Michigan* (1989). In *Doe*, a graduate student filed a First Amendment challenge to the university's anti-discrimination policy, alleging that the discussion of theories regarding "biological bases of individual differences in personality traits and mental abilities" might be subject to punishment as racist or sexist speech under the policy's terms. Among other conduct, the policy prohibited "[a]ny behavior, verbal or physical, that stigmatizes or victimizes an individual on the basis of race, ethnicity, religion, sex, sexual orientation, creed, national origin, ancestry, age, marital status, handicap or Vietnam-era veteran status" and "[c]reates an intimidating, hostile, or demeaning environment for educational pursuits, employment or participation in University sponsored extracurricular activities."

While recognizing that "most extreme and blatant forms of discriminatory conduct are not protected by the First Amendment," the federal district court found that the University of Michigan's code was unconstitutional. The court observed that the university was within its power to prohibit fighting words, incitement, obscenity, child pornography, libel, slander, and other speech beyond the First Amendment's protection, or to enact reasonable, content- and viewpoint-neutral time, place, and manner restrictions. But it could not "establish an anti-discrimination policy which had the effect of prohibiting certain speech because it disagreed with ideas or messages sought to be conveyed."

The district court's opinion noted the difficulty of drawing a line between protected speech and speech prohibited by the University of Michigan's policy:

During the oral argument, the Court asked the University's counsel how he would distinguish between speech which was merely offensive, which he conceded was protected, and speech which "stigmatizes or victimizes" on the basis of an invidious factor. Counsel replied "very carefully." The response, while refreshingly candid, illustrated the plain fact that the University never articulated any principled way to distinguish sanctionable from protected speech. Students of common understanding were necessarily forced to guess at whether a comment about a controversial issue would later be found to be sanctionable under the Policy. The terms of the Policy were so vague that its enforcement would violate the due process clause.

"While the Court is sympathetic to the University's obligation to ensure equal educational opportunities for all of its students," District Judge Avern Cohn concluded, "such efforts must not be at the expense of free speech."

Other courts have reached the same result in the years since, striking down similar anti-discrimination policies at the University of Wisconsin in 1991, Central Michigan University and Stanford University (the latter via California's "Leonard Law") in 1995, Pennsylvania's Shippensburg University in 2003, Texas Tech University in 2004, Temple University in 2008, and the University of the Virgin Islands in 2010.

This virtually unbroken string of speech-supportive rulings demonstrates that, just as for Barbara Papish, the First Amendment does not permit public college students to be punished for their ideas—even, and perhaps especially, when those ideas shock or offend.

Public colleges and discriminatory harassment

It's important to note that the First Amendment does *not* grant students a license to harass each other. In fact, colleges and universities that receive federal funding—which encompasses the vast majority of schools, both public and private—are *required* to address discriminatory harassment through federal anti-discrimination laws like Title VI, which prohibits discrimination on the basis of race, color, and national origin, and Title IX, which prohibits discrimination on the basis of gender.

But the crucial task here is to define "harassment" in a way that prohibits discrimination but also protects the expressive rights of the students. The Supreme Court provided guidance on what a constitutional definition of harassment should look like in 1999's *Davis v. Monroe County Board of Education*. In *Davis*, the Court ruled that colleges must take action against discriminatory conduct when it is "so severe, pervasive, and objectively offensive that it can be said to deprive the victims of access to the educational opportunities or benefits provided by the school." Expressive conduct that does not meet this standard does not constitute harassment, and is therefore protected by the First Amendment.

A 2003 advisory letter to university administrators issued by the Department of Education's Office for Civil Rights—the federal agency that enforces federal anti-discrimination laws on campus—offered more direction regarding how colleges and universities can satisfy their twin obligations to protect students from harassment and to uphold students' First Amendment rights:

> Some colleges and universities have interpreted OCR's prohibition of "harassment" as encompassing all offensive speech regarding sex, disability, race or other classifications. Harassment, however, to be prohibited by the statutes within OCR's jurisdiction, must include something beyond the mere expression of views, words, symbols or thoughts that some person finds offensive. Under OCR's standard, the conduct must also be considered sufficiently serious to deny or limit a student's ability to participate in or benefit from the educational program. Thus, OCR's standards require that the conduct be evaluated from the perspective of a reasonable person in the alleged victim's position, considering all the circumstances, including the alleged victim's age.

What do you think? Where should the line between harassment and freedom of speech be drawn on campus? What might the consequences be of getting it wrong in either direction?

Civility policies

Public college administrators can *hope* students will be polite when speaking to one another, but they can't *require* civility under threat of punishment.

In *College Republicans at San Francisco State University v. Reed* (2007), a federal district court issued a preliminary injunction preventing the California State University System from enforcing a system-wide civility policy because the policy posed a threat to student First Amendment rights.

The case was sparked by an "Anti-Terrorism Rally" held by the San Francisco State University (SFSU) chapter of the College Republicans, during which the group displayed—and then stepped on—large paper copies of the Hamas and Hezbollah flags, some of which bore the name "Allah." Here's the court's explanation of the key facts:

A few students in the large group that had gathered to watch the event voiced strong objections to the College Republicans stepping on flags that included the word "Allah." In response, the College Republicans allowed several students to use marking pens to try to cover or block out the word about which feelings were so strong. These attempts were not completely successful. Ultimately, the College Republicans permitted one of the offended students from the audience to take the Hamas flag off the stage. The Hezbollah flag remained.

As the rally progressed, SFSU students and members of the College Republicans continued a heated debate about the significance of the word "Allah" on the flags and the propriety of the way the College Republicans had chosen to communicate their political views. University Police were present in Malcolm X Square during the rally to ensure student safety, but it never became necessary for them to intervene. The rally came to a peaceful close—but the emotions it had ignited continued to fester.

In the weeks that followed, SFSU administrators received several complaints about the rally—one student called it "downright insulting and offensive"—and began formal disciplinary proceedings against the College Republicans. Although the charges were finally dismissed five months after the rally was held, two members of the student group filed a First Amendment challenge to the system-wide civility policy under which they had been charged.

In granting the injunction against the enforcement of the civility policy, the federal judge identified the limits that requiring "civility" imposes on student speech:

> [A] regulation that mandates civility easily could be understood as permitting only those forms of interaction that produce as little friction as possible, forms that are thoroughly lubricated by restraint, moderation, respect, social convention, and reason. The First Amendment difficulty with this kind of mandate should be obvious: the requirement "to be civil to one another" and the directive to eschew behaviors that are not consistent with "good citizenship" reasonably can be understood as prohibiting the kind of communication that it is necessary to use to convey the full emotional power with which a speaker embraces her ideas or the intensity and richness of the feelings that attach her to her cause. Similarly, mandating civility could deprive speakers of the tools they most need to connect emotionally with their audience, to move their audience to share their passion....

The conduct in which the College Republicans engaged during their anti-terrorism rally was indisputably expressive. And the subjects about which plaintiffs sought to express their views are as central to First Amendment sensibilities as any could be. This was core political expression in a classic public forum—indeed, in one of the forums where First Amendment rights are to enjoy their greatest protection.

How would you define civility? Is there a difference between civility as a social norm and civility as a government requirement? Should civility be enforced, or only encouraged?

"Free speech zones"

Another common restriction on student speech is the use of so-called "free speech zones." The term may *sound* appealing, but in practice, free speech zones operate more like free speech quarantines, providing just one area, often small and remote, where students are allowed to exercise their First Amendment rights.

Public colleges, like other government entities, may impose reasonable time, place, and manner restrictions on expressive activities, as long as those restrictions are viewpoint- and content-neutral, are narrowly tailored to serve a significant governmental interest, and leave open ample alternative channels for expression. But there's nothing reasonable about restricting student speech to one tiny area of a sprawling public campus, as did Modesto Junior College (MJC) in California.

On September 17, 2013—Constitution Day—MJC student Robert Van Tuinen tried to hand out copies of the U.S. Constitution to his fellow students outside of the school's tiny free speech zone. But he was stopped by campus law enforcement and MJC administrators for violating the school's free speech zone policy, which limited activities like Van Tuinen's to a 600-square-foot area that only two students could use at any given time. The policy also required five days' advance notice, a written application, and a copy of the applicant's student ID. Furthermore, each student could only use the free speech zone for eight hours per semester.

Imagine being a student at a school with such a policy. If you had nine hours' worth of things to say during a semester, or if you wanted to organize an immediate public rally in light of breaking news events, you'd be out of luck.

With FIRE's help, Van Tuinen filed a First Amendment lawsuit challenging the constitutionality of MJC's free speech zone policy. MJC settled the suit and revised the policy shortly thereafter. Similar free speech zones have been successfully challenged at the University of Cincinnati; Citrus College; the University of Hawaii, Hilo (where the free speech zone was, quite literally, a swamp);

California State Polytechnic University, Pomona; Blinn College; and Dixie State University. What's more, as of early 2018, nine states have passed legislation banning free speech zones from their public campuses altogether.

Security fees

Every year, student groups across the political spectrum invite speakers to campus for all manner of events—concerts, rallies, speeches, panel discussions, and so forth. Hearing from experienced or compelling voices from outside the confines of campus is a time-honored and important part of the student experience. A 2017 FIRE/YouGov poll of 1,250 American undergraduates found that 93 percent wanted their institutions to bring a variety of guest speakers to their campus, and 64 percent said they had changed their attitude or option after listening to a guest speaker.

But in recent years, some colleges have required student groups bringing in controversial speakers to shoulder hefty "security fees" to cover the expense of having campus security officers or law enforcement keep the peace in anticipation of protests or violence. In other words, the cost of overtime pay for campus security is passed on by the school to the student group that has invited the controversial speaker. Because the "security fee" effectively serves as a tax on controversial speakers, it's a First Amendment problem.

In *Forsyth County v. Nationalist Movement* (1992), the Supreme Court explained that "[l]isteners' reaction to speech is not a content-neutral basis for regulation.... Speech cannot be financially burdened, any more than it can be punished or banned, simply because it might offend a hostile mob." The chance that a controversial speaker might spur others who *disagree* with her message to violent protest doesn't justify imposing a cost on the speaker or those who invited her. In fact, requiring security fees can incentivize people who disagree with a speaker to threaten violence in the hopes that the need for added security will make the event unaffordable. As the Supreme Court put it in *Forsyth*, it's unacceptable under the First Amendment if "[t]hose wishing to express views unpopular with bottle throwers, for example, may have to pay more for their permit."

Nevertheless, colleges do routinely impose security fees on student groups bringing unpopular or controversial speakers to campus. For example, in 2015, the Kalamazoo Peace Center at Western Michigan University (WMU) invited rapper and activist Boots Riley to campus to speak about his work on social justice issues as part of its annual Peace Week event. Riley had been a participant in the Occupy movement in his hometown of Oakland, California. That worried WMU's public safety chief, whose system for determining security needs was far from objective;

he later admitted to a local news outlet that he made such decisions on an ad hoc basis after considering a speaker's identity and history.

Because of Riley's involvement with Occupy, WMU initially refused to allow the Kalamazoo Peace Center to bring him on campus, citing "public safety issues." After the students showed administrators that Riley had spoken elsewhere without problems, the school backed off on banning Riley outright, but said it would only allow Riley's appearance if the Peace Center ponied up $62 per hour to pay for a private security officer at the event.

Riley eventually spoke without incident to the Peace Center at an off-campus location the student group secured in lieu of paying for the school's security. Members of the Kalamazoo Peace Center filed a First Amendment lawsuit challenging WMU's insistence upon a security fee for Riley's appearance. WMU settled the suit and revised its policies a few months after the complaint was filed.

Other colleges and universities continue to try—and fail—to foist similar taxes on speakers from across the political spectrum, from "alt-right" provocateurs like Milo Yiannopoulos at the University of Alabama to a socialist student group at DePaul University.

Whenever a public university attempts to impose a financial cost upon a student group because of the content of its views, or those of its invited guest speakers, the First Amendment will have the final word.

Speech codes at your school

Every year, the Foundation for Individual Rights in Education (FIRE) rates and reviews speech policies maintained by more than 400 colleges and universities. You can see how your school fares by visiting FIRE's Spotlight Database, and learn more about campus speech codes by reviewing FIRE's *Correcting Common Mistakes in Campus Speech Policies* and *Spotlight on Speech Codes* report on thefire.org.

12.

Commerce & Communication

If you want to be important—wonderful. If you want to be recognized—wonderful. If you want to be great—wonderful. But recognize that he who is greatest among you shall be your servant. That's a new definition of greatness.
—Dr. Martin Luther King, Jr., "The Drum Major Instinct"

IN 2018, more than 100 million people listened to those powerful words, aired on television to mark the 50th anniversary of Dr. King's "Drum Major Instinct" sermon, which was originally delivered at Ebenezer Baptist Church in Atlanta in February 1968.

In this televised homage to humanism, scene after scene of people helping others served as a backdrop for the great civil rights leader's message. As reported by NBC News, they included "All-American depictions of young football players, fishermen, cowboys, a teacher, rescue workers and a fireman rescuing a child" and "pictures of U.S. Marines and a camouflage-clad soldier hugging his child." The visuals meshed well with King's message:

> [B]y giving that definition of greatness, it means that everybody can be great, because everybody can serve. You don't have to have a college degree to serve. You don't have to make your subject and your verb agree to serve. You don't have to know about Plato and Aristotle to serve. You don't have to know Einstein's theory of relativity to serve. You don't have to know the second theory of thermodynamics in physics to serve. You only need a heart full of grace, a soul generated by love.

Millions of young Americans had never heard those words. Millions of older Americans had forgotten them. It was a moving moment—thirty seconds, to be precise. It was also a 2018 Super Bowl ad for Ram Trucks. Price tag: $5 million. Ram's slogan, "Built to Serve," flashed across the screen as Dr. King's exhortation to serve others trailed off, neatly tying together a timeless message and a truck advertisement.

Was this a case of the company being civic-minded? After all, Dr. King's words received more attention on that day from that commercial than perhaps all of the other calendar days for that year combined. By that measure, it was a tribute to a great man—even if there was an occasional cutaway to a Ram truck roughing it through muddied waters.

Dr. King's daughter Bernice and the King Center saw it differently. For them, the ad was an outrage—a profanity committed for nothing more than commercial gain. It was, some of King's relatives said, anathema to everything Dr. King stood for, this commercialization of human values.

But that was hardly the end of the matter. As CNN reported, the King Estate (represented by King's two sons) viewed the advertisement through a different lens:

> Following the backlash, the King Estate said in a statement that it had reviewed the ad before it aired to make sure it met its standards and "found that the overall message of the ad embodied Dr. King's philosophy that true greatness is achieved by serving others."
>
> "Thus we decided to be a part of Ram's 'Built to Serve' Super Bowl program," the King Estate said.

So where do you stand? With the producers of the Ram commercial, Bernice King and the King Center, or his sons and the King Estate? What informs your decision?

Questions like this bring us to the topic of advertising and why and when (if at all) it should receive First Amendment protection. Keep this Super Bowl commercial in mind as we proceed, because it says much about commerce and communication in modern America and how they are linked, for better or for worse. As it stands, commercial speech currently receives less First Amendment protection than pure political speech, though the difference in their treatment by courts is becoming ever slighter.

THE SUBMARINE ADVERTISEMENT CASE

Mr. Chrestensen was a man with a nose for business and a subma-
rine, which he moored in New York's East River and opened to the
public for an admission charge. Anticipating substantial wartime
interest in viewing the inside of a submarine, he began distributing
handbills, but the law caught up with him.
—Alex Kozinski and Stuart Banner, "Who's Afraid of
Commercial Speech," Virginia Law Review 76, no. 4 (1990)

F.J. Chrestensen owned a World War I–era submarine. In 1940, hoping to make money off of his prize possession, he docked it at a pier on the East River in New York City and offered tours of the submarine. To advertise the tours, he distributed handbills on New York's city streets. That's when he ran afoul of a municipal ordinance that barred "distribution in the streets of commercial and business advertising matter."

Enter Lewis J. Valentine, New York City's police commissioner. Valentine wasn't big on the idea of such advertising; he warned Chrestensen he was in violation of the local law *unless* the handbills were devoted to "information or a public protest." Ever creative, Chrestensen came up with an idea. He redrafted his handbill. The admission fee was deleted from the front side. On the back side, he protested the City Dock Department's refusal to grant his submarine dockage.

Clever, right? Apparently, not clever enough, at least in the eyes of the police commissioner. As Valentine saw it, the front side still contained commercial advertising even though there was no admission price. That made it illegal. Chrestensen disagreed; he went to court claiming that he had lost $4,000 in profits because he had not been permitted to distribute the redesigned handbill. He alleged that the law as applied to him violated the due process clause of the Fourteenth Amendment.

The Federal District Court ruled in his favor and the Court of Appeals for the Second Circuit affirmed by a 2–1 margin. Valentine thereafter petitioned the Supreme Court to reverse the ruling and was granted a review.

The Court had this question to answer: Did the addition of information about a public protest on one side of an advertising handbill render the entire handbill protected under the Fourteenth Amendment?

The advertisement at issue in Valentine v. Chrestensen.

Writing for a unanimous Supreme Court in *Valentine v. Chrestensen* (1942), Justice Owen Roberts reversed the judgment favoring the constitutional claim raised by Chrestensen:

> This Court has unequivocally held that the streets are proper places for the exercise of the freedom of communicating information and disseminating opinion and that, though the states and municipalities may appropriately regulate the privilege in the public interest, they may not unduly burden or proscribe its employment in these public thoroughfares. We are equally clear that *the Constitution imposes no such restraint on government as respects purely commercial advertising. Whether, and to what extent,*

one may promote or pursue a gainful occupation in the streets, to what extent such activity shall be adjudged a derogation of the public right of user, are matters for legislative judgment [emphasis added]....

The respondent [Chrestensen] contends that, in truth, he was engaged in the dissemination of matter proper for public information, nonetheless so because there was inextricably attached to the medium of such dissemination commercial advertising matter. The court below appears to have taken this view since it adverts to the difficulty of apportioning, in a given case, the contents of the communication as between what is of public interest and what is for private profit. We need not indulge nice appraisal based upon subtle distinctions in the present instance nor assume possible cases not now presented. It is enough for the present purpose that the stipulated facts justify the conclusion that the affixing of the protest against official conduct to the advertising circular was with the intent, and for the purpose, of evading the prohibition of the ordinance. If that evasion were successful, every merchant who desires to broadcast advertising leaflets in the streets need only append a civic appeal, or a moral platitude, to achieve immunity from the law's command.

The decree is reversed.

Judgment was found against Chrestensen, and his First Amendment challenge denied.

Points to Consider

1. The first commercial speech case.

Halter v. Nebraska (1907) was the first commercial speech case to come before the Supreme Court. The case involved sellers of beer whose bottles had images of the American flag on them. In it, the Court upheld a Nebraska law that made it illegal to use the flag for commercial purposes.

2. The law professor who argued for protecting commercial speech.

The most extended and original argument for protecting commercial speech was formulated by Northwestern University Professor Martin Redish in an 1971 article for the *George Washington Law Review* entitled "The First Amendment in the Marketplace: Commercial Speech and the Values of Free Expression," and further developed in 2017 in an article for the *Cato Institute: Policy Analysis* titled "Commercial Speech and the Values of Free Expression." Redish argued that Constitutional protection for commercial speech was vital to citizens living in a capitalistic culture.

3. Political vs. commercial speech.

Notice that the New York City ordinance permitted political handbills but prohibited commercial ones. This is because political and religious speech have long been granted more protection than other forms of speech.

Justice Owen Roberts' opinion explored that dichotomy; he explained that, while the distribution of political handbills on the public streets is protected, "the Constitution imposes no such restraint on government as respects purely commercial advertising."

Why do you suppose that such a dichotomy exists? Do you think that all forms of political speech are always more important than commercial speech? How is commercial speech distinct from political speech or campaign materials?

What about editorial advertisements? In March of 1960, the Committee to Defend Martin Luther King and the Struggle for Freedom in the South took out a full-page advertisement in the *New York Times*. The ad solicited legal funds for Dr. King, who was facing an Alabama perjury indictment. It also detailed abuses against civil rights protestors under a banner headline that read, "Heed Their Rising Voices." As we discussed in Chapter 9, the Court in *New York Times, Co. v. Sullivan* (1964) ruled that such speech was protected under the First Amendment even though it was a paid advertisement, albeit a political one.

4. PSAs in advertisements.

Assume that Coors Brewing Company ran a commercial that contained messages such as: "drink responsibly," "don't drink and drive," and "if you're pregnant, do not drink." Assume that visuals were used to illustrate these messages and that the ad simply ended with the word "Coors." Would such a commercial be of *less* value to the public than a political advertisement urging people to "support world peace" and ending with the words "The Soros Foundation"? Does the identity of the messages' sponsors play a major role in your opinion?

5. Mixed commercial and political speech.

Justice Owen Roberts' opinion stated that "purely commercial advertising" was not entitled to constitutional protection. Was the advertising in *Valentine* purely commercial? The submarine ad in *Valentine* is somewhat similar to the Ram Trucks ad featuring Dr. King in that it is a mixture of political and commercial speech. Would you treat both as political speech (enhanced protection) or commercial speech (diminished protection)? What would it take to make either the Ram ad or the submarine handbill a form of political expression?

6. Fourteenth Amendment case.

Note that Chrestensen brought his case as a Fourteenth Amendment case (and not, formally speaking, a First Amendment case). Recall that the First Amendment became binding on the states by way of the Due Process Clause of the Fourteenth Amendment.

7. Standard of review.

The Court's opinion left determinations concerning the protection of commercial speech to "legislative judgment." By that measure, lawmakers would have almost absolute discretion to ban commercial speech. As you'll see later, this power has been limited by more recent cases.

PRESCRIPTION DRUG ADVERTISEMENTS

Two nonprofit organizations, the Virginia Citizens Consumer Council and the Virginia State AFL-CIO, joined by several individual prescription drug consumers, challenged a Virginia law that barred licensed pharmacists from advertising their prices for prescription drugs. When the case reached the Supreme Court in 1976, the Court had to grapple with the following question: Does a ban on advertising prescription drug prices by licensed pharmacists violate the First Amendment, even when the expression in question is commercial speech?

Writing for the Court in *Virginia State Board of Pharmacy v. Virginia Citizens Consumer Council, Inc.*, Justice Harry Blackmun declared:

> As to the particular consumer's interest in the free flow of commercial information, that interest may be as keen, if not keener by far, than his interest in the day's most urgent political debate. Appellees' case in this respect is a convincing one. Those whom the suppression of prescription drug price information hits the hardest are the poor, the sick, and particularly the aged. A disproportionate amount of their income tends to be spent on prescription drugs; yet they are the least able to learn, by shopping from pharmacist to pharmacist, where their scarce dollars are best spent. When drug prices vary as strikingly as they do, information as to who is charging what becomes more than a convenience. It could mean the alleviation of physical pain or the enjoyment of basic necessities.

Justice Blackmun went on to further elaborate the value of commercial speech for First Amendment purposes:

Moreover, there is another consideration that suggests that no line between publicly "interesting" or "important" commercial advertising and the opposite kind could ever be drawn. Advertising, however tasteless and excessive it sometimes may seem, is nonetheless dissemination of information as to who is producing and selling what product, for what reason, and at what price. So long as we preserve a predominantly free enterprise economy, the allocation of our resources in large measure will be made through numerous private economic decisions. *It is a matter of public interest that those decisions, in the aggregate, be intelligent and well informed. To this end, the free flow of commercial information is indispensable* [emphasis added].

So, what is commercial speech and how is it to be distinguished from political speech? Justice Blackmun answered the question this way: Commercial speech is speech that "propose[s] a commercial transaction."

With this case, the Court abandoned the rule announced in *Valentine v. Chrestensen* that purely commercial speech was entitled to no First Amendment protection. On this point, Justice Blackmun noted that there was no claim that "prescription drug price advertisements are forbidden because they are false or misleading in any way. Untruthful speech, commercial or otherwise, has never been protected for its own sake."

Justice William H. Rehnquist wrote the lone dissent, wherein he warned: "Under the Court's opinion, the way will be open not only for dissemination of price information, but for active promotion of prescription drugs, liquor, cigarettes, and other products the use of which it has previously been thought desirable to discourage." Note that, under *Valentine*, commercial speech that either involves an illegal activity (e.g., solicitation for prostitution) or is contrary to public policy (e.g., urging minors to smoke) is not protected.

Truthful or Misleading?

In *In re R.M.J.* (1982), the Court further clarified its position on misleading speech, declaring:

Commercial speech doctrine, in the context of advertising for professional services, may be summarized generally as follows: Truthful advertising related to lawful activities is entitled to the protections of the First Amendment. But when the particular content or method of the advertising suggests that it is inherently misleading, or when experience has proved that, in fact, such advertising is subject to abuse, the States may impose appropriate restrictions. Misleading advertising may be prohibited entirely.

The Problem of Too Little Information

What about disclosure? If an advertiser fails to disclose something about a product, might that be considered misleading and therefore unprotected speech? The Court addressed that question in *Zauderer v. Office of Disciplinary Counsel* (1985):

> [A]n advertiser's rights are adequately protected as long as disclosure requirements are reasonably related to the State's interest in preventing deception of consumers.

Points to Consider

1. Consumer vs. seller focus.

Alan Morrison, the public interest lawyer who successfully argued the *Virginia* case on behalf of consumers, later wrote:

> My basic idea behind the case that became *Virginia State Board of Pharmacy v. Virginia Citizens Consumer Council, Inc.* was that the emphasis under the First Amendment should be on the impact of denying consumers access to useful information, rather than on the restrictions on the seller or would-be speaker.

This interpretation extends First Amendment protection to those who want to receive truthful commercial information so that they might make better-informed decisions.

2. Modern advertising.

How does the idea that consumers' interest in advertising is related to receiving truthful commercial information square with the practices of modern-day advertising? Consider the following quote from David N. Martin: "Great advertising is a storyteller, a romantic voice, an emotional persuader....It must persuade in a way that romances and lures the customer unsuspecting into the brand's sticky web."

Is the type of advertising to which Martin refers synonymous with the kind of informed decision-making championed in *Virginia Pharmacy*? For example, does image advertising or lifestyle advertising actually help consumers make informed decisions? If not, are they entitled to protection under the rationale offered in *Virginia Pharmacy*?

3. Extending the reach of Virginia Pharmacy.

As Morrison saw it, the pharmacy case was but the first in a string of commercial speech cases he planned to bring:

> At the time the case was filed, I had just begun to serve as the director of the newly formed Public Citizen Litigation Group, with Ralph Nader as my boss. One of our goals was to increase the availability and afford-ability of legal services for ordinary people, and I had identified the total ban on all lawyer advertising as a promising area to challenge. The pre-scription drug ban on price advertising was chosen as our first adver-tising case because, while false advertising can be banned, the Virginia law applied to useful information whose truth (accuracy) could easily be verified. With a win here, we planned to move on to the lawyer adver-tising ban, with an intermediate stop in a case in which the local medical society threatened to discipline doctors if they provided factual infor-mation, such as where they went to medical school, whether they were board certified in a specialty, whether they spoke a foreign language, and whether they accepted Medicare and Medicaid.

4. Overbreadth doctrine.

Generally speaking, the overbreadth doctrine does *not* apply to commercial speech cases. In part, this is due to the lingering dichotomy between commercial speech (less protection) and political speech (more protection). Thus, the Court grants to the latter what it denies to the former.

5. Criticism of commercial speech doctrine.

Professor Steven Shiffrin, a noted First Amendment scholar, is an outspoken critic of giving commercial speech the kind of increased protection it has received in more recent times. Consider the following arguments he has made against such protection:

> Of course, commercial advertising serves an economic purpose in creat-ing demand, and it is understandable why, in the absence of more explicit fraud and deception, a legislature would decline to regulate. But it is unclear why this deluge of manipulation should enjoy constitutional protection. Indeed, whatever the economic advantages associated with commercial advertising, it comes with cultural and political costs.
>
> When US advertisers spend in excess of $180 billion on media advertisements in a single year, they inevitably promote a materialistic,

hedonistic culture. It encourages human beings in that culture to focus on possessing objects (and to revel in sensations) at the center of their lives. This conception of the good life might comport with the crassest form of hedonism, but there is more to life than pleasure seeking, including the service of others, the nurturing of relationships, the cultivation of character, and the development of a mature personality. In the end, it is preposterous to suppose that human beings achieve their dignity by securing material goods.

As Professor Shiffrin views it, commercial speech is far from being sufficiently beneficial to warrant constitutional protection; rather, it is actually *harmful* to a culture and therefore should be freely regulated by the state.

That's a moving argument, and it may well move you. But ask yourself this: Is that critique of commercial speech really a critique of something far bigger, namely modern American capitalism? If so, how would it ever be possible to regulate such speech and remain a capitalist society?

SEARCHING FOR A RULE: THE *CENTRAL HUDSON* TEST AND ITS EVOLUTION

While the ruling in *Virginia Pharmacy* held out new First Amendment hope for commercial speech, it lacked clarity when it came to formulating a rule that lawmakers could follow and judges could use in deciding a case. Is all commercial speech (save for speech that is false, is misleading, or involves unlawful activities) entitled to full protection? Four years after *Virginia Pharmacy*, the Supreme Court answered that question in *Central Hudson Gas & Electric Corporation v. Public Service Commission of New York* (1980).

As recounted in the First Amendment Encyclopedia, the facts were as follows: "In an effort to conserve energy and discourage consumption during the 1973 energy crisis, the Public Service Commission of New York had ordered all electric utilities in the state to cease advertising. Central Hudson Gas and Electric Corp. challenged the order in court as a restraint on free speech. Lower courts ruled that the government's interest in discouraging consumption outweighed the value of the speech."

The Supreme Court, in an 8–1 ruling, overruled the lower court and held that New York's ban on commercial speech violated the speech protections guaranteed by the First and Fourteenth Amendments. The Court declared the regulation overly broad.

Justice Lewis Powell, writing for the majority, set out a four-part test to determine when commercial speech should be protected. That test remains the law—though, as you will see, it has been applied in such a way as to make it more protective of speech than originally suggested.

Under the *Central Hudson* test, regulations affecting lawful and non-misleading speech is constitutional if:

1. The government has a *substantial* interest;
2. The regulation *directly and materially advances* the substantial interest of the government; and
3. The regulation is *narrowly tailored* to serve the government's interest.

The reason the Court developed this test was to provide some middle ground between the "no protection for commercial speech" rule of *Valentine v. Chrestensen* and the near-absolute protection customarily given to political speech. Thus, the *Central Hudson* rule was first seen as a kind of intermediate standard for reviewing commercial speech cases. On the one hand, it was not entirely deferential to the government as in *Valentine*. On the other hand, it was not as stringent in reviewing commercial speech regulations as it was when reviewing political speech regulations.

Under *Central Hudson*, if the government seeks to regulate or ban legal and non-misleading commercial speech, it must do two things: First, it must prove that it does so in the name of a very important or "substantial" government interest (e.g., protecting the public health). Second, it must prove that the law actually serves (i.e., it "directly advances") that substantial government objective.

The last part of the test requires that any law regulating non-misleading and legal commercial speech be drawn in such a way that it prohibits no more speech than is actually necessary.

The Move to Stricter Standards

Over the years, a majority of the Court began to interpret the *Central Hudson* test in such a way that it moved closer to the strict scrutiny test used in political speech cases.

The strict scrutiny test requires that the government show that it has a *compelling* need for regulating speech. This test is a difficult, if not nearly impossible, one for the government to satisfy.

In *44 Liquormart v. Rhode Island* (1996) Justice John Paul Stevens suggested a more protective approach for reviewing commercial speech cases, even though he claimed to hold true to the *Central Hudson* test:

> The First Amendment directs us to be *especially skeptical* [emphasis added] of regulations that seek to keep people in the dark for what the government perceives to be their own good. That teaching applies equally to state attempts to deprive consumers of accurate information about their chosen products....
>
> [T]he Court concluded that *"special care"* [emphasis added] should attend the review of such blanket bans, and it pointedly remarked that "in recent years this Court has not approved a blanket ban on commercial speech unless the expression itself was flawed in some way, either because it was deceptive or related to unlawful activity."

In a separate concurring opinion, Justice Clarence Thomas urged for a clear break from the past and the use of a more rigorous standard of review:

> In cases such as this, in which the government's asserted interest is to keep legal users of a product or service ignorant in order to manipulate their choices in the marketplace, the balancing test adopted in *Central Hudson Gas & Elec. Corp. v. Public Serv. Comm'n*...should not be applied, in my view. Rather, such an "interest" is per se illegitimate and can no more justify regulation of "commercial" speech than it can justify regulation of "noncommercial" speech....
>
> I do not see a philosophical or historical basis for asserting that "commercial" speech is of "lower value" than "noncommercial" speech. Indeed, some historical materials suggest to the contrary.

No Heightened Scrutiny

Writing in dissent in *Sorrell v. IMS Health, Inc.* (2011), a case involving a challenge to a state law that barred the sale, disclosure, and use of records that revealed the prescribing practices of individual doctors, Justice Stephen Breyer took exception to the idea that there should be added protection for commercial speech:

> The First Amendment does not require courts to apply a special "heightened" standard of review when reviewing such an effort....
>
> To apply a strict First Amendment standard virtually as a matter of course when a court reviews ordinary economic regulatory programs

(even if that program has a modest impact upon a firm's ability to shape a commercial message) would work at cross-purposes with…basic constitutional [principles]. Since ordinary regulatory programs can affect speech, particularly commercial speech, in myriad ways, to apply a "heightened" First Amendment standard of review whenever such a program burdens speech would transfer from legislatures to judges the primary power to weigh ends and to choose means, threatening to distort or undermine legitimate legislative objectives.…To apply a "heightened" standard of review in such cases as a matter of course would risk what then-Justice Rehnquist, dissenting in *Central Hudson*, described as a "retur[n] to the bygone era of *Lochner v. New York* (1905), in which it was common practice for this Court to strike down economic regulations adopted by a State based on the Court's own notions of the most appropriate means for the State to implement its considered policies."

FIVE BASIC POINTS

So what is the takeaway from all of this? Among other things, we have learned the following:

1. Definition: Commercial speech is speech that which "propose[s] a commercial transaction."
2. Exceptions: Commercial speech is unprotected if it involves an illegal activity or is false or misleading.
3. The overbreadth doctrine does not apply to commercial speech cases.
4. *Central Hudson* set forth a three-prong test to determine when the government can regulate lawful and non-misleading commercial speech: The government has a substantial interest; the regulation directly and materially advances the substantial interest of the government; and the regulation is narrowly tailored to serve the government's interest.
5. In more recent cases, the Court seems to have implemented the *Central Hudson* rule in such a fashion as to require "heightened" (or strict) scrutiny.

13

Free Speech Incorporated: When Money Speaks

We know that money talks, but that is the problem, not the answer.
—Anthony Lewis (1976)

To me, [many campaign financing laws are] nothing less than outright suppression of speech of the most odious nature.
—Floyd Abrams (2005)

IS MONEY SPEECH? Hold onto that question; it's an important one to which we will turn soon enough. Meanwhile, let's start with a few stories—true ones.

THE CONTRIBUTOR

Shaun McCutcheon's problem started when he tried to give away money. He believed in donating to charities like Feed the Children and giving to political causes and campaigns. He thought it would make America a better place. But if he acted on his political beliefs as he wanted to, he could find himself behind bars. The threat of a five-year penalty for contributing his own money to a political cause struck him as un-American. So he went to the Federal Election Commission (FEC) and then to court. The federal campaign law, he argued, abridged his First Amendment rights.

At 46, Shaun McCutcheon was no status quo man. "He wants change," Chris Brown, an Alabama Republican political consultant, told a *USA Today* reporter. "He wants guys who are going to shake it up." Much to the same effect, he described himself to two *Washington Post* reporters as "just another political activist trying to change the world." To that end, the politically active business-man contributed almost $384,000 to federal candidates, committees, and parties in the 2011–2012 election cycle, according to the Center for Responsive Politics. But McCutcheon wanted to do even more. Acting as an individual (and not a corpo-ration—an important distinction we'll visit later), he aimed to give more of his personal money to the Republican National Committee, the National Republican Senatorial Committee, and the National Republican Congressional Committee, as well to as to conservative candidates and political action committees (PACs). (PACs take center stage in many campaign finance discussions as they are orga-nizations that pool donations together and use that money to campaign for or against political candidates, legislative efforts, and other political initiatives.)

The problem: A federal campaign law, known as the Bipartisan Campaign Reform Act, barred him from giving as much money as he would like, both to dif-ferent PACs and in the aggregate. Enforced by the FEC, the law limits individuals to $48,600 in contributions to candidates and $74,600 in contributions to political parties, with an aggregate cap of $123,200.

He contributed a total of $33,088 to sixteen candidates during the 2011–2012 election cycle. He wanted to donate more—an additional $75,000 to party com-mittees and $1,776 to each of the additional twelve candidates he supported—but due to the aggregate limits imposed by the campaign finance law, he could not. For the 2013–2014 election cycle, he hoped to contribute more than $60,000 to candidates, plus $75,000 to three Republican national party committees. Such contributions for both cycles would have exceeded federal limits.

Were he to violate those limits, he would be guilty of a felony.

The idea of being criminally penalized for supporting a cause or campaign with his money did not sit well with McCutcheon. "It's a freedom of speech case about your right to spend your money on as many candidates as you choose," he told an Alabama reporter. Or, as *USA Today* quoted him: "If the government tells you that you can't spend your money where you want, there should be a real, real good reason."

Was there a "good reason"—a compelling reason—to abridge the First Amendment right asserted by Shaun McCutcheon?

THE REFORMER

The *New York Times* called Fred Wertheimer "the dean of campaign finance 'reformers.'" In 2008, *Legal Times* labeled the Brooklyn-born and Harvard Law

School–educated lawyer as one of greatest lawyers of the last thirty years. And in 2010, the *Hill* identified him as one of Washington's top grassroots lobbyists.

At eighty, the balding and white-mustached public interest advocate is as outspoken today as he was when he first came to Common Cause, the nonpartisan, grassroots organization dedicated to creating an "open, honest, and accountable government," in May 1971. During his long tenure at Common Cause, he has served as legal counsel, legislative director, vice president, and then president. In 1997, Wertheimer founded Democracy 21, a nonprofit group dedicated to removing the influence of private money from politics. One of its objectives is to provide the media and public with the latest information and analysis on money in politics and campaign finance reform efforts.

"There is a special class of citizens in this country today," is how he put it in a 2013 *USA Today* interview. "They are the huge donors to the Democrats and Republicans" who have "bought a premium place at the table when it comes to government decisions." And what do we know about them? "They spent $1 billion on presidential and congressional elections. And almost all of that money was in huge contributions, the kinds of contributions that buy influence." For Wertheimer, that money defines the privileged class that he criticizes: "That [money] puts those individuals and others in a special category—they have special access [and] special influence with government officials. And that access and influence invariably comes at the expense of ordinary Americans." According to the *Washington Post*, the 2016 election cost a grand total of $6.5 billion.

THE QUESTIONS

Do you agree with Shaun McCutcheon's assertion that limiting his contributions was "a freedom of speech case about your right to spend your money on as many candidates as you choose"? Or do you think Fred Wertheimer is correct when he says that big money corrupts politics and creates a privileged class who can afford to buy lawmakers?

To put it another way, is money speech when it's spent on political campaigns? That is:

- Can the federal and/or state governments regulate how much money you wish to contribute directly to a political candidate?
- Can they regulate how much money you wish to expend generally on a campaign?
- Can they require you to disclose your identity when you make a political contribution or expenditure?

These are the questions that led to *Buckley v. Valeo* (1976), in which the Supreme Court assessed whether the limits placed on electoral spending by the Federal Election Campaign Act of 1971 (and related IRS provisions) violated freedom of speech and association under the First Amendment.

THE CASE OF THE SENATOR WHO CHALLENGED CAMPAIGN FINANCE LAW

After the Watergate scandal shook American confidence in the electoral process, Congress began to take a serious look at campaign corruption and in 1974 amended the Federal Election Campaign Act of 1971. The amendments imposed restrictions on the amount an individual could donate to a given campaign and required reporting on donations above a certain dollar amount. Congress also established the Federal Election Commission (FEC) in order to enforce the statute.

Senator James L. Buckley (R-NY) led a group of lawmakers, political candidates, various contributors, and political groups in filing a First Amendment challenge to the new federal campaign law. Joining Senator Buckley's challenge was Eugene McCarthy, the former Democratic senator from Minnesota who had run against Lyndon Johnson for the Democratic Party nomination in the 1968 election. And one of the groups challenging the law was the American Civil Liberties Union, whose lawyer, Joel Gora, argued on its behalf in the Supreme Court.

On Thursday, January 30, 1976, the Supreme Court delivered a tome of surprising length and complexity to the legal and political circles that had eagerly awaited its ruling. Coming in at a total of 294 pages in the *United States Reports*, the *Buckley* decision consists of an unsigned *per curiam* opinion of the Court, an appendix to that *per curiam*, and opinions concurring and dissenting in part from five of the eight justices who participated in the deliberations. It is one of the longest published cases in Supreme Court history.

In the *per curiam* opinion, an eight-member Court ruled that restrictions on large campaign contributions are in the state's interest to prevent "corruption and the appearance of corruption spawned by the real or imagined coercive influence of large financial contributions on candidates' positions and on their actions if elected to office." The Court defined "corruption" as "large contributions... given to secure a political *quid pro quo* from current and potential office holders." Here are the major takeaway points from the *Buckley* decision:

- The Court distinguished campaign *contributions* from campaign *expenditures*. For example:

- You write a check for $50,000 to the Sam Smith campaign for Congress. This is a campaign contribution.
- You write a check for $50,000 to the Sam Smith Political Action Committee, which in turn spends the money on TV and radio ads, billboards, and lawn signs. This is an independent expenditure.

- The Court held that campaign *contributions* may be regulated. The rationale for regulating campaign contributions was "the appearance of corruption."
- In contrast, the Court struck down *expenditure* limitations (e.g., restrictions on spending by individuals and groups, personal candidate spending, and overall campaign spending) as unconstitutional.
- The Court upheld the constitutionality of disclosure requirements.
- The Court upheld the constitutionality of the presidential campaign *public funding* system, where candidates can elect to receive tax money to fund their campaigns.

Unquestionably, the most pivotal parts of the decision—those which garnered the most attention and criticism from jurists, scholars, lawyers, politicians, and pundits—were the Court's overall characterization of spending money as political speech, and the dichotomy the Court found between contributions and expenditures in terms of their differing treatment in First Amendment law.

Yes, Money Is Speech; It Implicates "Fundamental First Amendment Activities"

At the outset, the justices recognized that campaign contribution laws and expenditure limitations "operate in an area of the most fundamental First Amendment activities. Discussion of public issues and debate on the qualifications of candidates are integral to the operation of the system of government established by our Constitution."

The Court also stated that restricting the amount of money that can be spent on political campaign communication "necessarily reduces the quantity of expression by restricting the number of issues discussed, the depth of the exploration, and the size of the audience reached." This is so, it posited, "because virtually every means of communicating ideas in today's mass society requires the expenditure of money." Simply put, when it comes to political campaigning, money "talks."

Money "Talks" Differently

Nonetheless, for First Amendment purposes, the Court reasoned, money "talks" differently depending on the form of political communication that it takes.

The Court determined that money spent on campaign contributions "serves as a general expression of support for the candidate and his views" (i.e., symbolic political expression) and "affiliate[s] a person with a candidate" (i.e., political association). Thus, a limitation on the amount of money a person or group can contribute "involves little direct restraint" on political communication, because it "does not in any way infringe the contributor's freedom to discuss candidates and issues." The Court granted that the prevention of "the actuality and appearance of corruption resulting from large individual financial contributions" was a constitutionally sufficient reason for the contribution limitations.

By contrast, when in the form of a political expenditure, money "talks" as an expression of the spender. Independent expenditures explicitly advocate a person's views on the election or defeat of identified candidates (i.e., individual political expression), and group or non-candidate political committee expenditures effectively amplify the voices of their adherents (i.e., associational political expression). Accordingly, the Court explained, limitations imposed on expenditures by persons, groups, candidates, and political parties "represent substantial, rather than merely theoretical, restraints on the quantity and diversity of political speech."

When it came to the limitations on expenditures, however, the *Buckley* Court rejected the anti-corruption rationale it accepted with regard to contributions. When the Court imposed the strictest of constitutional review standards on all of the spending ceilings—for individual and group independent expenditures, for personal candidate expenditures, and for total candidate-campaign expenditures—the risk-of-corruption argument collapsed.

As long as spending remained truly independent (i.e., not directly coordinated by a candidate's campaign), the Court ruled that the absence of coordination with candidates and their campaign committees would reduce the risk of actual or apparent corruption. As far as personal-candidate and total-campaign expenditures were concerned, the anti-corruption rationale simply had no place.

WHAT IS CORRUPTION?

> *No one has a strong idea of what corruption is....Corruption is a real interest, but it is very hard to build on it theoretically and to expand it out to campaign finance....We do not have an account of corruption that can be generalized in a way that's very helpful to us.*
> —Robert Post, "Tanner Lectures" (2013)

In the seminal campaign-finance case *Buckley v. Valeo* (1976), the Court declared:

To the extent that large contributions are given to secure a political *quid pro quo* from current and potential office holders, the integrity of our system of representative democracy is undermined....Of almost equal concern as the danger of actual quid pro quo arrangements is the impact of the appearance of corruption stemming from public awareness of the opportunities for abuse inherent in a regime of large individual financial contributions.

In *Austin v. Michigan Chamber of Commerce* (1990), a slim majority did not rely on the *quid pro quo* corruption rationale used in *Buckley* to justify the restraint on corporate treasury spending, but rested instead on what Justice Thurgood Marshall's opinion for the Court called "a different kind of corruption"—namely, "the corrosive and distorting effects of immense aggregations of wealth that are accumulated with the help of the corporate form." Thus, *Austin* significantly moved away from a narrow view of corruption—an exchange of money for political favor—to a broader and more systemic understanding of corruption that focused on the potential of big money to undermine the integrity of the electoral process. Such a broad definition of corruption effectively granted lawmakers more leeway to regulate campaign finance.

Buttressing *Buckley*: The Burger and Rehnquist Courts

However unsatisfying the *Buckley* framework seemed to its critics, it proved to have staying power. Over the next 29 years—the remainder of the Burger Court era and the entirety of the Rehnquist Court era—the justices heard no fewer than fifteen campaign financing cases, thirteen of which involved challenges to federal or state regulations on campaign contributions and expenditures. In those thirteen cases, segments of the Court occasionally voiced opposition either to *Buckley*'s affirmation of contribution limitations or to its negation of expenditure limitations. But no majority of five justices ever coalesced around the reversal of either ruling.

Despite some significant doctrinal wrinkles written into the First Amendment law by way of various kinds of campaign finance cases, the Court reinforced, time and again, the contribution–expenditure dichotomy at the center of *Buckley*.

But would it continue to do so? The answer came when a movie gave rise to a landmark Supreme Court ruling.

HILLARY: THE MOVIE AND CITIZENS UNITED

David Bossie was the president of a Washington-based nonprofit corporation dedicated to conservative advocacy called Citizens United. Bossie had long been involved in scrutinizing alleged electoral improprieties committed by Democrats, including a stint working for Republican Senator Fred Thompson in investigating the Whitewater scandal. He was searching for an idea to make a conservative documentary—one that could rival the kind of documentaries produced by liberal filmmaker Michael Moore.

One of the most irresistible targets for a documentary was a politician whom Citizens United had attacked ever since she was America's First Lady—Hillary Rodham Clinton. Once Senator Clinton launched her campaign for the 2008 presidential election, Bossie determined to make her the incorrigible punching bag of his documentary.

Hillary: The Movie featured ninety minutes of news clips, foreboding music, and slashing critiques by a marquee list of conservative commentators aiming to highlight the Clintons' political scandals (including the Whitewater and the White House FBI files controversies), to savage Hillary's character, and to slice into her electoral chances. Typical of the film's vehement harangues was that of Dick Morris, a disaffected advisor to the Clinton administration: "She's deceitful, she'll make up any story, lie about anything, as long as it serves her purposes of the moment." Agreeing that Hillary was a liar, the right-wing firebrand Ann Coulter delivered the movie's only compliment: Hillary "looks good in a pantsuit."

Amidst all of the bashing, there was one declaration that *Hillary* carefully avoided: At no point did the film expressly advocate for the candidate's electoral defeat. To do so would clearly run afoul of federal election law.

David Bossie intended that the documentary run as an on-demand cable movie, free to viewers at Citizen United's expense, during the entire 2008 primary election period. There was, however, a legal catch.

As a nonprofit corporate PAC funded in part by donations from for-profit corporate entities, Citizens United was barred by election laws from financing the cablecast (or television advertisements for it) during the pre-election blackout period when such ads were barred. That is, if *Hillary* was classified as an "electioneering communication" within the meaning of federal campaign finance law, then its airing could be blocked.

To prevent such problems, the organization sought an FEC ruling that the movie was not subject to the rules of a federal election law that codified the ban on corporate-funded independent expenditures. The Commission denied Citizens United's claim, ruling that the film was an "electioneering communication." Hence, its showing during the election cycle could be banned. With that, Citizens United appealed, all the way to the Supreme Court.

The Roberts Court's *Citizens United* Ruling

On the morning of Thursday, January 21, 2010, Justice Anthony Kennedy announced the decision of a narrowly divided Court in *Citizens United v. Federal Election Commission*. His tempered description of the ruling and reasoning of the five majority justices was followed by about twenty minutes of Justice John Paul Stevens reading an impassioned dissenting statement from the bench.

The majority invalidated a portion of the Bipartisan Campaign Reform Act that barred corporations and unions from using their general treasury funds for express advocacy or electioneering communications. Kennedy's opinion (joined in pertinent part by Chief Justice Roberts and Justices Scalia, Thomas, and Alito) fervently embraced lofty and abstract First Amendment principles that tolerated no distinctions that would disfavor corporate speakers such as Citizens United, a nonprofit corporation. (People tend to overlook the fact that groups such as NAACP, the ACLU, Planned Parenthood, Harvard University, and People for the Ethical Treatment of Animals are nonprofit corporations, just like Citizens United.)

As Kennedy saw it, the contested electioneering ban regulated *political speech*, the type of speech that should be most highly protected by the First Amendment. He noted that as a content-based restriction on political speech, the restriction must be evaluated under strict scrutiny. "We find no basis," he wrote, "for the proposition that, in the context of political speech, the Government may impose restrictions on certain disfavored speakers," adding that "the First Amendment does not allow political speech restrictions based on a speaker's corporate identity."

The minority opinion, advanced by Stevens (joined by Justices Ginsburg, Breyer, and Sotomayor), was uninhibited. Almost twice as long as the majority opinion, the ninety-page rejoinder appeared to be his full-throated swansong, delivered only five months before he retired from the Court. He addressed the majority's rationales, point by point, in an effort to undermine and embarrass their proponents.

Both in substance and tone, the *Citizens United* majority and dissenting opinions revealed the heated nature of the debate over the First Amendment's meaning and the future of campaign finance reform.

Campaign Disclosure Law

Importantly, eight of the nine justices had upheld the election law's disclosure, disclaimer, and reporting requirements. This meant that the federal and state governments could still require people, groups, PACs, and corporations to disclose their identities when spending money on political campaigns.

The *Buckley* Court had stressed that disclosure requirements did not "prevent anyone from speaking." The Court explained that disclosure can be justified by a governmental interest in providing "the electorate with information" about election-related spending sources.

There was an exception to the disclosure rule, however. The *Citizens United* Court turned to this exception to reject facial challenges to the law. However, the Court acknowledged that as-applied challenges would be available if a group could show a "reasonable probability" that disclosing its contributors' names would "subject them to threats, harassment, or reprisals from either Government officials or private parties." Justice Clarence Thomas dissented from the notion that disclosure could be compelled:

> Congress may not abridge the "right to anonymous speech" based on the "'simple interest in providing voters with additional relevant information'....In continuing to hold otherwise, the Court misapprehends the import of "recent events" that some amici describe "in which donors to certain causes were blacklisted, threatened, or otherwise targeted for retaliation."...The Court properly recognizes these events as "cause for concern" but fails to acknowledge their constitutional significance. In my view, amici's submissions show why the Court's insistence on upholding [disclosure laws] will ultimately prove...misguided (and ill fated).

The Political Response to *Citizens United*

Within hours of the Court announcing its landmark ruling, *Citizens United* was tossed about like a football in a championship game. Politicians seized the opportunity in turn to declare their approval or dismay. Some examples:

- Senate Minority Leader Mitch McConnell (R-KY): "For too long, some in this country have been deprived of full participation in the political process. With today's monumental decision, the Supreme Court took an important step in the direction of restoring the First Amendment rights of [all] groups."
- Senator Patrick Leahy (D-VT): "There is clear reason for ordinary citizens to be concerned that this divisive ruling will, in reality, allow powerful corporations to drown out the voices of everyday Americans in future campaigns. This ruling is no doubt yet another victory for Wall Street, at the expense of Main Street America."
- President Barack Obama: "With its ruling today, the Supreme Court has given a green light to a new stampede of special interest money in

our politics. It is a major victory for big oil, Wall Street banks, health insurance companies and the other powerful interests that marshal their power every day in Washington to drown out the voices of everyday Americans. This ruling gives the special interests and their lobbyists even more power in Washington—while undermining the influence of average Americans who make small contributions to support their preferred candidates."

The Campaign to Amend the First Amendment

Outraged by *Citizens United*, a number of critics turned to Article V of the Constitution to amend the First Amendment. One of those was retired Supreme Court Justice John Paul Stevens, who proposed an amendment to the Constitution and elaborated on that proposal in his 2014 book *Six Amendments: How and Why We Should Change the Constitution*. That same year, 41 Senate Democrats proposed a constitutional amendment to overrule what to them had become the infamous *Citizens United* precedent.

In the midst of a June 3, 2014, Senate Judiciary Committee hearing on the measure, Republican Senator Ted Cruz turned to the Democrats and asked: "Where did the liberals go?...Why is there not a liberal standing here defending the Bill of Rights and the First Amendment?" Not a single Democratic senator spoke against the proposal. There was, however, one liberal who spoke out. Floyd Abrams, the famed First Amendment lawyer, argued against the proposed amendment. It failed in the Senate by a vote of 54–42.

THE *McCUTCHEON* CASE AND THE MOVE TO OVERRULE *BUCKLEY V. VALEO*

Against this backdrop, we return to the story of Shaun McCutcheon and his challenge to a campaign finance law that, in effect, limited the number of candidates to whom he could give money.

In September 2012, McCutcheon had given $33,088 to fifteen federal candidates and over $25,000 in non-candidate contributions during the 2011–2012 cycle. He also wanted to donate to an additional twelve federal candidates, bringing his contribution total over the federal aggregate limit on federal candidates. So he went to court and challenged the law on First Amendment grounds. When he lost his challenge in the Court of Appeals for the District of Columbia, he brought his case to the Supreme Court.

The idea that one could give money to fifteen candidates but not sixteen seemed, to some, the ideal framing to contest the contributions prong of *Buckley v.*

Valeo (1976). And given the Roberts Court's handiwork in *Citizens United*, the signs looked promising that *Buckley*'s limits on campaign contributions could be overruled.

But McCutcheon would have to contend with *stare decisis*. The words derive from the Latin maxim, *stare decisis et non quieta movere*. Translated, it means, "to stand by decisions and not disturb the undisturbed." In law, this is reflected in the doctrine of honoring precedent. Judges invoke *stare decisis* when an issue has been previously brought to the court and a ruling on it has been made. In such circumstances, judges generally adhere to the earlier ruling—though this is not always the case.

The doctrine of *stare decisis* was certainly an important issue in the lead-up to the *McCutcheon v. FEC* ruling. Would the justices of the Roberts Court hold to precedent and reaffirm *Buckley* as they had many times before? Or would they instead take their constitutional cue from Justice Thomas, who wanted to abandon campaign finance laws altogether and who had boldly declared in 1996, "I would reject the framework established by *Buckley v. Valeo*....In my view, the distinction [between contributions and expenditures] lacks constitutional significance, and I would not adhere to it."

Would the justices adopt the view espoused by the Cato Institute? In its *McCutcheon amicus* brief, the group argued that "[t]he *Buckley* distinction does not survive scrutiny under the factors that courts consider in applying *stare decisis*: how well-reasoned and old the original opinion is; how much people have relied on it; and how well the resulting legal rule works." Or would they instead be more influenced by what the government argued in its merits brief? The government reasoned: "In the nearly four decades since *Buckley*, this Court has consistently reaffirmed the foundational distinction between expenditure limits...and contribution limits."

Shaun McCutcheon's lawyer, Erin E. Murphy, was a former law clerk to Chief Justice John Roberts. The *McCutcheon* case was her first time arguing at the Supreme Court.

At the Supreme Court

McCutcheon v. FEC was the eleventh majority opinion on free expression that Chief Justice John Roberts had written in a First Amendment case. Since his appointment to the Court, Roberts had authored more such majority opinions than any of his colleagues—more than twice as many. Like Justices Oliver Wendell Holmes, Louis Brandeis, Hugo Black, and William Brennan, his name was becoming synonymous with the First Amendment. But unlike the liberal heroes of times past, several of his free expression rulings greatly pleased conservatives while appalling liberals. That was certainly true of his plurality opinion in *McCutcheon*, yet another First Amendment campaign finance case in which the Court divided 5–4 in its judgment, with Justices Ginsburg, Breyer, Sotomayor, and Kagan in forceful dissent.

By the chief justice's constitutional gauge, the aggregate contributions restrictions imposed a draconian restraint on pure political speech. "The Government may no more restrict how many candidates or causes a donor may support than it may tell a newspaper how many candidates it may endorse," he wrote. He also wondered whether the aggregate limits served the valid governmental purpose of preventing *quid pro quo* corruption. He wrote that "while preventing corruption or its appearance is a legitimate objective, Congress may target only a specific type of corruption—'*quid pro quo*' corruption." As Roberts saw it, *Citizens United* stood for the principle that the government's campaign finance efforts must focus on *quid pro quo* corruption. "The line between *quid pro quo* corruption and general influence," wrote Roberts in his *McCutcheon* opinion, "may seem vague at times, but the distinction must be respected in order to safeguard basic First Amendment rights. In addition, '[i]n drawing that line, the First Amendment requires us to err on the side of protecting political speech rather than suppressing it.' *Federal Election Comm'n v. Wisconsin Right to Life* (2007)."

For the plurality, the aggregate limit did not serve the purpose of preventing *quid quo pro* corruption. Hence, it did not satisfy the rigorous standard of review established in earlier cases. Moreover, the plurality ruled that the collective interest in combating corruption could only be justified provided it did not unnecessarily restrain an individual's freedom of speech. In this case, Roberts ruled that the aggregate limit was not sufficiently narrowly tailored to accomplish this goal. Justice Thomas concurred:

> I adhere to the view that this Court's decision in *Buckley v. Valeo* denigrates core First Amendment speech and should be overruled.... Contributions to political campaigns, no less than direct expenditures, "generate essential political speech" by fostering discussion of public issues and candidate qualifications.

Justice Breyer, on the other hand, dissented. He argued, "[T]oday's decision eviscerates our Nation's campaign finance laws, leaving a remnant incapable of dealing with the grave problems of democratic legitimacy that those laws were intended to resolve." In his view, the plurality opinion defined "corruption" far too narrowly. According to Justice Breyer:

The plurality's first claim—that large aggregate contributions do not "give rise" to "corruption"—is plausible only because the plurality defines "corruption" too narrowly. The plurality describes the constitutionally permissible objective of campaign finance regulation as follows: "Congress may target only a specific type of corruption—'*quid pro quo*' corruption." It then defines *quid pro quo* corruption to mean no more than "a direct exchange of an official act for money"—an act akin to bribery. It adds specifically that corruption does not include efforts to "garner 'influence over or access to' elected officials or political parties." Moreover, the Government's efforts to prevent the "appearance of corruption" are "equally confined to the appearance of *quid pro quo* corruption," as narrowly defined.

The conflict between the justices thus turned to the meaning of "corruption," with one side purportedly defining it too narrowly (so as to make it nearly toothless) and the other side purportedly defining it to broadly (so as to make it applicable to nearly all forms of contributions).

A FEW FINAL WORDS ABOUT CORPORATIONS

The following exchange is from a May 2018 interview for *SCOTUSblog*. In it, Ronald Collins interviewed UCLA law professor Adam Winkler in connection with his book *We the Corporations: How American Businesses Won Their Civil Rights* (2018). Read the excerpt and think about the role corporations have played in American history and how that has influenced government policies toward corporate speech:

> **Collins:** Your book offers a new wrinkle on the founding of America and the Jamestown story of 1607. Do tell.
>
> **Winkler:** Americans celebrate the liberty-seeking Pilgrims, but the first permanent English colony in the New World was thirteen years earlier in Jamestown, which was a corporate business venture. Indeed, the Virginia Company came to America to make money. The company also introduced democratic reforms, such as the first representative assembly, not in the spirit of popular sovereignty but to pursue profit.
>
> **Collins:** How do dissent in the colonies and the Boston Tea Party of 1773 fit into your narrative?
>
> **Winkler:** The American Revolution was also in small part a revolt against the world's most powerful corporation, the East India Company.

When the company's fortunes soured, the British government deemed the corporation too big to fail—and, as part of a massive bailout, gave the company for the first time the right to sell tea in the colonies without American middlemen. The Boston Tea Party was an uprising by merchants who, that night, went out to throw the East India Company's tea overboard.

Collins: Your book exposes a misleading argument presented to the Supreme Court by a railroad lawyer in the 1885 case *San Mateo County v. Southern Pacific Railroad Company*. Tell us a little bit about that disingenuous argument and how it played out in that case.

Winkler: In the 1880s, the Southern Pacific Railroad Company launched a remarkable series of what its lawyers called "test cases"—more than sixty in all—to win expansive rights for corporations under the 14th Amendment. Two of those cases made it to the Supreme Court. In the first, the railroad's lawyer, Roscoe Conkling, who had been one of the drafters of the 14th Amendment, told the justices the provision was written to protect not just the freed slaves but also business corporations. He even produced a musty old journal that he said was a never-published record of the drafting committee's deliberations. The journal was real, but historians who looked into the case years later quickly realized that the amendment had never been revised in the way Conkling claimed. As Howard Jay Graham, one of the leading historians on the 14th Amendment, concluded, Conkling had engaged in "a deliberate, brazen forgery" to win new rights for corporations.

Collins: The following year the Supreme Court decided *Santa Clara County v. Southern Pacific Railroad Company*. This time the inaccurate work was done by the court's Reporter of Decisions. Who was that man and how did his handiwork shape the history of American constitutional law?

Winkler: Another of the Southern Pacific's test cases reached the Supreme Court, but the justices declined to rule on the constitutional question, leading the colorful Justice Stephen Field to complain about the omission in a separate opinion. Then the case took a bizarre turn. The reporter of decisions, J.C. Bancroft Davis, included a headnote in the official published version of the opinion saying the court had held corporations were covered by the 14th Amendment. A few years later, Field, who was rumored to carry a gun beneath his robes and remains the only sitting justice ever arrested for a crime (and the charge was murder, no less), seized upon Davis' headnote. In a majority opinion on a separate issue, he wrote that the court had held that corporations had 14th Amendment rights in the Southern Pacific case—something he clearly knew to be untrue.

Collins: There is a fascinating discussion in your book about the 14th Amendment cases that were decided by the Supreme Court between 1868 and 1912. What happened?

Winkler: Once the Supreme Court extended 14th Amendment rights of equal protection and due process to corporations, businesses flooded the courts with constitutional challenges. The ensuing years would be known as the Lochner era, when the court broadly read the Constitution to protect business. Meanwhile, in cases like *Plessy v. Ferguson*, the justices refused to read the 14th Amendment to provide any meaningful protections for minorities. By 1912, the court had heard only 28 cases on the 14th Amendment rights of African-Americans—and an astonishing 312 cases on the 14th Amendment rights of corporations.

If nothing else, the evolution of the 14th Amendment reveals how its intended meaning can change, and change radically. But here, liberals, not conservatives, claim the historical high ground in calling for a return to the Amendment's "original meaning" (see Chapter 2).

14.

Public Employees & Free Speech

THERE IS AN old adage: "Tell your boss what you think of him and the truth will set you free."

The price of free speech is often quite high for public employees who criticize their employers, coworkers, or supervisors; question the wisdom of governmental policies; engage in controversial expression, even off-duty; or blow the whistle on corruption. Consider the following examples:

- A public school teacher, frustrated over misbehaving students, posts negative blog entries about them and their parents. The school catches wind of this and suspends her without pay.
- A police officer reacts on Facebook to another police shooting by saying he would have shot the suspect six times and is fired.
- A police officer faces retaliation after he criticizes a quota policy for arrests.
- A fire chief gives an interview to the press indicating that the fire department has insufficient resources, and is then fired.
- Three prison guards face retaliation after revealing that a fellow guard had brutalized an inmate.

These are actual scenarios experienced by public employees who faced retaliation after they spoke out. Under traditional First Amendment principles, the government may not punish individuals on the basis of the content or viewpoint of their expression—but a different principle applies to public employees.

The government has greater power and control over its employees' speech than it does over other citizens' speech. Stated another way, the government has greater power as an employer than it does as a sovereign. This can be troubling not only for the individual employee, but also for the public at large. Public employees often are in the best position to inform the general public about government corruption, malfeasance, or other problems. But this won't happen if they are silenced by the fear of losing their jobs.

THE TEACHER WHO SENT A LETTER TO THE LOCAL PAPER

As a state jurist, Justice Oliver Wendell Holmes famously wrote in *McAuliffe v. Town of New Bedford* (1892): "Petitioner may have a constitutional right to talk politics but not a constitutional right to be a policeman." The case involved police officer John J. McAuliffe, who was fired for engaging in political canvassing. The town had a rule limiting officers from doing so: "No member of the department will be permitted to be a delegate to or member of any political or partisan club.... No member of the department shall be allowed to solicit money or any aid, on any pretense, for any political purpose whatsoever."

When McAuliffe took his employer to court, the town prevailed on the basis that public employees willingly relinquished their free speech rights when they accepted public employment.

This limited view of public employees' free speech protections carried the day for the late nineteenth century and for much of the twentieth century. The Supreme Court gradually narrowed this broad proposition in a few loyalty oath cases in the 1960s, but the major change occurred with a case involving an Illinois teacher discharged for writing a letter to the editor for his local newspaper.

Marvin Pickering, a science teacher, believed that the school board was spending too much money on athletics, as opposed to academics. He also claimed in the letter that the superintendent had attempted to prevent faculty from speaking out on funding issues. The school board fired Pickering for his letter, saying it was detrimental to morale and showed disloyalty. Pickering challenged his firing all the way to the Supreme Court.

OPINION

Pickering v. Board of Education

(Abridged.)

391 U.S. 563 (1968)
Vote: 8–1

JUSTICE MARSHALL delivered the opinion of the Court.

[**Facts**] In February of 1961, the appellee Board of Education asked the voters of the school district to approve a bond issue to raise $4,875,000 to erect two new schools. The proposal was defeated. Then, in December of 1961, the Board submitted another bond proposal to the voters which called for the raising of $5,500,000 to build two new schools. This second proposal passed and the schools were built with the money raised by the bond sales. In May of 1964, a proposed increase in the tax rate to be used for educational purposes was submitted to the voters by the Board and was defeated. Finally, on September 19, 1964, a second proposal to increase the tax rate was submitted by the Board and was likewise defeated. It was in connection with this last proposal of the School Board that appellant wrote the letter to the editor that resulted in his dismissal.

The letter constituted, basically, an attack on the School Board's handling of the 1961 bond issue proposals and its subsequent allocation of financial resources between the schools' educational and athletic programs. It also charged the superintendent of schools with attempting to prevent teachers in the district from opposing or criticizing the proposed bond issue.

The Board dismissed Pickering for writing and publishing the letter. Pursuant to Illinois law, the Board was then required to hold a hearing on the dismissal. At the hearing, the Board charged that numerous statements in the letter were false and that the publication of the statements unjustifiably impugned the "motives, honesty, integrity, truthfulness, responsibility and competence" of both the Board and the school administration. The Board also charged that the false statements damaged the professional reputations of its members and of the school administrators, would be disruptive of faculty discipline, and would tend to foment "controversy, conflict and dissension" among teachers, administrators, the Board of Education, and the residents of the district. Testimony was introduced from a variety of witnesses on the truth or falsity of the particular statements in the letter with which the Board took issue. The Board found the statements to be false as charged. No evidence was introduced at any point in the proceedings as to the effect of the publication of the letter on the community as a whole or on the administration of the school system in particular, and no specific findings along these lines were made.

[**Balancing test**] The problem in any case is to arrive at a balance between the interests of the teacher, as a citizen, in commenting upon matters of public concern and the interest of the State, as an employer, in promoting the efficiency of the public services it performs through its employees.

An examination of the statements in appellant's letter objected to by the Board reveals that they, like the letter as a whole, consist essentially of criticism of the Board's allocation of school funds between educational and athletic programs, and of both the Board's and the superintendent's methods of informing, or preventing the informing of, the district's taxpayers of the real reasons why additional tax revenues were being sought for the schools. The statements are in no way directed towards any person with whom appellant would normally be in contact in the course of his daily work as a teacher. Thus, no question of maintaining either discipline by immediate superiors or harmony among coworkers is presented here. Appellant's employment relationships with the Board and, to a somewhat lesser extent, with the superintendent are not the kind of close working relationships for which it can persuasively be claimed that personal loyalty and confidence are necessary to their proper functioning.

[**A matter of public concern**] More importantly, the question whether a school system requires additional funds is a matter of legitimate public concern on which the judgment of the school administration, including the School Board, cannot, in a society that leaves such questions to popular vote, be taken as conclusive. On such a question free and open debate is vital to informed decision-making by the electorate. Teachers are, as a class, the members of a community most likely to have informed and definite opinions as to how funds allotted to the operation of the schools should be spent. Accordingly, it is essential that they be able to speak out freely on such questions without fear of retaliatory dismissal.

What we do have before us is a case in which a teacher has made erroneous public statements upon issues then currently the subject of public attention, which are critical of his ultimate employer but which are neither shown nor can be presumed to have in any way either impeded the teacher's proper performance of his daily duties in the classroom or to have interfered with the regular operation of the schools generally. In these circumstances we conclude that the interest of the school administration in limiting teachers' opportunities to contribute to public debate is not significantly greater than its interest in limiting a similar contribution by any member of the general public.

[**Holding**] In sum, we hold that, in a case such as this, absent proof of false statements knowingly or recklessly made by him, a teacher's exercise of his right to speak on issues of public importance may not furnish the basis for his dismissal from public employment. Since no such showing has been made in this case regarding appellant's letter, his dismissal for writing it cannot be upheld and the judgment of the Illinois Supreme Court must, accordingly, be reversed and the case remanded for further proceedings not inconsistent with this opinion.

Points to Consider

1. Marvin Pickering: A courageous litigant.

During the controversy, Marvin Pickering was blacklisted and could not get a teaching job in the state of Illinois. In order to support his family, he worked in a Campbell Soup Company factory for more than two years. After winning in the Supreme Court, he was reinstated as a Lockport Township High School teacher until he retired in 1997.

2. Justice Thurgood Marshall.

Justice Thurgood Marshall authored the Court's opinion in *Pickering*. Justice Marshall was a consistent defender of public employee free speech rights during his time on the Court. (He was also the lead counsel for the NAACP who successfully argued the case for the Brown family in 1954's *Brown v. Board of Education*.)

3. Public concern.

Justice Marshall wrote that "the problem in any case is to arrive at a balance between the interests of the teacher, as a citizen, in commenting upon matters of public concern and the interest of the State, as an employer, in promoting the efficiency of the public services it performs through its employees." This became known as the *Pickering* test.

The first step of the test is to identify whether the public employee spoke on a matter of public concern or importance, or whether the employee's speech was more of a private grievance. The second step of the test is known as the "balancing prong." In this step, the court balances the employee's right to free speech against the employer's efficiency interests.

In *Pickering*, the Court determined that the school board's allocation of money was an important issue for the community. Pickering's comments on the issue were therefore protected on the basis that they constituted speech on a matter of public concern.

4. Close working relationships.

In his letter to the editor, Marvin Pickering criticized the school board, not the teachers and administrators whom he worked with from day to day. The Court identified this as a key factor in striking the balance in favor of Pickering, rather than the school board. The outcome might have been different if Pickering had criticized his fellow teachers or his principal.

REFINING *PICKERING*

Connick v. Myers (1983)
The *Pickering* test was the governing law for decades. It considered:

1. Whether the speech touches on a matter of public concern; and
2. Whether the balance between the public employee's right to free speech and the public employer's efficiency interests weighs in favor of the public employee.

The Supreme Court clarified the *Pickering* balancing test in a 1983 decision involving a New Orleans District Attorney's Office. After District Attorney Harry Connick, Sr., transferred Assistant District Attorney Sheila Myers against her wishes, she circulated a questionnaire in the workplace that prompted her colleagues to comment on Connick's management practices. The questionnaire allegedly caused a "mini-insurrection," and Connick fired her for insubordination.

Myers' case against Connick reached the Supreme Court, which ruled for the district attorney by a 5–4 vote. The Court majority emphasized that government offices need to be able to function free from disruption and interference. "While as a matter of good judgment, public officials should be receptive to constructive criticism offered by their employees, the First Amendment does not require a public office to be run as a roundtable for employee complaints over internal office affairs," the majority explained.

The Court reasoned that federal courts often are not the appropriate forum for employer–employee disputes. The majority stated that the "common-sense realization that government offices could not function if every employment decision became a constitutional matter."

The Court also noted that Sheila Myers' speech impacted day-to-day close working relationships, unlike Marvin Pickering's expression. "When close working relationships are essential to fulfilling public responsibilities, a wide degree of deference to the employer's judgment is appropriate," the majority explained.

While the Court sided with the employer in *Connick*, they affirmed protections for speech on matters of "public concern." The Court defined speech on a matter of public concern as that "relating to any matter of political, social, or other concern to the community." In regards to the speech at issue, it stated: "Myers' questionnaire touched upon matters of public concern in only a most limited sense; her survey, in our view, is most accurately characterized as an employee grievance concerning internal office policy."

For his part, Harry Connick, Sr., (the father of the singer Harry Connick, Jr.) never understood why this case became a free speech dispute. Connick said:

> We should have won in the district court....If that case got to the Supreme Court, then any case involving a public employee could get to the Supreme Court....At oral arguments, I was thinking, "What in the hell are we doing in the Supreme Court?" This case had to do with an assistant D.A. refusing to be transferred for the good of the office. All of this free-speech foolishness was nonsense.

Rankin v. McPherson (1987)

A few years later, the Supreme Court determined in *Rankin v. McPherson* that a clerical employee in a Texas constable's office spoke on a matter of public concern when she told her boyfriend in a private conversation at work: "If they go for him, I hope they get him." The "him" was President Ronald Reagan. Clerical employee Ardith McPherson made this declaration after learning that John Hinckley, Jr., had shot Reagan. Constable Walter Rankin learned of the remark and called McPherson into his office. When she admitted to her comment, he fired her.

A bare majority of the Court sided with McPherson. Justice Thurgood Marshall, writing for the majority, first determined that McPherson's speech "clearly dealt with a matter of public concern"—dissatisfaction with the president and some of his economic policies.

The Court struck the balance between McPherson's expression on a matter of public concern and its impact on the workplace in favor of McPherson, writing: "Where, as here, an employee serves no confidential, policymaking, or public contact role, the danger to the agency's successful functioning from that employee's private speech is minimal."

In dissent, Justice Antonin Scalia wrote that the First Amendment should not allow a public employee to "ride with the cops and cheer for the robbers."

THE OUTSPOKEN PROSECUTOR WHO CAME TO THE DEFENSE OF A DEFENDANT

In 2006, the Supreme Court changed the equation with its opinion in *Garcetti v. Ceballos*. In *Garcetti*, Assistant District Attorney Richard Ceballos wrote a memo to his superiors recommending dismissal of criminal charges against a defendant because Ceballos believed that the search warrant leading to the charges contained perjured law enforcement testimony. Eventually, Ceballos' superiors stripped him of his supervisory duties and transferred him to a less desirable office location.

Ceballos sued, alleging retaliation on the basis that his speech was protected. As he saw it, speech about perjured law enforcement testimony would qualify as speech on a matter of public concern. He lost in federal district court but prevailed before the Ninth Circuit Court of Appeals. On further appeal, he lost again, this time before the U.S. Supreme Court. The Court determined that the matter of potential perjury was not enough to render Ceballos' speech protected under the First Amendment.

This decision fundamentally changed public employee free speech jurisprudence. Recall that in 1968, the Court had ruled in *Pickering v. Board of Education* that public employees had free speech rights to speak out on matters of public concern. With *Garcetti*, the Court created an additional threshold layer of analysis: the question of whether the employee spoke as an *employee* or as a *citizen*. If the employee spoke as an employee, or was engaged in official job duties when speaking, then the First Amendment would offer no protection. If the employee spoke more as a citizen, then the court would s apply the rest of the *Pickering* analysis.

It is hard to overstate the significance of the *Garcetti* decision. Many public employees, including many who have tried to blow the whistle on corruption, have lost their free speech cases because of this decision. Many employment lawyers refer to this phenomenon as being "Garcettized."

OPINION

Garcetti v. Ceballos

(Abridged.)

547 U.S. 410 (2006)
Vote: 5–4

JUSTICE KENNEDY delivered the opinion of the Court.

It is well settled that "a State cannot condition public employment on a basis that infringes the employee's constitutionally protected interest in freedom of expression." *Connick v. Myers* (1983). [**Issue**] The question presented by the instant case is whether the First Amendment protects a government employee from discipline based on speech made pursuant to the employee's official duties.

[**Facts**] Respondent Richard Ceballos has been employed since 1989 as a deputy district attorney for the Los Angeles County District Attorney's Office. During the period relevant to this case, Ceballos was a calendar deputy in the office's Pomona branch, and in this capacity he exercised certain supervisory responsibilities over other lawyers. In February 2000, a defense attorney contacted Ceballos about a pending criminal case. The defense attorney said there were inaccuracies in an affidavit used to obtain a critical search warrant. The attorney informed Ceballos that he had filed a motion to traverse, or challenge, the warrant, but he also wanted Ceballos to review the case. According to Ceballos, it was not unusual for defense attorneys to ask calendar deputies to investigate aspects of pending cases.

After examining the affidavit and visiting the location it described, Ceballos determined the affidavit contained serious misrepresentations. The affidavit called a long driveway what Ceballos thought should have been referred to as a separate roadway. Ceballos also questioned the affidavit's statement that tire tracks led from a stripped-down truck to the premises covered by the warrant. His doubts arose from his conclusion that the roadway's composition in some places made it difficult or impossible to leave visible tire tracks.

Ceballos spoke on the telephone to the warrant affiant, a deputy sheriff from the Los Angeles County Sheriff's Department, but he did not receive a satisfactory explanation for the perceived inaccuracies. He relayed his findings to his supervisors, petitioners Carol Najera and Frank Sundstedt, and followed up by preparing a disposition memorandum. The memo explained Ceballos' concerns and recommended dismissal of the case. On March 2, 2000, Ceballos submitted the memo to Sundstedt for his review. A few days later, Ceballos presented Sundstedt with another memo, this one describing a second telephone conversation between Ceballos and the warrant affiant.

Based on Ceballos' statements, a meeting was held to discuss the affidavit. Attendees included Ceballos, Sundstedt, and Najera, as well as the warrant affiant and other employees from the sheriff's department. The meeting allegedly became heated, with one lieutenant sharply criticizing Ceballos for his handling of the case.

Despite Ceballos' concerns, Sundstedt decided to proceed with the prosecution, pending disposition of the defense motion to traverse. The trial court held a hearing on the motion. Ceballos was called by the defense and recounted his observations about the affidavit, but the trial court rejected the challenge to the warrant.

[**Alleged retaliation**] Ceballos claims that in the aftermath of these events he was subjected to a series of retaliatory employment actions. The actions included reassignment from his calendar deputy position to a trial deputy position, transfer to another courthouse, and denial of a promotion. Ceballos initiated an employment grievance, but the grievance was denied based on a finding that he had not suffered any retaliation. Unsatisfied, Ceballos sued in the United States District Court for the Central District of California. He alleged petitioners violated the First and Fourteenth Amendments by retaliating against him based on his memo of March 2.

Petitioners responded that no retaliatory actions were taken against Ceballos and that all the actions of which he complained were explained by legitimate reasons such as staffing needs. They further contended that, in any event, Ceballos' memo was not protected speech under the First Amendment. Petitioners moved for summary judgment, and the District Court granted their motion. Noting that Ceballos wrote his memo pursuant to his employment duties, the court concluded he was not entitled to First Amendment protection for the memo's contents. It held in the alternative that even if Ceballos' speech was constitutionally protected, petitioners had qualified immunity because the rights Ceballos asserted were not clearly established.

The Court of Appeals for the Ninth Circuit reversed, holding that "Ceballos's allegations of wrongdoing in the memorandum constitute protected speech under the First Amendment."

We granted certiorari and we now reverse.

As the Court's decisions have noted, for many years "the unchallenged dogma was that a public employee had no right to object to conditions placed upon the terms of employment—including those which restricted the exercise of constitutional rights." *Connick.*

When a citizen enters government service, the citizen by necessity must accept certain limitations on his or her freedom. See, e.g., *Waters v. Church* (1994) ("[T]he government as employer indeed has far broader powers than does the government as sovereign"). Government employers, like private employers, need a significant degree of control over their employees' words and actions; without it, there would be little chance for the efficient provision of public services. *Connick* ("[G]overnment offices could not function if every employment decision became a constitutional matter"). Public employees, moreover, often occupy trusted positions in society. When they speak out, they can express views that contravene governmental policies or impair the proper performance of governmental functions.

[**Citizen v. employee**] At the same time, the Court has recognized that a citizen who works for the government is nonetheless a citizen. The First Amendment limits the ability of a public employer to leverage the employment relationship to restrict, incidentally or intentionally, the liberties employees enjoy in their capacities as private citizens. So long as employees are speaking as citizens about matters of public concern, they must face only those speech restrictions that are necessary for their employers to operate efficiently and effectively.

With these principles in mind we turn to the instant case. Respondent Ceballos believed the affidavit used to obtain a search warrant contained serious misrepresentations. He conveyed his opinion and recommendation in a memo to his supervisor. That Ceballos expressed his views inside his office, rather than publicly, is not dispositive. Employees in some cases may receive First Amendment protection for expressions made at work. See, *e.g.*, *Givhan v. Western Line Consol. School Dist.* (1979). Many citizens do much of their talking inside their respective workplaces, and it would not serve the goal of treating public employees like "any member of the general public," *Pickering v. Board of Education* (1968), to hold that all speech within the office is automatically exposed to restriction.

The controlling factor in Ceballos' case is that his expressions were made pursuant to his duties as a calendar deputy. That consideration—the fact that Ceballos spoke as a prosecutor fulfilling a responsibility to advise his supervisor about how best to proceed with a pending case—distinguishes Ceballos' case from those in which the First Amendment provides protection against discipline. [**Holding**] We hold that when public employees make statements pursuant to their official duties, the employees are not speaking as citizens for First Amendment purposes, and the Constitution does not insulate their communications from employer discipline.

Ceballos wrote his disposition memo because that is part of what he, as a calendar deputy, was employed to do. It is immaterial whether he experienced some personal gratification from writing the memo; his First Amendment rights do not depend on his job satisfaction. The significant point is that the memo was written pursuant to Ceballos' official duties. Restricting speech that owes its existence to a public employee's professional responsibilities does not infringe any liberties the employee might have enjoyed as a private citizen. It simply reflects the exercise of employer control over what the employer itself has commissioned or created.

This result is consistent with our precedents' attention to the potential societal value of employee speech. Refusing to recognize First Amendment claims based on government employees' work product does not prevent them from participating in public debate. The employees retain the prospect of constitutional protection for their contributions to the civic discourse. This prospect of protection, however, does not invest them with a right to perform their jobs however they see fit.

["**no relevant analogue**"] Employees who make public statements outside the course of performing their official duties retain some possibility of First Amendment protection because that is the kind of activity engaged in by citizens who do not work for the government. The same goes for writing a letter to a local newspaper, see *Pickering*, or discussing politics with a co-worker, see *Rankin v. McPherson* (1987). When a public employee speaks pursuant to employment responsibilities, however, there is no relevant analogue to speech by citizens who are not government employees.

Proper application of our precedents leads to the conclusion that the First Amendment does not prohibit managerial discipline based on an employee's expressions made pursuant to official responsibilities. Because Ceballos' memo falls into this category, his allegation of unconstitutional retaliation must fail.

We reject the notion that the First Amendment shields from discipline the expressions employees make pursuant to their professional duties. Our precedents do not support the existence of a constitutional cause of action behind every statement a public employee makes in the course of doing his or her job.

The judgment of the Court of Appeals is reversed, and the case is remanded for proceedings consistent with this opinion.

Points to Consider

1. Bessie Givhan's case.

In *Garcetti*, the Court emphasizes that a public employee may retain some free speech protections, even for speech that takes place at work. The Court cited the example of Bessie Givhan, a public school teacher who was dismissed after speaking out against racial discrimination in her principal's office. The Supreme Court ruled in *Givhan v. West Line Consolidated School District* (1979) that her speech to the principal was a form of protected expression.

2. Whistleblowing laws.

One consequence of *Garcetti* is that whistleblowing employees may not have any free speech protection. Justice Kennedy tries to soften that blow by saying that there are laws that may provide protection to whistleblowers. Many experts have countered that such laws do not provide sufficient coverage for public employees who blow the whistle on workplace corruption.

3. No relevant analogue.

Many lower courts have seized upon the Court's language in *Garcetti* of "no relevant analogue." In other words, when there is a "citizen analogue" (or similar avenue for a citizen to speak) to the public employee speech, then the employee has a better chance of claiming that she or he is speaking as a citizen. When there is no relevant citizen analogue, then the employee is likely speaking only as an employee, not as a citizen.

4. Exception for academic freedom?

In his dissenting opinion, Justice David Souter warned that the Court's ruling in *Garcetti* could threaten academic freedom. Justice Souter pointed out that the official job duties of a professor employed by a public university include speech related to scholarship and teaching, writing that he had "to hope that today's majority does not mean to imperil First Amendment protection of academic freedom in public colleges and universities, whose teachers necessarily speak and write 'pursuant to official duties.'"

In his majority opinion, Justice Kennedy acknowledged Justice Souter's concern, and explicitly reserved the question of "whether the analysis we conduct today would apply in the same manner to a case involving speech related to scholarship or teaching." It remains a contested question as to whether and how *Garcetti* applies to faculty at public colleges and universities.

Two federal courts of appeals, the Fourth Circuit in *Adams v. Trustees of the University of North Carolina Wilmington* (2011) and the Ninth Circuit in *Demers v. Austin* (2013), have rejected *Garcetti* in the context of public university professors because of academic freedom concerns. The U.S. Supreme Court has not yet resolved the issue.

5. Truthful testimony.

Not all employee speech is considered to fall under the *Garcetti* rule. For example, the Supreme Court ruled that the First Amendment protected a public employee who was terminated after giving truthful testimony in a court hearing. In *Lane v. Franks* (2014), the Court explained that "[t]ruthful testimony under oath by a public employee outside the scope of his ordinary job duties is speech as a citizen for First Amendment purposes." The Court reasoned that it was not part of Lane's regular duties to provide court testimony.

6. Social media and public employees.

Many of the current public employee free speech cases involve public employees who are terminated or disciplined for posting comments on social media that are offensive, harmful, or otherwise disliked by their employers. *Garcetti* usually does not strip them of protection for such posts if they are made off-duty and are not part of the employee's official job duties. That does not mean that the First Amendment will always protect public employees when they engage in speech outside of work. Public employees have frequently been fired for posting negative comments about their superiors or coworkers.

Comments on social media may be the new watercooler talk, but it is hard to erase digital trails. Employees' intemperate online expression often provides fodder for public employers to successfully punish employees. After all, public employers don't like to see their dirty laundry aired in public, and some public employees use very bad judgment in making comments detrimental to their employers' interests.

15.

Press Freedoms in the Modern World

Our liberty depends on freedom of the press, and that cannot be limited without being lost.
—Letter from Thomas Jefferson to James Currie (1786)

One of the things I'm going to do if I win....I'm going to open up our libel laws so when they write purposely negative and horrible and false articles, we can sue them and win lots of money. We're going to open up those libel laws. So when the New York Times writes a hit piece which is a total disgrace or when the Washington Post, which is there for other reasons, writes a hit piece, we can sue them and win money instead of having no chance of winning because they're totally protected.
—Donald J. Trump (2016)

DONALD TRUMP, the 45th president of the United States, has called the press "an enemy of the people," "truly dishonest people," and the purveyor of "fake news." The Committee to Protect Journalists awarded him one of its "Press Oppressor" awards along with the likes of President Recep Tayyip Erdoğan of Turkey, President Abdel Fattah el-Sisi of Egypt, President Xi Jinping of China, and President Vladimir Putin of Russia.

Both as a candidate and as president, Trump has called for a change in libel laws, attempted to prevent critics from engaging with his Twitter feeds, banned reporters from certain press conferences, and promoted "Fake News" awards concerning several noted journalists.

Think what you will of Donald Trump, but know that where there is executive power, there will always be the temptation (often actualized) to abuse that power and go after the press. A little taste of history is illustrative.

EXECUTIVE ABRIDGEMENTS OF THE PRESS

John Adams, our second president and the leader of the Federalist Party, signed into law the Sedition Act of 1798, which criminalized "the writing, printing, uttering or publishing any false, scandalous and malicious writing or writings against the government of the United States, or either house of the Congress of the United States, or the President of the United States."

The Federalists used the Sedition Act of 1798 as an oppressive tool to silence Democratic-Republican newspaper editors, such as Benjamin Bache (see Chapter 1), William Duane, and Matthew Lyon.

In 1798, Congressman Matthew Lyon, who also owned a newspaper in his home state of Vermont, faced prosecution under the Sedition Act for writing the following passage about President Adams and the Federalists:

> As to the executive, when I shall see the efforts of that power bent on the promotion of the comfort, the happiness, and accommodation of the people, that executive shall have my zealous and uniform support: but whenever I shall, on the part of the Executive, see every consideration of the public welfare swallowed up in a continual grasp for power, in an unbounded thirst for ridiculous pomp, foolish adulations, and selfish avarice....I shall not be their humble advocate.

There are, to be sure, many more historical examples. For example:

- In 1859, presidential hopeful Abraham Lincoln purchased the *Illinois Staats-Anzeiger*, a German-language newspaper, and demanded that it endorse the Republican Party through the 1860 election.
- President Woodrow Wilson fought (and lost) for the inclusion of a provision in the Espionage Act of 1917 that would have expanded his power to censor the press. Wilson believed press censorship was "absolutely necessary to the public safety."
- President Richard Nixon's administration and his Justice Department unsuccessfully prosecuted the press with a vengeance in the "Pentagon Papers case" (*New York Times Co. v. United States* [1971])
- During President Barack Obama's time in office, federal prosecutors

invoked the Espionage Act to prosecute whistle blowers and leakers in nine different cases. Historian Lloyd C. Garner referred to President Obama's treatment of these reporters as "The War on Leakers."

PRIOR RESTRAINTS ON THE PRESS

Perhaps the greatest threat to the press from a First Amendment perspective is prior restraint—preventing the press from publishing certain material. The great English poet John Milton warned against the dangers of prior restraint (though he didn't use that term) when he criticized the English licensing law of 1643—a law that required a printer to obtain a license before printing material. Milton famously wrote in *Areopagitica* (1644):

> And though all the winds of doctrine were let loose to play upon the earth, so Truth be in the field, we do injuriously, by licensing and pro-hibiting to misdoubt her strength. Let her and Falsehood grapple; who ever knew Truth put to the worse, in a free and open encounter.

In the 1700s, the English writer and legal theorist Sir William Blackstone con-sidered freedom of expression chiefly to mean freedom from prior restraints on speech. He wrote in his *Commentaries on the Law of England*: "The liberty of the press is indeed essential to the nature of a free state: but this consists in laying no *previous* restraints upon publications, and not in freedom from censure for crimi-nal matter when published."

The Supreme Court initially adopted the Blackstonian view of the First Amendment in *Patterson v. Colorado* (1907). Justice Oliver Wendell Holmes wrote for the Court:

> [T]he main purpose of such constitutional provisions is "to prevent all such previous restraints upon publications as had been practiced by other governments," and they do not prevent the subsequent punish-ment of such as may be deemed contrary to the public welfare.

However, the Court later applied the First Amendment both to prior restraints on speech and to subsequent punishments.

The Court reiterated the danger of prior restraints in *Near v. Minnesota* (1931). The case involved an attempt to declare publisher Jay Near's *Saturday Press* a "public nuisance." Minnesota law provided that a judge could issue an injunction to stop the publication of a newspaper as a public nuisance if it was a "malicious, scandalous and defamatory newspaper, magazine or other periodical."

Writing for the Court, Chief Justice Charles Evans Hughes called the law "the essence of censorship." He added: "The fact that the liberty of the press may be abused by miscreant purveyors of scandal does not make any the less necessary the immunity of the press from previous restraint in dealing with official misconduct." In other words, prior restraint on speech was something not in the spirit of the First Amendment and freedom of speech. Hughes noted a few narrow exceptions when the government could issue a prior restraint:

> No one would question but that a government might prevent actual obstruction to its recruiting service or the publication of the sailing dates of transports or the number and location of troops. On similar grounds, the primary requirements of decency may be enforced against obscene publications. The security of the community life may be protected against incitements to acts of violence and the overthrow by force of orderly government.

THE SECURITY EXCEPTION: THE MILITARY ANALYSTS WHO LEAKED 43 VOLUMES OF CLASSIFIED DOCUMENTS

Perhaps the most powerful argument a governmental entity can advance to justify a prior restraint is national security. The United States Government used this argument in *New York Times Co. v. United States* (1971), better known as the "Pentagon Papers" case.

The "Report of the Office of the Secretary of Defense Vietnam Task Force"— better known as the "Pentagon Papers"—was a secret government study detailing U.S. involvement in Vietnam from 1945 to 1967. There were only fifteen copies of the report. Daniel Ellsberg, a RAND Corporation employee, had access to the report and released it to the *New York Times* and the *Washington Post.*

The voluminous study contained 2.5 million words and weighed sixty pounds, according to Floyd Abrams, who was one of the attorneys for the *New York Times.*

The *New York Times* received a court order to cease publication at the request of the Justice Department, citing the Espionage Act. The Supreme Court considered whether there was sufficient justification for prior restraint.

OPINION

New York Times Co. v. United States

(Abridged.)

403 U.S. 713 (1971)
Vote: 6–3

PER CURIAM.

We granted certiorari in these cases in which the United States seeks to enjoin the New York Times and the Washington Post from publishing the contents of a classified study entitled "History of U.S. Decision-Making Process on Viet Nam Policy."

"Any system of prior restraints of expression comes to this Court bearing a heavy presumption against its constitutional validity." *Bantam Books, Inc. v. Sullivan* (1963); see also *Near v. Minnesota* (1931). The Government "thus carries a heavy burden of showing justification for the imposition of such a restraint." *Organization for a Better Austin v. Keefe* (1971). The District Court for the Southern District of New York in the *New York Times* case, and the District Court for the District of Columbia and the Court of Appeals for the District of Columbia Circuit in the *Washington Post* case, held that the Government had not met that burden. We agree.

The judgment of the Court of Appeals for the District of Columbia Circuit is therefore affirmed. The order of the Court of Appeals for the Second Circuit is reversed and the case is remanded with directions to enter a judgment affirming the judgment of the District Court for the Southern District of New York. The stays entered June 25, 1971, by the Court are vacated. The judgments shall issue forthwith.

JUSTICE BLACK, concurring.

I adhere to the view that the Government's case against the Washington Post should have been dismissed, and that the injunction against the New York Times should have been vacated without oral argument when the cases were first presented to this Court. I believe that every moment's continuance of the injunctions against these newspapers amounts to a flagrant, indefensible, and continuing violation of the First Amendment. In my view, it is unfortunate that some of my Brethren are apparently willing to hold that the publication of news may sometimes be enjoined. Such a holding would make a shambles of the First Amendment.

Our Government was launched in 1789 with the adoption of the Constitution. The Bill of Rights, including the First Amendment, followed in 1791. Now, for the first time in the 182 years since the founding of the Republic, the federal courts are asked to hold that the First Amendment does not mean what it says, but rather means that the Government can halt the publication of current news of vital importance to the people of this country.

[**Main purpose of the First Amendment**] In seeking injunctions against these newspapers, and in its presentation to the Court, the Executive Branch seems to have forgotten the essential purpose and history of the First Amendment. When the Constitution was adopted, many people strongly opposed it because the document contained no Bill of Rights to safeguard certain basic freedoms. They especially feared that the new powers granted to a central government might be interpreted to permit the government to curtail freedom of religion, press, assembly, and speech. In response to an overwhelming public clamor, James Madison offered a series of amendments to satisfy citizens that these great liberties would remain safe and beyond the power of government to abridge. Madison proposed what later became the First Amendment in three parts, two of which are set out below, and one of which proclaimed:

> "The people shall not be deprived or abridged of their right to speak, to write, or to publish their sentiments, *and the freedom of the press, as one of the great bulwarks of liberty, shall be inviolable.*" (Emphasis added.)

The amendments were offered to curtail and restrict the general powers granted to the Executive, Legislative, and Judicial Branches two years before in the original Constitution. The Bill of Rights changed the original Constitution into a new charter under which no branch of government could abridge the people's freedoms of press, speech, religion, and assembly. Yet the Solicitor General argues and some members of the Court appear to agree that the general powers of the Government adopted in the original Constitution should be interpreted to limit and restrict the specific and emphatic guarantees of the Bill of Rights adopted later. I can imagine no greater perversion of history. Madison and the other Framers of the First Amendment, able men that they were, wrote in language they

earnestly believed could never be misunderstood: "Congress shall make no law…
abridging the freedom…of the press.…" Both the history and language of the
First Amendment support the view that the press must be left free to publish news,
whatever the source, without censorship, injunctions, or prior restraints.

["**Bare the secrets of government**"] In the First Amendment, the Founding
Fathers gave the free press the protection it must have to fulfill its essential role
in our democracy. The press was to serve the governed, not the governors. The
Government's power to censor the press was abolished so that the press would
remain forever free to censure the Government. The press was protected so that it
could bare the secrets of government and inform the people. Only a free and unrestrained press can effectively expose deception in government. And paramount
among the responsibilities of a free press is the duty to prevent any part of the
government from deceiving the people and sending them off to distant lands to
die of foreign fevers and foreign shot and shell. In my view, far from deserving
condemnation for their courageous reporting, the New York Times, the Washington Post, and other newspapers should be commended for serving the purpose
that the Founding Fathers saw so clearly. In revealing the workings of government that led to the Vietnam war, the newspapers nobly did precisely that which
the Founders hoped and trusted they would do.

[**Justification: national security**] We are asked to hold that, despite the First
Amendment's emphatic command, the Executive Branch, the Congress, and the
Judiciary can make laws enjoining publication of current news and abridging freedom of the press in the name of "national security." The Government does not
even attempt to rely on any act of Congress. Instead, it makes the bold and dan-
gerously far-reaching contention that the courts should take it upon themselves to
"make" a law abridging freedom of the press in the name of equity, presidential
power and national security, even when the representatives of the people in Congress have adhered to the command of the First Amendment and refused to make
such a law.

To find that the President has "inherent power" to halt the publication of news
by resort to the courts would wipe out the First Amendment and destroy the fundamental liberty and security of the very people the Government hopes to make
"secure." No one can read the history of the adoption of the First Amendment
without being convinced beyond any doubt that it was injunctions like those
sought here that Madison and his collaborators intended to outlaw in this Nation
for all time.

[**"Security" as a justification is too vague**] The word "security" is a broad, vague generality whose contours should not be invoked to abrogate the fundamental law embodied in the First Amendment. The guarding of military and diplomatic secrets at the expense of informed representative government provides no real security for our Republic. The Framers of the First Amendment, fully aware of both the need to defend a new nation and the abuses of the English and Colonial governments, sought to give this new society strength and security by providing that freedom of speech, press, religion, and assembly should not be abridged. This thought was eloquently expressed in 1937 by Mr. Chief Justice Hughes—great man and great Chief Justice that he was—when the Court held a man could not be punished for attending a meeting run by Communists.

> "The greater the importance of safeguarding the community from incitements to the overthrow of our institutions by force and violence, the more imperative is the need to preserve inviolate the constitutional rights of free speech, free press and free assembly in order to maintain the opportunity for free political discussion, to the end that government may be responsive to the will of the people and that changes, if desired, may be obtained by peaceful means. Therein lies the security of the Republic, the very foundation of constitutional government."

Points to Consider

1. *Justice Hugo Black.*

Justice Hugo Black, a former member of the Ku Klux Klan as a young man in his home state of Alabama, became one of the country's foremost defenders of constitutional freedoms. He was well known for carrying around a pocket copy of the Constitution and for his passionate defense of the First Amendment. He was fond of saying that "'no law' means no law" when referring to the text of the First Amendment.

His concurring opinion in the Pentagon Papers case shows Black articulating the values of a free society and a press that truly serves as the watchdog of that free society. Consider his line: "The press was protected so that it could bare the secrets of government and inform the people."

2. *Daniel Ellsberg.*

The leaker in the Pentagon Papers case, Daniel Ellsberg, took a huge risk in releasing the study to the newspapers. Ellsberg was indicted for violating the Espionage Act, conspiracy, misappropriation, and other charges. And the government was not exactly playing by the rules. At Ellsberg's trial, presided over by U.S. District Court Judge William Matthew Byrne, Jr., Judge Byrne dismissed the charges because of gross government misconduct, including a break-in at the office of Ellsberg's psychiatrist.

Ellsberg has authored books about the Pentagon Papers case: *Papers on the War* (1972) and *Secrets: A Memoir of Vietnam and the Pentagon Papers* (2002). He is a vocal supporter of Edward Snowden, who leaked evidence of the National Security Agency's secret mass surveillance system.

3. Alexander Bickel and Floyd Abrams.

The *New York Times* had a "dream team" of attorneys, including Alexander Bickel, a distinguished Yale Law School professor, and Floyd Abrams, then a young attorney who went on to become the preeminent First Amendment lawyer in the nation.

Floyd Abrams has argued several First Amendment cases before the Supreme Court, including *Nebraska Press Association v. Stuart* (1976), *Landmark Communications, Inc. v. Virginia* (1978), *Herbert v. Lando* (1979), *Smith v. Daily Mail Publishing Co.* (1979), *CBS v. FCC* (1981), *Metromedia v. City of San Diego* (1981), and *McConnell v. FEC* (2003). He also has written several books on the First Amendment, including *Speaking Freely: Trials of the First Amendment* (2005), *Friend of the Court: On the Front Lines with the First Amendment* (2013), and *The Soul of the First Amendment* (2017).

4. *The* Washington Post.

The *Washington Post* also published the Pentagon Papers and was included in the case. The *Washington Post*'s efforts were led by Katharine Graham, the first female publisher of a major U.S. newspaper, and Ben Bradlee, the paper's executive director. In 2017, Steven Spielberg produced and directed *The Post*, a movie about the paper's publication of the Pentagon Papers. Meryl Streep played Graham and Tom Hanks played Bradlee in the movie.

GAG ORDERS: FREE PRESS AND FAIR TRIALS

A special type of prior restraint against the press is called a gag order. This type of prior restraint usually comes in the form of an order issued by a judge attempting to prevent further dissemination of information about a pending case—usually a criminal case.

The Supreme Court condemned such gag orders in *Nebraska Press Association v. Stuart* (1976). The case involved a judicial gag order issued by Nebraska trial court judge Hugh Stuart, who was upset about press coverage of the trial of Edwin Simants. Simants stood accused of killing six members of a family in Sutherland, Nebraska, and Judge Stuart thought that press coverage of the murder trial implied guilt and would make a fair trial by jury impossible.

OPINION

Nebraska Press Association v. Stuart

(Abridged.)

427 U.S. 539 (1976)
Vote: 9–0

CHIEF JUSTICE BURGER delivered the opinion of the Court.

The respondent State District Judge entered an order restraining the petitioners from publishing or broadcasting accounts of confessions or admissions made by the accused or facts "strongly implicative" of the accused in a widely reported murder of six persons. We granted certiorari to decide whether the entry of such an order on the showing made before the state court violated the constitutional guarantee of freedom of the press.

[**Facts**] On the evening of October 18, 1975, local police found the six members of the Henry Kellie family murdered in their home in Sutherland, Neb., a town of about 850 people. Police released the description of a suspect, Erwin Charles Simants, to the reporters who had hastened to the scene of the crime. Simants was arrested and arraigned in Lincoln County Court the following morning, ending a tense night for this small rural community.

The crime immediately attracted widespread news coverage, by local, regional, and national newspapers, radio and television stations. Three days after the crime, the County Attorney and Simants' attorney joined in asking the County Court to enter a restrictive order relating to "matters that may or may not be publicly reported or disclosed to the public," because of the "mass coverage by news media" and the "reasonable likelihood of prejudicial news which would make difficult, if not impossible, the impaneling of an impartial jury and tend to prevent a fair trial." The County Court heard oral argument but took no evidence; no attorney for members of the press appeared at this stage. The County Court granted the prosecutor's motion for a restrictive order and entered it the next day, October 22. The order prohibited everyone in attendance from "releas[ing] or authoriz[ing] the release for public dissemination in any form or manner whatsoever any testimony given or evidence adduced"; the order also required members of the press to observe the Nebraska Bar Press Guidelines.

Simants' preliminary hearing was held the same day, open to the public but subject to the order. The County Court bound over the defendant for trial to the State District Court. The charges, as amended to reflect the autopsy findings, were that Simants had committed the murders in the course of a sexual assault.

[**The press intervenes**] Petitioners—several press and broadcast associations, publishers, and individual reporters—moved on October 23 for leave to intervene in the District Court, asking that the restrictive order imposed by the County Court be vacated. The District Court conducted a hearing, at which the County Judge testified and newspaper articles about the *Simants* case were admitted in evidence. The District Judge granted petitioners' motion to intervene and, on October 27, entered his own restrictive order. The judge found "because of the nature of the crimes charged in the complaint that there is a clear and present danger that pre-trial publicity could impinge upon the defendant's right to a fair trial." The order applied only until the jury was impaneled, and specifically prohibited petitioners from reporting five subjects: (1) the existence or contents of a confession Simants had made to law enforcement officers, which had been introduced in open court at arraignment; (2) the fact or nature of statements Simants had made to other persons; (3) the contents of a note he had written the night of the crime; (4) certain aspects of the medical testimony at the preliminary hearing; and (5) the identity of the victims of the alleged sexual assault and the nature of the assault. It also prohibited reporting the exact nature of the restrictive order itself. Like the County Court's order, this order incorporated the Nebraska Bar-Press Guidelines. Finally, the order set out a plan for attendance, seating, and courthouse traffic control during the trial.

[**Sixth Amendment v. First Amendment**] The problems presented by this case are almost as old as the Republic. Neither in the Constitution nor in contemporaneous writings do we find that the conflict between these two important rights was anticipated, yet it is inconceivable that the authors of the Constitution were unaware of the potential conflicts between the right to an unbiased jury and the guarantee of freedom of the press. The unusually able lawyers who helped write the Constitution and later drafted the Bill of Rights were familiar with the historic episode in which John Adams defended British soldiers charged with homicide for firing into a crowd of Boston demonstrators; they were intimately familiar with the clash of the adversary system and the part that passions of the populace sometimes play in influencing potential jurors. They did not address themselves directly to the situation presented by this case; their chief concern was the need for freedom of expression in the political arena and the dialogue in ideas. But they recognized that there were risks to private rights from an unfettered press.

The trial of Aaron Burr in 1807 presented Mr. Chief Justice Marshall, presiding as a trial judge, with acute problems in selecting an unbiased jury. Few people in the area of Virginia from which jurors were drawn had not formed some opinions concerning Mr. Burr or the case, from newspaper accounts and heightened discussion both private and public. The Chief Justice conducted a searching *voir dire* of the two panels eventually called, and rendered a substantial opinion on the purposes of *voir dire* and the standards to be applied. Burr was acquitted, so there was no occasion for appellate review to examine the problem of prejudicial pretrial publicity. Mr. Chief Justice Marshall's careful *voir dire* inquiry into the matter of possible bias makes clear that the problem is not a new one.

The speed of communication and the pervasiveness of the modern news media have exacerbated these problems, however, as numerous appeals demonstrate. The trial of Bruno Hauptmann in a small New Jersey community for the abduction and murder of the Charles Lindberghs' infant child probably was the most widely covered trial up to that time, and the nature of the coverage produced widespread public reaction. Criticism was directed at the "carnival" atmosphere that pervaded the community and the courtroom itself. Responsible leaders of press and the legal profession—including other judges—pointed out that much of this sorry performance could have been controlled by a vigilant trial judge and by other public officers subject to the control of the court.

The excesses of press and radio and lack of responsibility of those in authority in the *Hauptmann* case and others of that era led to efforts to develop voluntary guidelines for courts, lawyers, press, and broadcasters. In the wake of these efforts, the cooperation between bar associations and members of the press led to the adoption of voluntary guidelines like Nebraska's.

In practice, of course, even the most ideal guidelines are subjected to powerful strains when a case such as Simants' arises, with reporters from many parts of the country on the scene. Reporters from distant places are unlikely to consider themselves bound by local standards. They report to editors outside the area covered by the guidelines, and their editors are likely to be guided only by their own standards. To contemplate how a state court can control acts of a newspaper or broadcaster outside its jurisdiction, even though the newspapers and broadcasts reach the very community from which jurors are to be selected, suggests something of the practical difficulties of managing such guidelines.

The problems presented in this case have a substantial history outside the reported decisions of courts, in the efforts of many responsible people to accommodate the competing interests. We cannot resolve all of them, for it is not the function of this Court to write a code. We look instead to this particular case and the legal context in which it arises.

[**The Sixth Amendment right to a fair trial**] The Sixth Amendment in terms guarantees "trial, by an impartial jury…" in federal criminal prosecutions. Because "trial by jury in criminal cases is fundamental to the American scheme of justice," the Due Process Clause of the Fourteenth Amendment guarantees the same right in state criminal prosecutions. *Duncan v. Louisiana* (1968).

> "In essence, the right to jury trial guarantees to the criminally accused a fair trial by a panel of impartial, 'indifferent' jurors.…'A fair trial in a fair tribunal is a basic requirement of due process.' *In re Murchison* (1955)" *Irvin v. Dowd* (1961).

In the overwhelming majority of criminal trials, pretrial publicity presents few unmanageable threats to this important right. But when the case is a "sensational" one, tensions develop between the right of the accused to trial by an impartial jury and the rights guaranteed others by the First Amendment.

In *Sheppard v. Maxwell* (1966), the Court focused sharply on the impact of pretrial publicity and a trial court's duty to protect the defendant's constitutional right to a fair trial. With only Mr. Justice Black dissenting, and he without opinion, the Court ordered a new trial for the petitioner, even though the first trial had occurred 12 years before.

Because the trial court had failed to use even minimal efforts to insulate the trial and the jurors from the "deluge of publicity," the Court vacated the judgment of conviction and a new trial followed, in which the accused was acquitted.

Pretrial publicity even pervasive, adverse publicity—does not inevitably lead to an unfair trial. The capacity of the jury eventually impaneled to decide the case fairly is influenced by the tone and extent of the publicity.

The costs of failure to afford a fair trial are high. In the most extreme cases, like *Sheppard* and *Estes v. Texas* (1965), the risk of injustice was avoided when the convictions were reversed. But a reversal means that justice has been delayed for both the defendant and the State; in some cases, because of lapse of time retrial is impossible or further prosecution is gravely handicapped. Moreover, in borderline cases in which the conviction is not reversed, there is some possibility of an injustice unredressed. The "strong measures" outlined in *Sheppard v. Maxwell* are means by which a trial judge can try to avoid exacting these costs from society or from the accused.

The state trial judge in the case before us acted responsibly, out of a legitimate concern, in an effort to protect the defendant's right to a fair trial. What we must decide is not simply whether the Nebraska courts erred in seeing the possibility of real danger to the defendant's rights, but whether in the circumstances of this case the means employed were foreclosed by another provision of the Constitution.

[**Reliance on the *Near* decision**] In *Near v. Minnesota ex rel. Olson* (1931), the Court held invalid a Minnesota statute providing for the abatement as a public nuisance of any "malicious, scandalous and defamatory newspaper, magazine or other periodical." Near had published an occasional weekly newspaper described by the County Attorney's complaint as "largely devoted to malicious, scandalous and defamatory articles" concerning political and other public figures. Publication was enjoined pursuant to the statute. Excerpts from Near's paper, set out in the dissenting opinion of Mr. Justice Butler, show beyond question that one of its principal characteristics was blatant anti-Semitism.

Mr. Chief Justice Hughes, writing for the Court, noted that freedom of the press is not an absolute right, and the State may punish its abuses. He observed that the statute was "not aimed at the redress of individual or private wrongs." He then focused on the statute:

> "[T]he operation and effect of the statute in substance is that public authorities may bring the owner or publisher of a newspaper or periodical before a judge upon a charge of conducting a business of publishing scandalous and defamatory matter...and unless the owner or publisher

is able…to satisfy the judge that the [matter is] true and…published with good motives…his newspaper or periodical is suppressed.…This is of the essence of censorship."

The Court relied on *Patterson v. Colorado ex rel. Attorney General* (1907): "[T]he main purpose of [the First Amendment] is 'to prevent all such previous restraints upon publications as had been practiced by other governments.'"

[**Reliance on the Pentagon Papers decision**] More recently in *New York Times Co. v. United States* (1971), the Government sought to enjoin the publication of excerpts from a massive, classified study of this Nation's involvement in the Vietnam conflict, going back to the end of the Second World War. The dispositive opinion of the Court simply concluded that the Government had not met its heavy burden of showing justification for the prior restraint. Each of the six concurring Justices and the three dissenting Justices expressed his views separately, but "every member of the Court, tacitly or explicitly, accepted the *Near* and *Keefe* (1971) condemnation of prior restraint as presumptively unconstitutional." *Pittsburgh Press Co. v. Human Rel. Comm'n* (1973). The Court's conclusion in *New York Times* suggests that the burden on the Government is not reduced by the temporary nature of a restraint; in that case the Government asked for a temporary restraint solely to permit it to study and assess the impact on national security of the lengthy documents at issue.

[**On prior restraints**] The thread running through all these cases is that prior restraints on speech and publication are the most serious and the least tolerable infringement on First Amendment rights. A criminal penalty or a judgment in a defamation case is subject to the whole panoply of protections afforded by deferring the impact of the judgment until all avenues of appellate review have been exhausted. Only after judgment has become final, correct or otherwise, does the law's sanction become fully operative.

A prior restraint, by contrast and by definition, has an immediate and irreversible sanction. If it can be said that a threat of criminal or civil sanctions after publication "chills" speech, prior restraint "freezes" it at least for the time.

The damage can be particularly great when the prior restraint falls upon the communication of news and commentary on current events. Truthful reports of public judicial proceedings have been afforded special protection against subsequent punishment.

The Nebraska courts in this case enjoined the publication of certain kinds of information about the *Simants* case. There are, as we suggested earlier, marked differences in setting and purpose between the order entered here and the orders in *Near*, *Keefe*, and *New York Times*, but as to the underlying issue—the right of the press to be free from *prior* restraints on publication—those cases form the backdrop against which we must decide this case.

We turn now to the record in this case to determine whether, as Learned Hand put it, "the gravity of the 'evil,' discounted by its improbability, justifies such invasion of free speech as is necessary to avoid the danger." *United States v. Dennis* (1950). [**Key test from the opinion**] To do so, we must examine the evidence before the trial judge when the order was entered to determine (a) the nature and extent of pretrial news coverage; (b) whether other measures would be likely to mitigate the effects of unrestrained pretrial publicity; and (c) how effectively a restraining order would operate to prevent the threatened danger. The precise terms of the restraining order are also important. We must then consider whether the record supports the entry of a prior restraint on publication, one of the most extraordinary remedies known to our jurisprudence.

[**The duty of the trial judge**] In assessing the probable extent of publicity, the trial judge had before him newspapers demonstrating that the crime had already drawn intensive news coverage, and the testimony of the County Judge, who had entered the initial restraining order based on the local and national attention the case had attracted. The District Judge was required to assess the probable publicity that would be given these shocking crimes prior to the time a jury was selected and sequestered. He then had to examine the probable nature of the publicity and determine how it would affect prospective jurors.

Our review of the pretrial record persuades us that the trial judge was justified in concluding that there would be intense and pervasive pretrial publicity concerning this case. He could also reasonably conclude, based on common human experience, that publicity might impair the defendant's right to a fair trial. He did not purport to say more, for he found only "a clear and present danger that pre-trial publicity *could* impinge upon the defendant's right to a fair trial." (Emphasis added.) His conclusion as to the impact of such publicity on prospective jurors was of necessity speculative, dealing as he was with factors unknown and unknowable.

[**Mitigating the effects of pretrial publicity**] We find little in the record that goes to another aspect of our task, determining whether measures short of an order restraining all publication would have insured the defendant a fair trial. Although the entry of the order might be read as a judicial determination that other measures would not suffice, the trial court made no express findings to that effect; the Nebraska Supreme Court referred to the issue only by implication.

[**Less restrictive alternatives**] Most of the alternatives to prior restraint of publication in these circumstances were discussed with obvious approval in *Sheppard v. Maxwell*: (a) change of trial venue to a place less exposed to the intense publicity that seemed imminent in Lincoln County; (b) postponement of the trial to allow public attention to subside; (c) searching questioning of prospective jurors; (d) the use of emphatic and clear instructions on the sworn duty of each juror to decide the issues only on evidence presented in open court. Sequestration of jurors is, of course, always available. Although that measure insulates jurors only after they are sworn, it also enhances the likelihood of dissipating the impact of pretrial publicity and emphasizes the elements of the jurors' oaths.

We have therefore examined this record to determine the probable efficacy of the measures short of prior restraint on the press and speech. There is no finding that alternative measures would not have protected Simants' rights, and the Nebraska Supreme Court did no more than imply that such measures might not be adequate. Moreover, the record is lacking in evidence to support such a finding.

[**Effect of prior restraint**] We must also assess the probable efficacy of prior restraint on publication as a workable method of protecting Simants' right to a fair trial, and we cannot ignore the reality of the problems of managing and enforcing pretrial restraining orders.

Given these practical problems, it is far from clear that prior restraint on publication would have protected Simants' rights.

The record demonstrates, as the Nebraska courts held, that there was indeed a risk that pretrial news accounts, true or false, would have some adverse impact on the attitudes of those who might be called as jurors. But on the record now before us it is not clear that further publicity, unchecked, would so distort the views of potential jurors that 12 could not be found who would, under proper instructions, fulfill their sworn duty to render a just verdict exclusively on the evidence presented in open court. We cannot say on this record that alternatives to a prior restraint on petitioners would not have sufficiently mitigated the adverse effects of pretrial publicity so as to make prior restraint unnecessary. Nor can we conclude that the restraining order actually entered would serve its intended purpose. Reasonable minds can have few doubts about the gravity of the evil pretrial publicity can work, but the probability that it would do so here was not demonstrated with the degree of certainty our cases on prior restraint require.

Our analysis ends as it began, with a confrontation between prior restraint imposed to protect one vital constitutional guarantee and the explicit command of another that the freedom to speak and publish shall not be abridged. We reaffirm that the guarantees of freedom of expression are not an absolute prohibition under all circumstances, but the barriers to prior restraint remain high and the presumption against its use continues intact. We hold that, with respect to the order entered in this case prohibiting reporting or commentary on judicial proceedings held in public, the barriers have not been overcome; to the extent that this order restrained publication of such material, it is clearly invalid. To the extent that it prohibited publication based on information gained from other sources, we conclude that the heavy burden imposed as a condition to securing a prior restraint was not met and the judgment of the Nebraska Supreme Court is therefore

Reversed.

Points to Consider

1. Chief Justice Warren Burger.

Chief Justice Warren Burger, who authored this opinion, wrote many important opinions regarding the freedom of the press for the Court. He penned the Court's decision in *Miami Herald Publishing Co. v. Tornillo* (1974), striking down a Florida law that required newspapers to give equal time to political candidates. He also authored the Court's decision in *Smith v. Daily Mail Publishing Co.* (1979), ruling that the press could not be punished for publishing the name of a juvenile offender.

2. Judge Hugh Stuart.

Judge Hugh Stuart was the district court judge who narrowed the gag order on the press initially issued by a county judge. However, Stuart's order still imposed limitations on what the press could print about the Simants murder trial. Stuart once said: "I modified the county judge's order because I thought it was too broad. I was trying to achieve a balance between the First Amendment right to a free press and the Sixth Amendment right to an impartial jury."

3. Aftermath: Erwin Charles Simants.

Simants was ultimately found not guilty by reason of insanity and committed to Nebraska's state psychiatric hospital in Lincoln. While the Lincoln Regional Center has since found that Simants' schizophrenia is in full remission and that he "has not demonstrated any agitation, anger, paranoia or delusional thinking and has been in remission for a long period of time," a state court has found him to still be a danger to the public every year at his competency hearing.

4. Sam Sheppard case.

One of the cases Chief Justice Burger relied upon was *Sheppard v. Maxwell* (1966). In that decision, the Court reversed the conviction of Dr. Sam Sheppard, a Cleveland-based physician convicted of murdering his wife, because of the trial's "carnival atmosphere" and excessive pretrial publicity. "Bearing in mind the massive pretrial publicity, the [trial] judge should have adopted stricter rules governing the use of the courtroom by newsmen," wrote Justice Tom Clark for the Court.

In 1966, a jury found Sheppard not guilty in a retrial. His trial is rumored to have inspired a television series and movie, both titled *The Fugitive*.

5. Fair trial versus free press.

In *Nebraska Press Association*, Chief Justice Burger expressed sensitivity toward criminal defendants' Sixth Amendment rights. The Sixth Amendment provides a litany of protections, including the right to an open trial, to a speedy trial, to confront one's accusers, to an impartial jury, to notice, and to the assistance of counsel. Collectively, it is often said that the Sixth Amendment protects the right to a fair trial.

As the Court ruled in *Nebraska Press Association*, the Sixth Amendment right to a fair trial should not lead to judges gagging the press. The press, after all, is the entity that ensures that individuals are informed about the workings of the criminal justice system.

6. Gag orders on trial participants.

The *Nebraska Press Association* case involved gagging the news media. This type of gag order is rarely, if ever, justifiable.

However, courts have greater power to control the conduct of actual trial participants. Judges sometimes do issue orders prohibiting attorneys in their courtroom from talking about the case publicly. Attorneys don't forfeit all of their free speech rights, but, as officers of the court, they are not entitled to the same level of free speech protections as they are outside the context of their representative capacities.

Some constitutional experts object to this. For example, constitutional law expert Erwin Chemerinsky has called such gag orders on trial participants "almost always unconstitutional."

7. Who qualifies for protection under this clause of the First Amendment?

Recall the questions posed in Chapter 2: Do redistributors of the news such as the conservative *Drudge Report* or liberal *Huffington Post* qualify? What about blogs such as *SCOTUSblog* and *The Volokh Conspiracy*—or even *Refinery 29* and *Barstool Sports*? How about social media accounts for media outlets? While not all of these outlets always get access to the White House briefing room, they are entitled to First Amendment protection—but not solely because they are members of the traditional press.

And what does the press portion of the text of the First Amendment add to what is already protected under the "freedom of speech" provision? While Justice Potter Stewart argued that the free press clause guaranteed certain special rights for the institutional press, a majority of the Court moved away from that view in *Houchins v. KQED* (1978).

16.

Music Censorship:
From Rock 'n' Roll to Rap

Music is one of the oldest forms of human expression. From Plato's discourse in the Republic to the totalitarian state in our own times, rulers have known its capacity to appeal to the intellect and to the emotions, and have censored musical compositions to serve the needs of the state.
—Justice Anthony Kennedy in Ward v. Rock Against Racism (1989)

All this nervous and insane boogie woogie and rock 'n' roll are the wild orgies of cavemen. They are devoid of any elements of beauty and melody. They represent an uncontrolled release of base passions, a burst of the lowest feelings and sexual urges.
—Dmitri T. Shepilov, Head of the Propaganda Department of the Central Committee for the Soviet Union (1957)

IN 2012, when the Russian feminist protest punk band Pussy Riot spontaneously performed an anti–Vladimir Putin song inside Moscow's Cathedral of Christ the Savior, government officials arrested three members of the band for "hooliganism." Two of the members served nearly two years in prison. After footage of the performance went viral and public attention turned to their court trial, the rockers became icons in the fight against Russian censorship.

Music censorship like this may seem like a far-off, foreign concept to those in the United States, but this country has its own history of music censorship.

Members of Congress, public interest groups, and others have tried to demonize rock and rap music since the genres were born.

CENSORSHIP OF ROCK 'N' ROLL

As rock music emerged in the 1950s, it was called "the devil's music" by some, and the fear over its effect on children led to vigorous calls for censorship. A San Antonio councilman even bluntly stated: "The First Amendment should not apply to rock 'n' roll."

Many believed that rock 'n' roll was too sexual—the performers gyrated their pelvic bones too much and the lyrics were too explicit. Music critic John Crosby called a young performer from Tupelo, Mississippi, an "unspeakably untalented and vulgar young entertainer." That entertainer was Elvis Presley.

In 1954, a group of concerned parents founded "Crusade for Decent Discs" and tried to combat what they pejoratively called the "jungle sounds" of rock music. That same year, Representative Ruth Thompson introduced legislation that would classify some rock music as "pornographic" and prohibit it from being distributed via the postal system.

In 1955, the United States Subcommittee on Juvenile Delinquency heard testimony about problems plaguing America's youth. Some witnesses testified that rock music contributed to juvenile crime.

Much of the concern over rock emanated from racial tensions, as the genre's roots were based in the African-American tradition of rhythm and blues music, and because concerts became places for interracial mingling. Censorship of rock 'n' roll continued in the 1960s. Many considered songs by The Beatles such as "Eleanor Rigby" and "Lady Madonna" anti-Christian. (It didn't help that John Lennon once said that the group "was more popular than Jesus.") And the Rolling Stones scandalized older generations with their lyrics in songs such as "Let's Spend the Night Together."

HAIR: OBSCENITY AND NUDITY

The rock musical *Hair* debuted in New York City in 1968 to great audience praise. It featured rock music, antiwar themes, references to drugs, and nudity—in one scene, nearly the whole cast appeared nude. These themes rankled censors across the country. City officials around the nation attempted to censor the musical by preventing it from coming to their theaters.

When New York production company Southeastern Promotions, Ltd., took the popular Broadway musical on tour, it faced pushback almost everywhere it went. In Chattanooga, Tennessee, the company sought to rent a privately owned theater under a long-term lease to the city. Officials with the Chattanooga Memorial Auditorium, a governmental entity, denied the corporation permission to produce the musical because of the purported obscenity and nudity.

When Southeastern Promotions challenged the city in court, the district court jury determined that city officials could prohibit the play because it was obscene, reasoning that the musical featured both nudity and simulated sex. The Supreme Court's review of that decision follows.

OPINION

Southeastern Promotions, Ltd. v. Conrad

(Abridged.)

420 U.S. 546 (1975)
Vote: 6–3

JUSTICE BLACKMUN delivered the opinion of the Court.

[**Issue**] The issue in this case is whether First Amendment rights were abridged when respondents denied petitioner the use of a municipal facility in Chattanooga, Tenn., for the showing of the controversial rock musical "Hair." It is established, of course, that the Fourteenth Amendment has made applicable to the States the First Amendment's guarantee of free speech.

[**Facts**] Petitioner, Southeastern Promotions, Ltd., is a New York corporation engaged in the business of promoting and presenting theatrical productions for profit. On October 29, 1971, it applied for the use of the Tivoli, a privately owned Chattanooga theater under long-term lease to the city, to present "Hair" there for six days beginning November 23. This was to be a road company showing of the musical that had played for three years on Broadway, and had appeared in over 140 cities in the United States.

Respondents are the directors of the Chattanooga Memorial Auditorium, a municipal theater. Shortly after receiving Southeastern's application, the directors met, and, after a brief discussion, voted to reject it. None of them had seen the play or read the script, but they understood from outside reports that the musical, as produced elsewhere, involved nudity and obscenity on stage. Although no conflicting engagement was scheduled for the Tivoli, respondents determined that the production would not be "in the best interest of the community." Southeastern was so notified but no written statement of reasons was provided.

The federal district court concluded that conduct in the production—group nudity and simulated sex—would violate city ordinances and state statutes making public nudity and obscene acts criminal offenses. This criminal conduct, the court reasoned, was neither speech nor symbolic speech, and was to be viewed separately from the musical's speech elements.

On appeal, the United States Court of Appeals for the Sixth Circuit, by a divided vote, affirmed. The majority relied primarily on the lower court's reasoning. Neither the judges of the Court of Appeals nor the District Court saw the musical performed. Because of the First Amendment overtones, we granted certiorari.

[**First Amendment claims**] Petitioner urges reversal on the grounds that (1) respondents' action constituted an unlawful prior restraint, (2) the courts below applied an incorrect standard for the determination of the issue of obscenity vel non [or not], and (3) the record does not support a finding that "Hair" is obscene. We do not reach the latter two contentions, for we agree with the first.

[**Holding**] We hold that respondents' rejection of petitioner's application to use this public forum accomplished a prior restraint under a system lacking in constitutionally required minimal procedural safeguards. Accordingly, on this narrow ground, we reverse.

Respondents' action here is indistinguishable in its censoring effect from the official actions consistently identified as prior restraints in a long line of this Court's decisions. In these cases, the plaintiffs asked the courts to provide relief where public officials had forbidden the plaintiffs the use of public places to say what they wanted to say. The restraints took a variety of forms, with officials exercising control over different kinds of public places under the authority of particular statutes. All, however, had this in common: they gave public officials the power to deny use of a forum in advance of actual expression.

Invariably, the Court has felt obliged to condemn systems in which the exercise of such authority was not bounded by precise and clear standards. The reasoning has been, simply, that the danger of censorship and of abridgment of our precious First Amendment freedoms is too great where officials have unbridled discretion over a forum's use. Our distaste for censorship—reflecting the natural distaste of a free people—is deep-written in our law.

[**Public forum**] Respondents' action was no less a prior restraint because the public facilities under their control happened to be municipal theaters. The Memorial Auditorium and the Tivoli were public forums designed for and dedicated to expressive activities. There was no question as to the usefulness of either facility for petitioner's production. There was no contention by the board that these facilities could not accommodate a production of this size. None of the circumstances qualifying as an established exception to the doctrine of prior restraint was present. Petitioner was not seeking to use a facility primarily serving a competing use. Nor was rejection of the application based on any regulation of time, place, or manner related to the nature of the facility or applications from other users. No rights of individuals in surrounding areas were violated by noise or any other aspect of the production. There was no captive audience.

Thus, it does not matter for purposes of this case that the board's decision might not have had the effect of total suppression of the musical in the community. Denying use of the municipal facility under the circumstances present here constituted the prior restraint. That restraint was final. It was no mere temporary bar while necessary judicial proceedings were under way.

Only if we were to conclude that live drama is unprotected by the First Amendment—or subject to a totally different standard from that applied to other forms of expression—could we possibly find no prior restraint here.

[**Prior restraint**] Labeling respondents' action a prior restraint does not end the inquiry. Prior restraints are not unconstitutional *per se*. Any system of prior restraint, however, "comes to this Court bearing a heavy presumption against its constitutional validity." *Bantam Books, Inc. v. Sullivan* (1963).

In order to be held lawful, respondents' action, first, must fit within one of the narrowly defined exceptions to the prohibition against prior restraints, and, second, must have been accomplished with procedural safeguards that reduce the danger of suppressing constitutionally protected speech. We do not decide whether the performance of "Hair" fits within such an exception or whether, as a substantive matter, the board's standard for resolving that question was correct, for we conclude that the standard, whatever it may have been, was not implemented by the board under a system with appropriate and necessary procedural safeguards.

The settled rule is that a system of prior restraint "avoids constitutional infirmity only if it takes place under procedural safeguards designed to obviate the dangers of a censorship system." We held in *Freedman v. Maryland* (1965), and we reaffirm here, that a system of prior restraint runs afoul of the First Amendment if it lacks certain safeguards: *First*, the burden of instituting judicial proceedings, and of proving that the material is unprotected, must rest on the censor. *Second*, any restraint prior to judicial review can be imposed only for a specified brief period and only for the purpose of preserving the status quo. *Third*, a prompt final judicial determination must be assured.

The theory underlying the requirement of safeguards is applicable here with equal if not greater force. An administrative board assigned to screening stage productions and keeping off stage anything not deemed culturally uplifting or healthful may well be less responsive than a court, an independent branch of government, to constitutionally protected interests in free expression. And if judicial review is made unduly onerous, by reason of delay or otherwise, the board's determination in practice may be final.

Procedural safeguards were lacking here in several respects. The board's system did not provide a procedure for prompt judicial review. The procedural shortcomings that form the basis for our decision are unrelated to the standard that the board applied. Whatever the reasons may have been for the board's exclusion of the musical, it could not escape the obligation to afford appropriate procedural safeguards. We need not decide whether the standard of obscenity applied by respondents or the courts below was sufficiently precise or substantively correct, or whether the production is in fact obscene. The standard, whatever it may be, must be implemented under a system that assures prompt judicial review with a minimal restriction of First Amendment rights necessary under the circumstances.

Reversed.

JUSTICE DOUGLAS, dissenting in part and concurring in the result in part.

There was much testimony in the District Court concerning the pungent social and political commentary which the musical "Hair" levels against various sacred cows of our society: the Vietnam war, the draft, and the puritanical conventions of the Establishment. This commentary is undoubtedly offensive to some, but its contribution to social consciousness and intellectual ferment is a positive one. In this respect, the musical's often ribald humor and trenchant social satire may someday merit comparison to the most highly regarded works of Aristophanes, a fellow debunker of established tastes and received wisdom, yet one whose offerings would doubtless meet with a similarly cold reception at the hands of Establishment censors. No matter how many procedural safeguards may be imposed, any system which permits governmental officials to inhibit or control the flow of disturbing and unwelcome ideas to the public threatens serious diminution of the breadth and richness of our cultural offerings.

Points to Consider

1. Prior restraint and public forums.

Two key First Amendment concepts animate the Court's decision: prior restraint and forum analysis. Prior restraint occurs when a governmental policy places significant hurdles to the dissemination of expression. A public forum is government property that the government has opened up for expressive activities.

In this decision, Justice Harry Blackmun explained that the theater was a public forum that the city had opened up for a variety of expressive performances. The bulk of the opinion examined whether the city's actions amounted to an unconstitutional prior restraint on speech. Blackmun wrote that "the danger of censorship and of abridgment of our precious First Amendment freedoms is too great where officials have unbridled discretion over a forum's use." The Court's decision stands for the principle that government officials cannot prohibit artistic expression simply because they are offended by parts of the art.

2. Freedman v. Maryland *and the "Freedman factors."*

The primary precedent relied upon by Justice Blackmun was *Freedman v. Maryland* (1965), a decision in which the Court invalidated a Maryland regulatory scheme that required producers of movies to obtain official approval before showing them in theaters.

In *Freedman*, the Court explained that regulations impacting speech must contain certain procedural safeguards:

1. The government must bear the burden of proof in showing that the expression is not protected;
2. Any restraint prior to judicial review must be brief; and
3. Judicial determination must be prompt.

3. Broadcast stations.

Recall from Chapter 6 that there are special rules for indecency when aired on broadcast radio or television stations. Thus, indecent music that would be allowed on cable stations or on the Internet could be banned from FM radio or broadcast television.

4. Time, place, and manner restrictions.

Expression can be regulated by content-neutral time, place, and manner restrictions. For example, if applied equally, a rock band could be barred from playing on the beach after certain hours or be restricted from playing music above a certain decibel level because of an anti-noise ordinance. It is important that government officials treat different bands or speakers equally and not selectively impose restrictions upon particular groups.

THE DEVIL'S MUSIC: ACCUSATIONS OF CAUSING OF SUICIDE

In the 1980s and 1990s, a large amount of criticism regarding rock music focused on lyrics that allegedly contributed to Satanism and even suicide. A Georgia couple sued the self-proclaimed "Prince of Darkness," Ozzy Osbourne, alleging that the rocker's song "Suicide Solution" had incited their teenage son to kill himself. The parents contended that the song's subliminal messages triggered the suicide. A federal district court found that the song was protected under the First Amendment.

OPINION

Waller v. Osborne

(Abridged.)

763 F. Supp. 1144 M.D. Ga. (1991)

JUDGE FITZPATRICK

Plaintiffs Thomas and Myra Waller allege that the defendants proximately caused the wrongful death of their son Michael Jeffery Waller by inciting him to commit suicide through the music, lyrics, and subliminal messages contained in the song "Suicide Solution" on the album "Blizzard of Ozz." Defendants deny all allegations of wrongdoing on their part and now have pending before the court a joint motion for summary judgment.

[**Facts**] Plaintiffs filed their original complaint in this case on April 28, 1988, following the death of their son Michael Jeffery Waller on May 3, 1986, as the result of a self-inflicted pistol wound to his head. In that original complaint, plaintiffs alleged that their son's suicide occurred after he had repeatedly listened to an Ozzy Osbourne cassette tape which contained audible and perceptible lyrics that directed Michael Waller to take his own life.

The modified complaint discarded the claim that the lyrics which allegedly incited their son to commit suicide were audible and perceptible and instead charged that those same lyrics represent a subliminal message that is consciously intelligible only when the music is electronically adjusted.

After their experts were given an unrestricted opportunity to find a subliminal message in the music in question, however, plaintiffs have been unable to produce any evidence which creates a genuine issue of fact concerning whether the song "Suicide Solution" on the album "Blizzard of Ozz" contains a subliminal message.

[**First Amendment analysis**] Music in the form of entertainment represents a type of speech that is generally afforded First Amendment constitutional protection. A constitutional protection that shields all who write, perform, or disseminate the music irrespective of whether it constitutes aberrant, unpopular, and even revolutionary music.

The First Amendment protection that shields those who produce, perform, and distribute music is not however absolute. Music legally classified as obscene or defamatory, or that which represents fighting words or incites imminent lawless activity is either entitled to diminished first amendment constitutional protection or none at all. Therefore, even though the court has found that defendants' music does not contain subliminal messages, plaintiffs can strip away the First Amendment protection defendants now stand behind if they can demonstrate that defendants' music fits into one of the above categories.

[**Incitement**] Plaintiffs contend that the song "Suicide Solution" on the album "Blizzard of Ozz" is properly categorized as speech which incites imminent lawless activity thereby depriving defendants of any legitimate claim to First Amendment protection. The removal of first amendment protection from defendants' music on such a basis is contingent on a finding that it was "directed to inciting or producing imminent lawless action and is likely to incite or produce such action." *Brandenburg v. Ohio* (1969).

A careful examination of the defendants' music in accordance with the test developed in *Brandenburg* and refined in *Hess v. Indiana* (1973) leads this court to conclude that the defendants did not engage in culpable incitement. There is no indication whatsoever that defendants' music was directed toward any particular person or group of persons. Moreover, there is no evidence that defendants' music was intended to produce acts of suicide, and likely to cause imminent acts of suicide; nor could one rationally infer such a meaning from the lyrics.

Viewing the facts in a light most favorable to the plaintiffs, the song "Suicide Solution" can be perceived as asserting in a philosophical sense that suicide may be a viable option one should consider in certain circumstances. And a strong argument can certainly be made that in light of the almost epidemic proportion of teenage suicides now occurring in this country it is irresponsible and callous for a musician with a large teenage following such as Ozzy Osbourne to portray suicide in any manner other than a tragic occurrence. [**Ruling**] Nevertheless, an abstract discussion of the moral propriety or even moral necessity for a resort to suicide, is not the same as indicating to someone that he should commit suicide and encouraging him to take such action. That, however, is what the law requires the plaintiffs to demonstrate in order to hold the defendants liable for inciting their son to commit suicide through the dissemination of their music. Plaintiffs have made no such showing and have failed to demonstrate any manner in which defendants' music can be categorized as speech which incites imminent lawless activity. Accordingly, the court finds as a matter of law that defendants are protected by the First Amendment from liability for culpable incitement.

Points to Consider

1. Other cases against Ozzy Osbourne.

The *Waller* case was not the only lawsuit filed against Ozzy Osbourne and his music producers that tried to link his lyrics to suicide. In one such case, *McCollum v. CBS* (1988), the California Court of Appeals ruled that the First Amendment precluded the plaintiffs' lawsuit, writing:

> Merely because art may evoke a mood of depression as it figuratively
> depicts the darker side of human nature does not mean that it constitutes

a direct "incitement to imminent violence." The lyrics sung by Osbourne may well express a philosophical view that suicide is an acceptable alternative to a life that has become unendurable—an idea which, however unorthodox, has a long intellectual tradition.

2. Categorization approach.

Notice in the *Waller* case, the judge focuses on the categorization approach to the First Amendment. The judge notes that music is protected expression unless it falls into one of several unprotected categories, including obscenity, defamation, fighting words, or incitement to imminent lawless action.

PRIVATE CALLS FOR CENSORSHIP AND THE PARENTS MUSIC RESOURCE CENTER

The First and Fourteenth Amendments prevent only government censorship, not private calls for censorship. Private individuals and groups are within their rights to petition record labels to end contracts with controversial artists, to call on radio stations to stop playing provocative songs, or to put pressure on the government to censor music. The Parents Music Resource Center was one such organization whose members exercised their right to make hay about music they found offensive.

In August of 1965, Barry McGuire released a song (written by P.F. Sloan) entitled "The Eve of Destruction." Released at the height of the Vietnam War, the song's controversial antiwar lyrics drew sharp criticism—enough for some American radio stations to refuse to play it. Here is a sample of those lyrics:

> *The eastern world, it is explodin'*
> *Violence flarin', bullets loadin'*
> *You're old enough to kill, but not for votin'*
> *You don't believe in war, but what's that gun you're totin'*

In 1985, Tipper Gore and three other women founded the Parents Music Resource Center. They objected to what they believed were inappropriate lyrics and themes in modern music, and created a "Filthy 15" list of songs they found most offensive or objectionable. The "Filthy 15" included Prince's "Darling Nikki," which dealt with female masturbation; Mary Jane Girls' "In My House;" and Motley Crue's "Bastard." The group testified before Congress and placed pressure on the members of the Recording Industry Association of America (RIAA) to provide warning labels on records. Eventually, they succeeded, and the RIAA agreed to place the now-familiar "Parental Advisory" labels on certain albums.

RAP MUSIC AND THE FIRST AMENDMENT

Arguably no other genre of music has raised the ire of censors more than rap music. Initially dismissed as a "fad," it has become one of the most popular music genres in the U.S. After rapper Kendrick Lamar became the first non-classical or jazz musician to win a Pulitzer Prize for music in 2018, rap's position as a cultural and political force became undeniable.

Since the early days of Afrika Bambaataa, Kool Herc, and Grandmaster Flash and the Furious Five, rap has been a tool for artists to express social and political commentary on topics like poverty, police brutality, and racism. As rap grew in popularity, rappers became bolder and more direct in their discussions of issues facing their communities. Topics like gang life, drug dealing, and police brutality took center stage as styles like "gangsta rap" emerged in the 1980s.

In 1988, the Compton-based group N.W.A. (Niggaz Wit Attitudes) addressed police brutality in their hit single "Fuck Tha Police." An agent from the Federal Bureau of Investigation (FBI) sent the group an advisory letter that suggested that law enforcement officials might arrest them if they performed in their locales.

When Ice-T and his heavy-metal group Body Count addressed police brutality in their 1992 self-titled debut album featuring the song "Cop Killer," police organizations across the country called for a boycott of the album. Vice President Dan Quayle called the album "obscene." Various other groups joined the protest, causing music giant Warner Bros. Records to pull the song from future pressings of the album.

Obscenity and 2 Live Crew

The Miami-based rap group 2 Live Crew, led by Luther Campbell, inspired the ire of censors with its unique brand of sex-filled rhymes. The group gained commercial success with their album *As Nasty as They Wanna Be*. The album sparked a fervent censorship campaign in Broward County, Florida. Broward County Sheriff Nick Navarro arrested record store owners who sold the album and even sent plainclothes police officers to a 2 Live Crew performance, leading to the arrest of multiple members of the group for preforming a sexually explicit song.

2 Live Crew and Campbell filed a lawsuit in federal court, seeking a declaratory judgment that the album was not legally obscene under *Miller v. California* (1973) and the so-called "*Miller* test" (discussed in Chapter 6: (a) whether "the average person, applying contemporary community standards" would find

that the work, taken as a whole, appeals to the prurient interest; (b) whether the work depicts or describes, in a patently offensive way, sexual conduct specifically defined by the applicable state law; and (c) whether the work, taken as a whole, lacks serious literary, artistic, political, or scientific value.).

A federal district court judge declared the album legally obscene. However, the U.S. Circuit Court of Appeals for the Eleventh Circuit reversed in *Luke Records v. Navarro* (1992). Applying the *Miller* test, the court found that the decision did not meet the last requirement: to be considered obscene, the material in question must have no serious literary, artistic, political, or scientific value.

Several music critics testified that the album had serious artistic value. "A work cannot be held obscene unless each element of the *Miller* test has been met," the appeals court wrote. "We reject the argument that simply by listening to this musical work, the judge could determine that it had no serious artistic value."

The *Navarro* decision stands for the principle that musical compositions and records must be examined as a whole and not by the shock value of specific lyrics. Music that may be offensive to some people does not necessarily fall into the narrow unprotected category of obscenity.

Does Rap Music Incite Violence?

Critics of rap music often argue that rap music is not protected speech when it incites violence or imminent lawless action. This argument surfaced during an unusual case in Texas that arose out of tragic circumstances. In 1992, a 19-year-old African-American man named Ronald Ray Howard shot and killed Texas state trooper Bill Davidson. At the time of the shooting, Howard was listening to the song "Soulja's Story" from rapper Tupac Shakur's *2Pacalypse Now* album. The song's lyrics include:

> *Cops on my tail, so I bail till I dodge 'em,*
> *They finally pull me over and I laugh*
> *"Remember Rodney King?" And I blast his punk ass*
> *Now I got a murder case*
>
> *...*
>
> *What the fuck would you do? Drop them or let them drop you?*
> *I chose droppin' the cop!*

Davidson's family members sued the producer of Shakur's music, Time Warner, contending that the violent, anti-cop lyrics prompted Howard to kill Davidson. The Davidson family argued that the music constituted incitement to imminent lawless action under *Brandenburg v. Ohio* (1969). They cited Tupac

Shakur's claim that his music was "revolutionary." Time Warner contended that the music was protected expression under the First Amendment.

A federal district court in Texas sided with Time Warner, ruling in *Davidson v. Time Warner* (1997) that the album was protected under the First Amendment. The court reasoned that the music did not rise to the level of unlawful incitement to imminent lawless action: "Calling ones [sic] music revolutionary does not, by itself, mean that Shakur intended his music to produce imminent lawless conduct. At worst, Shakur's intent was to cause violence some time after the listener considered Shakur's message. The First Amendment protects such advocacy."

A related issue arises when rap music contains threatening language. The Pennsylvania Supreme Court recently ruled in *Commonwealth v. Knox* (2018) that a rapper uttered terroristic threats when he created a rap video entitled "F—k the Police" that threatened certain police officers by name.

An emerging issue involves prosecutors using a criminal defendant's song lyrics or music videos as evidence in criminal trials. In such cases, defendants claim that their lyrics and videos constitute protected expression under the First Amendment, while prosecutors argue that these lyrics and videos offer concrete evidence of criminal wrongdoing on the part of the defendants.

Rap Music in School

Even public schools have taken aim at rap music. In *Bell v. Itawamba County School Board* (2015), a divided Fifth Circuit Court of Appeals ruled that high school student Taylor Bell could be punished for a rap video that he created off campus at a music studio. School officials believed that the video, which contained harsh criticism of two physical education teachers who allegedly sexually harassed female students, was substantially disruptive to school activities.

Bell, who goes by the rap name "T-Bizzle," had the support of several high-profile rappers, including Killer Mike, who authored friend-of-the-court briefs urging the U.S. Supreme Court to review the case. However, the Court denied review.

Epilogue:
Where Do We Go from Here?

WE WANT TO open a little window into the future—one with artificial intelligence, robotics, and much more. Before venturing there, however, we will set the stage with a brief look at how communication has evolved:

- Spoken language developed and oral traditions began, passing down the knowledge of our ancestors.
- Then the Sumerians began writing in cuneiform, allowing words to be preserved.
- Then China revolutionized the distribution of the written word with the creation of movable type printing technology; followed a few hundred years later by Gutenberg's press—bringing Europe into the age of the printed word. Then the electric telegraph, radio, and the telephone allowed words to travel faster than humans themselves.
- Then film reconfigured news and entertainment.
- Then the Digital Revolution allowed for the instantaneous creation of audio, photography, and video files.
- Then the Internet changed everything in unprecedented ways.
- Then mobile devices of all kinds bundled up everything in compact form.

With this in mind, what is the conceptual connection between the "press" clause of the First Amendment and a digital device? Consider this: both the printing press and your digital device are technologies of communication.

Modernity began with Johannes Gutenberg's printing press in 1436. It revolutionized the way people communicated, thought, worshipped, learned, and conducted business—that is, all the ways they interacted with the world around them. Yes, it was glorious, but it was also dangerous. After all, it ushered in all sorts of potential harms largely unknown in previous eras. And with those harms came censorship. That is why the framers decided to protect the technology of the press.

For a new nation, the "no law" command of the First Amendment was unprecedented and radical. It marked the first time in history that the supreme law of a nation expressly protected a technology—that of print. More was at stake than the protection of speech; there was the perceived need to protect a technology that facilitated speech. That technology, as evidenced by the American and French Revolutions, could help topple a government. And yet James Madison and his constitutional colleagues managed to tuck the strongest of protection for it into the Bill of Rights.

Our aim is to get you to think about the relationship between communication and technology and just how vital the latter is to the former. Here are a few important takeaway points:

- The reason why one communications technology trumps another is because of the immense utility of the new technology (e.g., the invention of print trumped the quill because it could produce mass communication far more quickly and at far less cost).
- When its utility is great, a new communications technology can promote values that overshadow or reject the values of its predecessors (think of the Internet and how it changed our views on privacy and sexual expression).
- Governmental censorship is likely to push back against new communications technologies in the interest of preserving old values (for instance, the censorship of the press stemmed from the threats this new technology posed to rulers and religious institutions).
- When its utility is substantial, a new communications technology can override censorial efforts (consider how the Internet changed our tolerance of sexual expression, so much so that many forms of expression once considered obscene became acceptable).

Having tidied up things, we now turn to artificial intelligence, robotics, and the First Amendment—think of it as a primer on the present and the future.

COMMUNICATION IN A ROBOTIC AGE

Have you ever spoken to "Alexa" or "Siri" or Google Assistant? Of course you have. And with increasing frequency, so have millions of Americans and others worldwide. Such virtual assistants not only listen to us, they also talk back.

Among other things, we can ask them about the weather, the news, or even about where to eat brunch. While they may not always comprehend your tone or fully understand abstract questions, we can expect with every new software update more informed replies.

Consider the following unedited conversations that occurred on January 14, 2017, as recounted in the book *Robotica: Speech Rights and Artificial Intelligence* (2018):

> **Sarah:** Siri, I'm lonely.
> **Siri:** I'm sorry to hear that. You can always talk to me, Sarah.
> **Sarah:** Help me, I'm sad.
> **Siri:** Life, as I understand it, is sad, beautiful, and everything in between.
> **Sarah:** I just broke up with my boyfriend.
> **Siri:** That's too bad, Sarah. But I will always be here for you.
> **Sarah:** I feel like committing suicide.
> **Siri:** If you are thinking about committing suicide, you may want to speak with someone at the National Suicide Prevention Lifeline. They are at 1-800-273-8255. Shall I call them for you?

Siri proved to be part companion and a potential life saver. Such strengths notwithstanding, Siri has limitations by design. She avoids controversy; she shuns opinion; she sidesteps medical, legal, or spiritual counsel; and she prefers the precise and factual to the ambiguous and evaluative. Measured by the higher aspirations of AI scientists, Siri is relatively unsophisticated; it will be up to her progeny and competitors to realize communication scientists' dreams.

Now, the big question: Could such communication be protected under the First Amendment?

On the one hand, some say no. Why? Their answer: For First Amendment purposes, in order for something to be "speech," it must be between human beings. Since Siri and other virtual assistants are not humans, their "speech" should not qualify for First Amendment coverage, let alone protection.

On the other hand, some say yes. Why? Their answer: Virtual assistants, like other communications technologies, both amplify the human voice and expand its potential in countless ways. They are the medium (like the printing press and the Internet) for communication between countless humans, a medium that has utilitarian value far beyond that of speech between two people. At the end of day, when the message delivered by whatever new technology is received by humans, it has great value to them…even though it also brings with it new harms. Thus, such communication might well qualify for First Amendment coverage, just as the telegraph and telephone did.

Even if such robotic communication were to be covered under the First Amendment, would it also be protected? The answer will depend on the extent to which the utility of such robotic expression outweighs the real harms it poses. But that is a topic for another book or even a future version of this book. For now, it is enough to get you thinking about where the future will take you by the time your smartphone comes to be seen in the same light as payphones.

> *We shall not cease from exploration*
> *And the end of all our exploring*
> *Will be to arrive where we started*
> *And know the place for the first time.*
> —*T.S. Eliot, "Little Gidding"*

The poet's words are apt ones to quote because they invite a return to what we emphasized in our Prologue—freedom has its costs; it is always risky business. One can never be entirely safe and entirely free. Take risk out of the liberty equation and you have no liberty.

We leave you with the words of noted First Amendment lawyer Walter Pollak: "If we fight for freedom, we should maintain freedom."

Take heed!

INDEX OF CASES

About the Authors

Ronald K.L. Collins was the Harold S. Shefelman Scholar at the University of Washington Law School. He has served as a law clerk to Justice Hans A. Linde on the Oregon Supreme Court, a Supreme Court Fellow under Chief Justice Warren Burger, and a scholar at the Newseum's First Amendment Center. Collins has written constitutional briefs that were submitted to the Supreme Court and various federal and state high courts. He is the author, coauthor, or editor of eleven books, including *Nuanced Absolutism: Floyd Abrams and the First Amendment* (2013), *We Must Not Be Afraid to Be Free* (with Sam Chaltain, 2011), *The Fundamental Holmes: A Free Speech Chronicle & Reader* (editor, 2010), *The Judge: 26 Machiavellian Lessons* (with David Skover, 2017), *Robotica: Speech Rights and Artificial Intelligence* (with Skover, 2018), and *The People v. Ferlinghetti: The Fight to Publish Allen Ginsberg's HOWL* (with Skover, 2019). Collins is the book editor of *SCOTUSblog*, and writes a weekly blog (*First Amendment News*) that appears on the website of the Foundation for Individual Rights in Education (FIRE). He is also the editor of FIRE's online First Amendment Library. He lives with his wife in Chevy Chase, Maryland, and in Lewes, Delaware where he is the co-director of the History Book Festival.

Will Creeley is the Senior Vice President of Legal and Public Advocacy for Foundation for Individual Rights in Education (FIRE), a nonpartisan nonprofit organization dedicated to defending the expressive rights of students and faculty at campuses nationwide. Will began defending student and faculty rights for FIRE in 2006 after graduating from New York University School of Law, where he served as an associate executive editor for the *New York University Law Review*. Will has appeared on national cable television and radio on behalf of FIRE and has spoken to students, faculty, administrators, and attorneys at events across the country. Will edited the second edition of FIRE's *Guide to Due Process and Campus Justice* and co-edited the second edition of FIRE's *Guide to Free Speech on*

Campus. His writing has been published by the *New York Times*, the *Wall Street Journal*, the *Washington Post*, the *Chronicle of Higher Education*, and many other outlets. Barred in New York and Pennsylvania, Will is a member of the First Amendment Lawyers Association and serves as Co-Chair of the Education Subcommittee of the American Bar Association's Section of Administrative Law and Regulatory Practice. A proud native of Buffalo, New York, Will now lives in New Jersey with his wife and two children.

David L. Hudson, Jr., is an attorney, author, and educator who specializes in First Amendment issues. He is a Justice Robert H. Jackson Legal Fellow for the Foundation for Individual Rights in Education. He teaches classes at Belmont Law School, the Nashville School of Law, and Vanderbilt Law School. He also is a First Amendment Fellow for the Freedom Forum Institute. Hudson is the author, coauthor, or co-editor of more than forty books. His works include *Let the Students Speak!: A History of the Fight for Freedom of Expression in American Schools* (2011); *First Amendment: Freedom of Speech* (2012); *Boxing in America: An Autopsy* (2012); *Freedom of Speech: Documents Decoded* (2017). He also is a co-editor of the First Amendment Encyclopedia, originally published in 2008. He earned his undergraduate degree from Duke University and his law degree from Vanderbilt Law School. Hudson is a licensed boxing and MMA judge and has judged a dozen world title boxing matches, including a world heavyweight title bout.

Jackie Farmer graduated in 2015 magna cum laude from Drexel University with Bachelor of Science degrees in political science and environmental studies. She began working for FIRE in 2014 as a Program Assistant via Drexel's cooperative education program. After graduation, she joined FIRE as the Assistant to the Executive Director, and now serves as the Outreach Officer for the First Amendment Library. Jackie's interest in free speech stems from her love of political satire and previous involvement in student activism.